Foundations of the Extra Lesson

Foundations of the Extra Lesson

Beyond What is Seen in the Exercises

by Joep Eikenboom

Rudolf Steiner College Press

Publication of this book was made possible
by a grant from the Waldorf Curriculum Fund.

Cover art: Erica Eikenboom
Cover design: Claude Julien and John Wihl

Permision to reproduce illustrations has been graciously granted by:
Verlag am Goetheanum for drawings by Daniel van Bemmelen
Walter Keller Verlag for the painting by Katherina Eisleben

© 2007 Joep Eikenboom

All Rights Reserved. No part of this book may be copied in any form without the written consent of the publisher.

ISBN 978-0-945803-83-6

The content of this book represents the view of the author and should not be taken as the official opinion or policy of Rudolf Steiner College or Rudolf Steiner College Press.

Book orders may be made through
the Bookstore at Rudolf Steiner College
Tel: 916-961-8729, Fax: 916-961-3032,
Catalog and online orders: www.steinercollege.edu
E-mail:orders@steinercollege.edu.

Rudolf Steiner College Press
9200 Fair Oaks Blvd.
Fair Oaks, CA 95628, U.S.A.

*This book is dedicated
to the angel of the Dordtse Vrije School
(the Waldorf School in Dordrecht, the Netherlands)
and my colleagues and the children there
who during the last twenty years have made it possible
for me to research Audrey McAllen's work.*

Acknowledgments

My thanks to

Audrey McAllen for her patience in answering my hundreds of questions.

Liane Collot d'Herbois for inviting me to tea several times and giving me indications on color and painting.

Monica Ellis, Mary Jo Oresti, Rachel Ross, Ingun Schneider, Uta Stolz, Ernst Westermeier, and Mary E. Willby for exchanging ideas, experiences, and knowledge.

Erica, my wife, who was the first to ask me to become an Extra Lesson educational support teacher and who has encouraged me in this work ever since.

Hannah, who as a small girl showed me the relation between the Extra Lesson exercises and the different stages of human movement development.

Claude Julien and Judy Blatchford for their support and patience, making the text into a legible manuscript in English and a professional book.

Ingun Schneider for her careful reading of the manuscript and her additions and corrections thereof.

Verlag am Goetheanum and Walter Keller Verlag for giving their kind permission to reproduce illustrations by Rudolf Steiner, Daniel van Bemmelen, and Katherina Eisleben.

Contents

Foreword i

Preface iii

Introduction 1

1 Human Development 5

2 Lectures on the Senses and Supersensible Currents 15

3 Right-angled Triangle and Threefold Spiral Exercises 31

4 Two Painting Exercises 43

5 Copper Ball and Moving Straight Line and Lemniscate Exercises .. 55

6 Eye Color Affinity: Blue Moon and Red Sun Drawing 69

7 The Qualities of the Colors 85

8 Colors in the Extra Lesson Painting Exercises 105

9 Mirroring and the Imprinting Process 113

10 Handedness Pattern Assessment and Flower Rod Exercise 135

11 The Cube as Reversal of Three-dimensional Space 145

12 The Divine Architecture of the Structural Physical Body 157

Appendices:
   A. Notes on *The King of Ireland's Son*, Joep Eikenboom 167
   B. Intrusion of the Adversarial Powers, Audrey McAllen 179
   C. The Physical Body as Educator of the Soul, Audrey McAllen 185
   D. Earth as a Picture of the Human Being, Audrey McAllen 193

Bibliography 203

Index 209

About the author

Foreword

The exercises developed by Audrey McAllen in The Extra Lesson are studied and practiced in Waldorf schools throughout the world. Training programs for teachers focusing on this remarkable work are currently offered in at least eight countries in Europe, North America, Australia and South America.

Joep Eikenboom has devoted himself to decades of practical educational support in the Waldorf classroom using these exercises and to deep study of the spiritual science of Rudolf Steiner on which they are based. The insights he gained have allowed him to make enormous contributions not only to our understanding of the spiritual background of The Extra Lesson but also towards connecting this foundation to its manifestation in the specific exercises.

The elaboration of these pedagogical insights could not have come at a more crucial time. The decade of the 1990s was already referred to as "the nano-second nineties." Today both the Self-help and Business sections of bookstores display a myriad of titles addressing the subject of change and its almost frightening acceleration in our time. For those with eyes to see, it has become apparent that an education system that attempts to cram children with content, or to prepare them for technologies that become obsolete overnight, is itself outdated.

An emphasis on the development of faculties and capacities makes far more sense in our modern situation. The cultivation of imagination, whole-system thinking and love of learning are essential for our future. It is precisely with this challenge to develop faculty that The Extra Lesson begins, outlining necessary conditions for this development and detailing difficulties.

Joep Eikenboom's presentation is a valuable resource towards helping to remove psychic and bodily hindrances to this development–a task that in Steiner's Deeper Insights Into Education is declared to be the province, not of the doctor, but of the teacher. It continues Audrey McAllen's work in addressing the pivotal existential question and dilemma of incarnation itself, namely "How do 'I' get into my body?"

Gayle Davis

Preface

My purpose in writing this book is to make available the anthroposophical sources and concepts upon which Audrey McAllen's Extra Lesson work has been built. In the 1960s Audrey was asked by Norbert Glas, the school doctor at the Wynstones Waldorf School in Gloucester, England, to work with some of the students. He himself had not found any medical or constitutional indication for their learning problems. Through her careful work, she attained considerable success with these children, and her friends Else Göttgens and Annerie Marx later encouraged her to publish the exercises she developed. The first edition of the Extra Lesson book, however, contained little background information. Audrey assumed her Waldorf-teacher colleagues had access to the same anthroposophical background information she had.

The exercises by Audrey as published in *The Extra Lesson* are not just an example of what an individual teacher can develop when confronted with the needs of her students. Audrey developed an archetypal concept, deeply rooted in Rudolf Steiner's anthroposophy, which goes far beyond the level of the individual. The exercises address the spirit forces within the body and integrate the movements of the students into the universal movements of the earth. Her work, in my opinion, carries seeds for far future times of which we can now only dimly imagine the value and necessity. We need, however, to preserve and nurture these seeds so that these concepts will not be lost. Practicing the exercises oneself will reveal their effectiveness; studying the concepts from which these exercises are developed will deepen our understanding of *why* they work.

In the content of this book, I am pleased to pass on the background information Audrey McAllen herself gave in lectures and conversations. I have tried to distill her answers to hundreds of questions by telephone and fax, and from innumerable notes that Audrey handed on, as her legacy. This material has been filtered through my twenty years of research and experience with the Extra Lesson exercises in my role as an educational support teacher and a class teacher in the Waldorf movement.

I encourage every reader to explore and research the Extra Lesson concept and Rudolf Steiner's anthroposophical spiritual science in order to further this valuable work.

Audrey McAllen at 28

Audrey McAllen at 70

Introduction

When in the early 1940s Audrey McAllen studied to become a Waldorf teacher, Rudolf Steiner's education lectures *Foundations of Human Experience* (also published as *Study of Man*), given to the teachers when the first Waldorf School in Stuttgart was founded, had not yet been translated into English. Miss Elly Wilke lectured on "The Understanding of the Human Being," a subject that covered the anthroposophical insights into the human body, soul, and spirit. Audrey McAllen was twenty-one years old at the time. Miss Wilke's teaching was based on Rudolf Steiner's lectures (given in Berlin in 1909, 1910, and 1911), now published in *A Psychology of Body, Soul, and Spirit*. In the four 1909 lectures, Steiner spoke about the senses and the human physical body built up by flowing spiritual currents. Later, when Audrey McAllen was asked to work with children with learning difficulties, these same lectures became the inspiring source out of which Audrey developed the Extra Lesson.

To understand the foundation of the Extra Lesson—the concepts that lie behind this body of exercises—one needs to go back to the roots and study these lectures, think them over again and again, and "forget" their content. At least this is what Rudolf Steiner advises us to do: study anthroposophy, meditate on it repeatedly, and then forget the content (see *Balance in Teaching*). As a result of this process, intuition for what to do with children we work with will rise from the subconscious realms of one's will forces: one's sense perceptions will become sharper, observation will be directed to the needs of the children, and one will develop new exercises. In following Steiner's advice, one will work consciously with the different soul activities: day-wake consciousness, dreaming consciousness, and sleeping consciousness. After studying in the day-wake consciousness, repetitively meditating on the content will connect it with the dream consciousness of the feeling life. Then out of the sleeping subconscious state, from the soul activity of the will, new and fruitful intuitions and thoughts will arise (see *Foundations of Human Experience*, lecture 6).

As educational support teachers working with the Extra Lesson, we owe it to anthroposophy, to Waldorf education, to Rudolf Steiner, and to the Extra Lesson to really take up this intuitive process and bring the work into the future. The author of this book is sharing his research on the sources of Audrey McAllen's work, knowing that this is only just a beginning but hoping that this work will encourage colleagues to continue developing the Extra Lesson concept.

Audrey McAllen developed the body of exercises published in *The Extra Lesson* out of her knowledge of anthroposophy and her experience as a Waldorf teacher. The reader of this book on the foundations of that work is assumed to be familiar with basic anthroposophical concepts given by Rudolf Steiner and to have actively experienced the Extra Lesson exercises. The following is offered as a brief orientation to the ground on which this book is based.

The Fourfold Human Being
Spiritual science takes into account the invisible, supersensible aspects of the human being and the world, without neglecting the findings of natural science.

> The first member of the human being is the *physical body*. This is what is visible. All that is visible in the human being and in the world consists of mineral elements, is subject to the laws of physical existence, and is lifeless. The physical element of the human body is the corpse; its substances will fall back into their realm of existence, the mineral realm.

> A second essential principle gives life to the human body, to animals, and to plants. This Rudolf Steiner calls the life body or *etheric body*. This body maintains life, growth, and reproduction.

> Consciousness lives in the soul, with its activities of thinking, feeling, and willing. Spiritual science gives this complex the name *astral body*, meaning star body. It is the vehicle of pain, pleasure, perception, feeling, and impulse. The human being shares this astral element with the animals.

> The fourth member gives the human being his or her unique biography. It is the *Ego*, the divine element in the human being, that develops during several different incarnations. The Ego works in and purifies the other members of human nature.

In his early book *The Education of the Child*, Rudolf Steiner gives a compact outline of his view on education. This little booklet was written in 1907, over ten years before the first Waldorf school was founded in Stuttgart, Germany.

The Threefold Human Being
The soul of the human being, with its activities of thinking, feeling, and willing, reveals and expresses itself in the human structure.

> The nervous system and the brain form the bodily vessel for the soul activity of thinking. Here the human being is awake and conscious.

The feeling life—love, hate, desire, dislike, and so on—is centered in the vessel of the rhythmic processes of breathing and heartbeat. Every emotion of the inner life immediately affects the rhythmic system.

When people want to move, do things, come into action, they need the limbs and the metabolic processes.

The will forces are not centered in the human brain. In the brain, the *concepts* of the will impulses become conscious. In the deep subconscious realms of the metabolic processes, in the muscles of the movement system, the human will lives. Warmth forms the bridge between the soul and the body, between the warm enthusiasm that lives in the soul and the warmth produced inside the physical body. Rudolf Steiner strongly stresses that it is not the motor nerves that transmit will impulses. Rather, these nerves are involved in the perception of movement.

The threefold aspect of soul was known in the world religions. In Hinduism, there are Brahma, Shiva, and Vishnu; in Egypt, they worshiped Osiris, Isis, and Horus; Christianity knows the Holy Trinity of Father, Son, and Holy Spirit.

A most beautiful representative of the threefold aspect of soul is the form of the baroque concertos (Vivaldi, Bach) and the classical sonata (Haydn, Mozart, Beethoven). The early concertos and sonatas have three movements. In the classical sonata form the first movement has a threefold structure where two themes are introduced in the "exposition." In the "development," the two themes seem to be in dialogue. The third section or "recapitulation" restates the themes of the exposition, usually in the same order; the second theme is now heard in the tonic. This structure of the first movement shows us the process of thinking, where in an inner discussion different points of view are considered and a conclusion is drawn. The second movement is often in a slow tempo and a minor key. The third movement is often in a *presto* tempo, typically a dance such as a gigue or a rondo. This is the will element. We can recognize in this musical form the hidden human nature that is revealed to us by spiritual science.

Evolution of the World and the Human Being

In his book *An Outline of Esoteric Science*, Rudolf Steiner describes evolution from a spiritual point of view. With the help of other spiritual beings, human beings develop an Ego. Eventually every individual will become totally responsible for his or her role in evolution. High divine beings guide this process as loving parents educate and protect their children.

Other spiritual beings obstruct human development—like beavers building dams in a stream. There are beings that have intruded into the human soul and implanted the seed of a lower ego. This gave the human being independence at a premature stage of development, and along with it, egoism and desire. This element in development is indicated in the first book of the Bible in the story of the snake in Paradise called Lucifer (Genesis 3).

Another group of spiritual beings is at work in the subconscious levels of the life body. There they shrink the life forces, as a drought causes deserts. In the human soul, this lack of life forces causes materialism. These beings are known under the Persian name Ahriman, and they are discussed further in this book.

Child Development

As an educational support teacher, one needs to be familiar with the results of mainstream scientific research—especially the development in the first seven years, the aspects of neurological and movement development, early childhood movement patterns, integration of midline barriers, and the development of dominance. An Extra Lesson teacher will have learned to feel total respect for the insights scientists have developed in this realm. As an anthroposophist, the Extra Lesson teacher has to learn the spiritual laws hidden behind these physical facts, so that supporting the children addresses their total beings of body, soul, and spirit.

Housekeeping detail:
As in Audrey McAllen's books, to avoid awkward constructions, we are using "she" to refer to a teacher and "he" to refer to a child.

Chapter 1

Human Development

In the first chapter of his book *The Spiritual Guidance of the Individual and Humanity*, Rudolf Steiner describes spiritual forces forming the body of the child in the first three years of life. Higher spiritual members of the human being have the task of building up the body. These spiritual members are closely connected with the spiritual world. In the first year, the bodily system with which the child learns to walk is further developed and exercised. It is the sensory organization that gives the child the ability to stand up, to balance, and to perceive its movement in space. The main senses involved in this process are the sense of self-movement and the sense of balance. In the second year, the speech organs and all systems connected with them are further developed and the child learns to speak. In the third year, the brain is differentiated and finely developed. This gives the child an increasing capacity to think.

Then comes the moment the child starts to say "I." The individuality learns to find an inner relation to the bodily systems. The first form of memory appears, which makes the child conscious of being an ego. This individuality is the personal lower ego, connected with the blood, which now becomes the main influence in life. The higher spiritual forces that played their main role in the first three years, which one could name the higher Ego, withdraw their activity to the background. They continue in their function of guiding the bodily senses, all in the subconscious of the human soul.

We have to keep in mind that the lower ego is diluted by the luciferic forces, as the Buddha said: the wheel of incarnation is caused by egoism. Those who have had the opportunity to closely observe little children will remember the innocence in the eyes of the young child playing and exploring the world. This innocence in the gaze changes after the child says "I." The child starts to find out and test its behavioral boundaries with grownups and playmates. This happens when the lower ego comes in—a new step in development.

Rudolf Steiner writes that when, as an adult, someone wants to develop higher spiritual forces on an inner spiritual path, this requires reactivation of the forces that built up the physical body during the first three years and then withdrew. Steiner points the way by quoting the Biblical verse: unless you turn and become like children, you will never enter the kingdom of heaven (Matt. 18:3). It is very likely that old eastern spiritual schools—for example, in Yoga and Tai Chi—originally exercised these bodily senses to develop higher spiritual enlightenment.

Karl König's book *The First Three Years of the Child* is based on the indications given in *The Spiritual Guidance of the Individual and Humanity* by Steiner. König describes in detail the important developmental steps of the young child. He also shares his research into the metamorphoses of the bodily senses into the higher senses. For the educational support teacher, kindergarten teacher, and grades teacher, this is highly valuable material.

The higher Ego is composed of the spiritual members of the human being: spirit self, life spirit, and spirit man. The activity of the spiritual organ of the sixteen-petaled lotus flower (chakra near the larynx) forms and completes the nervous system. The twelve-petaled lotus flower (chakra near the heart) forms and completes the total muscular system including the muscles of the larynx and the rest of the speech organs. The two-petaled lotus flower (chakra at the brow between the eyes) forms the two hemispheres of the brain, the instrument for thinking (see *A Psychology of Body, Soul, and Spirit* Part I).

The Extra Lesson exercises help children to recapitulate the developmental steps of the first seven years: the development of the senses, spatial awareness, and body geography. The structure and vertical position of the physical body give human beings the ability to orient themselves in and become conscious of three-dimensional space. In this vertical position human eyes focus to combine information from left and right sense organs, giving the human being a unique position in the world of creation. Mammals such as the horse and the dog have their eyes on the sides of their head. Even cats and owls, whose eyes face forward, do not focus in the way that human beings do. This focusing of the eyes gives the gaze a three-dimensional perspective. With this, a consciousness of self is developed.

The divine Hierarchies at work behind the evolution of the earth had a plan, an architectural blueprint, of what the human being would be like. The physical body was planned to become a cup for the human ego to incarnate into. Physical body, etheric body, and astral body were prepared by the hierarchies during the Earth's developmental stages known as Old Saturn, Old Sun, and Old Moon. The Hierarchies offered this bodily organization to the human being. The architectural blueprint of the human body included the idea of the vertical position of the skeleton with the twelve ribs of the rib cage, the twenty-eight vertebrae, the twelve cranial nerves, the muscles, etc. This physical structure was prepared by the Hierarchies as their imaginations, inspirations, and intuitions: the imaginative picture of the skeleton and brain, the inspiring music-forming muscles (muscle tone), the intuitive will intentions forming the nerve-sense system. In *An Outline of Esoteric Science*, Rudolf Steiner describes in detail the different stages of evolutionary development of the cosmos and the roles of the different Hierarchies.

Rudolf Steiner, in lecture 5 of *TheWorld of the Senses and the World of the Spirit*, describes how the blueprint of the human body of bones, nerves, and muscles was darkened and filled with substance through the intrusion of Lucifer at the Fall. As a result of the luciferic influence in evolution, the spiritual imaginations, inspirations, and intuitions of the Hierarchies were filled with matter. At that time the human being was given the metabolic and glandular systems, the different organs with the metabolic processes, and also the sense activity connecting the inner soul life with the outer world. This was all caused by the intrusion of Lucifer. In the Bible, this process is described in the sentence: Therefore the Lord God sent him forth from the garden of Eden, to till the ground from which he was taken (Gen. 3:23). The so-called gate of the Garden of Eden, in which the human being lived before, can be understood as the human sense organs. Through sense perception we live in the outside world. We are not able to see the inside of ourselves. The sense perceptible world is brought to us by Lucifer, the result of eating the apple of the Tree of Knowledge. The white daylight that awakens our daily consciousness hides from us the reality of the spiritual beings working behind the sense perceptible world. Through this situation the human being is, however, able to develop a self-consciousness, an individuality. It gave the human being independence from spiritual beings—freedom. (And the Lord God said, "Behold, the man has become like one of us"—Gen. 3:22.) Humankind had to pay a price for all that. Because of this, humanity suffers from illness, pain, and death:

> In the sweat of your face you shall eat bread, till you return to the ground, for out of it you were taken; you are dust, and to dust you shall return.
>
> Genesis 3:19

On this subject, the Judeo-Christian tradition corresponds with Buddhism. Before he became a Buddha, the Bodhisattva, Prince Siddhartha, recognizes that the cause of suffering (illness, old age, and death) is birth, and birth is caused by desire for sense impressions. The sense world is created by Mara, the Lord of Misfortune, Sin, Destruction, and Death—the ruler of desire. Mara is the Buddhist name for the luciferic forces we mentioned earlier. In Greek mythology the story of Prometheus gives a similar archetypal picture. Every day an eagle, the symbol of passion, eats from Prometheus' liver, which causes tremendous pain. This is the price the human being, who has descended from paradise, has to pay for his freedom.

Two Mystery Streams

In human cultural history, one can differentiate two streams. The first was developed primarily in Ancient India, Egypt, and Southern Europe. The Jewish and Christian cultures carry elements of this cultural and historic stream. Initiates in this stream were brought to clairvoyance by developing their inner soul life. In the mystery schools, students were prepared to meet the forces living in the subconscious of the soul. They would meet greed, egoism, and jealousy and needed to learn to conquer these soul tendencies. One can think of Buddha's eightfold path towards enlightenment and the story of Saint Francis. This is the cultural stream from the East and South.

The second cultural stream developed primarily in Ancient Persia and later in the north and west of Europe in the Celtic and German mysteries. These mysteries focused on the forces that created and continue to be connected with the outer physical sense world. Initiates were trained to develop courage to clairvoyantly meet the spiritual forces behind the outer world of sun, wind, thunder and lightning, and so on. The Celtic missionaries that visited the European continent in the ninth century were from this initiation stream. Their influence was undermined by the official Roman Catholic Church, but worked on in the hidden activity of King Arthur and the Knights of the Round Table, the medieval minstrels and troubadours, the Cathars, Templars, and Rosicrucians.

In the different Grimms' fairy tales, one will learn to distinguish these inner and outer paths of development by the numbers used. The threefold soul can enter the inner, personal realm where it will meet the sevenfold aspects of the constitution. The other path leads via the twelvefold sense organization into the outer world indicated by the numbers twelve or six. The twelve labors of Hercules and the story of Theseus are related to the outer aspect of the twelve signs of the zodiac. Even the differences between the Christmas story in the Gospels of St. Luke and St. Matthew can be seen in this light. The shepherds represent the inner mystery stream, the three kings the outer mysteries. At the birth of the archetypal Ego of Humankind, these two streams united.

Structural and Constitutional Physical Body

Following the spiritual insights of Rudolf Steiner, Audrey McAllen taught us to differentiate between the structural physical body of nerves, bones, and muscles and the constitutional physical body—that is, the metabolic system with its organs and processes and the sense perceptive activities. The structural physical body has the element of objectivity: every human being on the earth has the same physical structure. Without this objective archetypal structure one would not be able to do medical surgery procedures. The processes of the constitutional element, however, are highly individual. Everybody has individual DNA. Transplanting organs can be problematic. Processes such as metabolism, illness, temperament, and constitutional types are subjective and individualized.

Rudolf Steiner said it is only the constitutional physical body that is perishable. The structural physical body of nerves, muscles, and bones has eternal value, for they are imaginations, inspirations, and intuitions of the gods—however, filled in with matter. After death, the matter will disappear, but the quality of the thoughts, feelings, and deeds of the human being will remain and start to spiritually radiate as imaginations, inspirations, and intuitions.

In a lecture about mental illnesses ("Subconscious Impulses in the Human Soul"), Rudolf Steiner speaks very specifically about the constitutional aspect of the human being. He says that the ego is working in the blood and enters the body through the solar plexus and its ganglion system. It is this part of the nervous system that is connected with the organs of the metabolic system. Through the connection between the solar plexus and the metabolic processes, the ego is anchored in the lower part of the body. It is that ego element in the human being that is influenced and infected by evil luciferic forces. These forces gave the human being the seed of the ego too early, thereby drawing the ego too deeply into the astral body, offering self-consciousness and freedom. The price of this is that the lower ego has become a carrier of evil forces such as sneakiness, cunning, untruthfulness, and egoism.

The astral body of the constitution is connected with the spinal nerves and, through these, with the rhythmic system. The lower astral body also carries luciferic and ahrimanic elements that manifest as superficiality, illogicalness, mania, strong melancholy, or hypochondria.

All this is connected with that part of the physical body that Audrey McAllen named the constitutional body. This is the carrier of the individual karmic element that is connected with destiny and illness. Therefore we can say that the constitutional element is the realm of the medical profession, for illness is always related to the personal destiny, karma.

In a healthy condition, the lower ego and astral organization are anchored in the organs and processes of the metabolic system of the physical and etheric bodies. Hence, all the luciferic or ahrimanic elements stay in the sub-conscious, from which they cause illness or personality problems. When these forces disengage themselves too early from their bodily tasks, before the time of death, they will cause soul problems or even mental illness. Anthroposophical medical psychiatry has elaborated Rudolf Steiner's indications; it relates depression and mania, hysteria, obsession, and psychosis to the processes in the liver, gall bladder, lungs, kidney, or heart.

In contrast to this, there is the structural physical body that is the carrier of the pure higher Ego and astral forces, as planned by the Hierarchies during the creation of the human being. Rudolf Steiner says (*Foundations of Esotericism* lecture 12):

> The spinal cord, with the brain, is the organ of the ego. This is surrounded by the threefold protective sheath of the astral, etheric, and physical bodies. After the organ for the ego (spinal cord and brain) has been prepared, the ego laid itself in the bed made ready for it, and spinal cord and brain appear as organs in the service of the ego. The fourfold human being is put together in this way. It is the Pythagorean square:
> 1. The spinal cord and brain are the organs of the ego.
> 2. The warm blood and the heart are the organ of the astral body.
> 3. The solar plexus is the organ of the etheric body.
> 4. The physical body is the complicated physical apparatus.
>
> Thus has the fourfold human being been constructed. The physical body, etheric body, and astral body have built up the human being from without. This unites with what works from within, the Ego.

Here Rudolf Steiner describes the human organization from the standpoint of the structural body. Note that in this passage Rudolf Steiner names the spinal cord and brain as vessel for the Ego, not the blood as he speaks of it in other places. He speaks in this context of the higher Ego that carries consciousness. Studying Rudolf Steiner's different indications, one always has to keep in mind from what point of view and to what audience he was speaking. One can learn to develop a feeling for how different elements (here structural and constitutional) are interconnected.

The structural body is the form of the human being created by the formative forces of the zodiac. These forces come from high spiritual beings and are reflected in the human organization; in bones, nervous system, muscles, and the sensory system.

The processes of the constitutional body are connected with forces from the planets. Illness, however, is caused by the influence Lucifer has on the astral body. This influence is reflected into the etheric body of the individual. Perhaps one could characterize the relation between the structural and constitutional physical bodies with the following words from the Gospel of Matthew (6:22–23):

> The eye is the lamp of the body. So, if your eye is sound, your whole body will be full of light; but if your eye is not sound, your whole body will be full of darkness, how great is the darkness!

In the first seven years, children are busy individualizing their physical bodies. Steiner described this in *The Education of the Child*. From the structural physical aspect, we focus on the objective steps in the motor and neurological development. These developmental steps have an objective and archetypal hierarchical order, common for every human being. The movement development of every child will start with early childhood movement patterns and will develop gradually the different new stages of symmetrical movement patterns, laterality, and dominance. At the same time, the structure of the nervous system and the two sides of the brain will grow and become more and more complex. In the last stage, the corpus callosum will bridge the two sides that then will be able to work independently, yet simultaneously. In the three different large stages of development of the first seven years, the midline barriers will play an important role until they are overcome and integrated. The development of dominance will be the last stage of the structural physical aspect of the incarnation process.

The individuality with its personal destiny will express itself in the development of the constitutional aspect of the physical body. The individuality needs to build up a new body and transform the inherited body that was given at birth. New individual substances need to be created. The liver plays an especially important role in this process of transformation and metabolism. The individual aspect expresses itself in the development of speech as the different sounds each baby's voice produces. These can be quite varied and personal. The way the child speaks will also be distinctive and will express the character and temperament of the individuality. The constitution of the child will be an expression of the individual/personal element, its weakness and its strength.

The moment the 2½–3-year-old child starts saying "I," we know that the individuality identifies itself with the structural aspect of the physical body. Until this time, the development of the child was led by the higher Ego. From now on, the lower aspect of the personal ego will play a far more important role. Karl König describes the development of walking, speaking, and thinking through the wisdom of the higher Ego in *The First Three Years of the Child*. From the spiritual world and under the guidance of spiritual beings, forces are penetrating the child that make it possible to overcome gravity, form the larynx, and shape the brain, so they can become tools for the individuality to express his or her thoughts, feelings, and will.

The individuality will have certain talents and faculties. The structural development of movement and the nerve system will bring skills for manifesting the child's talents. The end result of a proper first seven years' development is that these two aspects of the physical body, the structural and constitutional sides, match. They belong to one another just as the two halves of a mold are brought together to form a sculptural figure. The interlinking element between the structural and the constitutional physical body is warmth, the body temperature of 98.6°F (37°C). Warmth is a remembrance of the early evolutionary stage of the earth, called Old Saturn. The warmth of the blood is a metamorphosis of the warmth on Old Saturn. During that time, the first seeds of the human physical body, which have become the basis of the senses, were laid down. The bodily temperature of 98.6°F (37°C) is common to every human being. It is archetypal and therefore connected with the structural element, yet it is also connected with the blood and the constitution.

An architect creates a floor plan for a house and may build twenty houses on a street using the same plan. However, each house will have a personal aspect when people move in with their own furniture and decor. Each of the twenty houses will be different because of this personal aspect. This is the cup and the content, the hardware and the software, the structural and constitutional aspects of the physical body.

Audrey McAllen described very clearly, with illustrations, children's drawings expressing both the stages of the structural development and the process of the work of the formative forces from the constitutional aspect in her book, *Reading Children's Drawings* (chapter 2). The following outline, given by Audrey McAllen in a lecture for educational support teachers in the Netherlands in 1988, gives an overview of the structural and constitutional elements.

Structural Physical Body	Constitutional Physical Body
Remembrance of the Old Saturn Period—warmth connects these two aspects of the human body 98.6°F (37°C).	
Forces from the zodiac	Forces from planets
Nerves, muscles, and bones	Etheric life processes, sense perception
TWOFOLD HUMAN	THREEFOLD HUMAN
Head—trunk	Thinking—feeling—willing
(Represented in left side of body)	(Represented in right side of body)

1. ——————————— 0–2.5 yrs. ———————————

Creeping, crawling, standing Spatial orientation	Development of speech between the astral and ether bodies
Self-awareness through gravity Horizontal midline barrier Will	

2. ——————————— 2.5–5 yrs. ———————————

Sidedness Symmetrical or vertical midline barrier Body geography	Creative play, playing and speaking together Social element, middle system

3. ——————————— 5–7 yrs. ———————————

Dominance	Growth into the limbs Children now need real craft work
This is represented in the drawing of the house, the twofoldness of spirit-soul and physical-life bodies.	Drawing of a human body as a picture of the threefoldness of the soul (head, chest and metabolic-limb system)
Development of skills	Development of faculties

(added by the author)

School readiness (skills are developed)	School ripeness (organs and soul are ripe)

From Audrey McAllen's notebooks

1. Here we have the two aspects: the incarnating human soul (upper triangle) and the human organization (lower triangle) created by the Hierarchies on Old Saturn, Old Sun and Old Moon.

2. When these elements interpenetrate, the human soul becomes conscious of itself.

3. To retain its consciousness of self, the human soul must penetrate the human being. It can only do this if it reflects the world.

4. The world itself is a product of Old Saturn, Old Sun, and Old Moon.

   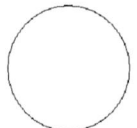

5. The world is reflected in the human being by the eye. The human soul becomes conscious of this reflection through thinking.

6. When the human soul can reflect the world, it becomes endowed with Egohood; that is, it has the possibility of knowing itself as a spiritual being among other spiritual beings. But there has been an interference. The soul does not penetrate the human being by itself; Luciferic beings also come in. The human being is dirtied and no longer reflects the world.

7. To remedy this, the World Spirit must clean the human being. First from within, that is by penetrating the human being (the Three Years of Christ after the Baptism). Then by penetrating the world (the Resurrection and Ascension).

8. The human soul becomes conscious of its own Ego being, if through its own efforts it begins to reflect the world. The world's true pattern is also in the human being; when the soul follows the world patterns laid down in the human being, it reflects the world pattern and will know itself. When the human soul goes its own way, it follows the forces of interference, becoming their prey and losing its will to their desires in return for illusionary ego experiences.

Chapter 2

Lectures on the Senses and Supersensible Currents

In the lectures given in Berlin in October 1909, mentioned earlier as being the roots of the Extra Lesson, Rudolf Steiner gave what he considered to be the foundations of anthroposophy. He started with two and a half lectures on the fundamentals of the senses; in the balance of the four lectures, he spoke of the spiritual currents forming the human physical body.

The Sense Organs

In the first two lectures, Rudolf Steiner explains how different supersensible bodies of the human being are active in the sense organs, in a different way for each organ. Those organs that are sensing the condition of the human body itself are connected with the highest spiritual members of the human being. Actually, these high spiritual members are not even individualized by the human being at this present stage of development of humankind; they are still under the guidance of high spiritual beings. This corresponds with the fact that in the human being these bodily senses are at work in the subconscious of the soul life. Generally, we are not aware of our bodily condition, our movements, and our position in space. The bodily senses that support us are: the sense of life, the sense of balance, and the sense of self-movement.

The sense of life gives us information about how we feel inside our body; how does our body fit us today? This is the feeling of being alive, the vital sense. Our highest member, Spirit Man (Rudolf Steiner in 1909 used the theosophical term *Atman*), penetrates the etheric body, controlling it by cramping it together. Through this activity, the physical body is brought into tension. As a result, the astral body of the human being is pressed out of the physical and etheric bodies, like water that is squeezed out of a sponge. It is the astral body that is connected with the soul life. In the astral body the sensations perceived through the life sense express themselves as feelings of power, exhaustion, pain, and so on. This information generally stays in the subconscious of the soul; for example, one is not aware of shoes or clothes that fit well. Likewise, information about the bodily condition usually comes into consciousness when something is not right. When in pain, one often holds the body in a contracted, cramped gesture.

In the sense of self-movement, a second high spiritual member of the human being is active: the Life Spirit (or *Buddhi*). Within the etheric body, this member brings about balance. When this balance is disturbed by a physical movement made by the human being, the Life Spirit will restore this imbalance immediately by having the astral body make a counter movement. This counterflow occurs for every movement we make. Whenever we nod our head, blink an eye, or move a leg, the astral body in the sense of self-movement will make a movement in the opposite direction. This is an important law we need to be aware of (especially when working with movement exercises) to understand the movement problems we observe. In this sense organization, most of the information from the sense of self-movement is also processed in the subconscious of the soul.

In the sense of balance, the spiritual member called Spirit Self (or *Manas*) is at work. The Spirit Self penetrates and expands the etheric body so that the astral body is able to free itself and connect with the surrounding three-dimensional physical world. The organ of the three semicircular canals in the inner ear is the physical manifestation of this expansion of the etheric body into the three directions of space. We can learn from this that the highest spiritual forces are deeply connected with the most physical and bodily elements.

In the first three years of life, the child develops and exercises these three bodily senses. The learning process of standing upright and walking depends especially on the sense of balance (vestibular system) and the sense of self-movement (proprioception)—self awareness. In Rudolf Steiner's time, the early years of the 20th century, these senses were unknown, or at least not very much researched yet. I think one may say that in those days Rudolf Steiner was ahead of time with this research on the human sensory organization.

Later in this lecture cycle, Rudolf Steiner speaks about the senses of hearing, speech, and thought. He explains that the auditory senses require more than just the ear. The ear gives us the perception of sound. To perceive spoken language, the human being develops a different sense organ: the sense of speech. The word *bus* is more than just the combination of the three different sounds B-U-S. With the word, one immediately perceives the meaning of the word. At one level higher than the sense of speech is the sense organ with which the human being perceives the concepts of a fellow human being. Sometimes we are not able to reproduce verbatim what has been said, but we can reproduce the main concept. These three auditory senses are very important to recognize and understand when one is teaching children to write and read.

Rudolf Steiner indicates that in these three senses the individuality of the human being is not active either. He describes in detail how the Angels, Archangels, and Archai work in the complex processing of listening: perceiving speech and concepts or ideas. The angels help the human being to perceive sound. They live in the element of air. The archangels, as folk spirits connected with the different languages around the world, help the human being to perceive the spoken word. They live in the fluid element of the etheric bodies. The Archai help the human being to perceive thoughts, ideas, or concepts.

Here again, Rudolf Steiner showed how detailed his insights are. Speaking about a separate sense organ for perceiving language and a separate sense organ for perceiving thought content is revolutionary—and very helpful. It can give us an idea of how deaf people can understand words and concepts through sign language. They do not need their sense of hearing for that. Not so long ago, it was thought that deaf children should not learn sign language. This policy hindered the mental development of these children enormously. It is important for teachers to learn about the three different auditory senses. They all play their part in the process of teaching a child to read and write: to learn the different sounds connected with the letters, to learn to analyze the sounds in a spoken word and write them down, to read words and analyze them, and to be able eventually to understand the concept expressed in the sentences in a book.

The six sense organs discussed so far are not penetrated by the individual or personal forces of a human being. They are all under the guidance of higher hierarchies. The middle four senses (sense of smell, sense of taste, sense of sight, and sense of warmth) are all connected with a different soul member of the individual, although the process of sensing itself takes place in the subconscious. Especially in the senses of smell, taste, and sight, we can experience how we are able to direct them personally.

Also important for the work of teachers, educational support teachers, and any other therapist is how in these lectures Rudolf Steiner explains the working of the sense of warmth. When the temperature in the room is higher than our own body temperature, we will let warmth stream into us. In a sauna the temperature is between 86° and 212°F (30°–100°C), in a Turkish bath around 113°F (45°C). As this warmth streams into our physical and etheric bodies, they expand; at the same time, the astral body streams outward in a countermovement to the instreaming warmth. If the temperature of an object we touch, or the room around us, is lower than the temperature of our body, we let warmth stream out of our body, and an astral stream goes into our body; then the physical and ether bodies contract (gooseflesh). This also happens when we go from a colder room to a warmer or vice versa. We experience the difference in temperature through the movement of our astral body that is counter to the movement of warmth. This is our inner thermometer; we only have this sense impression when warmth moves.

Working therapeutically with children, we need to take care that the room is sufficiently warm, even a bit warmer than we usually would have it. In this nice warm room, the child will be able to let warmth stream into his body, and his astral forces will stream out of his body. The child will relax, the ether body will expand, and the forces that were too strongly involved in the support of the physical body and habit patterns will begin to be released. The soul-spirit of the child will become able to penetrate the body, and the child will gradually let go of old habit patterns he held on to.

Rudolf Steiner mentions the sense of touch but in these lectures does not talk about this sense in relation to a particular organ. He says that every sense organ has an element of touch in it. In later lectures, he is more specific about this sense organ. Here he again points to the astral body making the countermovement in relation to the physical. When we touch something, our skin is pushed back a little, but the astral body will fill in this space. By doing this, the astral body feels that we are touching something.

In these 1909 lectures, Rudolf Steiner does not differentiate the ego sense as he does in a June 20, 1916 lecture on the twelve senses (published in English in *Cosmic Being and Egohood*). Instead he links it with an eleventh, twelfth, and thirteenth sense: the spiritual organs of perception—of Imagination, Inspiration, and Intuition—also called the two-petaled, sixteen-petaled, and twelve-petaled lotus flowers or chakras. He explains that when one is not clairvoyant, these senses pour their activity inward, into the inner soul life of the human being. By means of these three spiritual senses, the outer sense perceptions are processed as sensation (*Empfindung*), feeling, and formation of thoughts in the inner soul life. That is the inner processing of all sense perceptions inside the soul based on the work of these three astral sense organs. Even more subtle soul activities are brought about by the other lotus flowers or chakras.

As mentioned before, Steiner describes (*The Spiritual Guidance of the Individual and Humanity*) how in the small child (0–3 yrs) these spiritual sense organs build up the bodily system that enables the child to stand up, learn to speak, and think. When the child starts saying "I," these spiritual forces withdraw into the background. Then they play their role in the subconscious. Those who decide to follow a path of spiritual development will learn to use these same forces withdrawn into the subconscious area of the human organization. Steiner says this is the true meaning of the saying: "Truly, I say to you, unless you turn and become like children, you will never enter the kingdom of heaven." (Matt. 18:3) What we see here is that the total physical structure of the human being is built up by the highest spiritual forces that work deeply into the physical bodily organization.

In the year following his 1909 lectures in Berlin, Rudolf Steiner speaks in detail about the inner processes of the soul life. These lectures have the title "Psychosophy" and are now published as the second part of *A Psychology of Body, Soul, and Spirit*. These lectures give the fundamentals for a spiritual scientific psychology. They contain the basic elements for a picture of the soul forces of antipathy and sympathy given by Rudolf Steiner in 1919 to the teachers at the beginning of the Waldorf School in *Study of Man* (also published as *Foundations of Human Experience*).

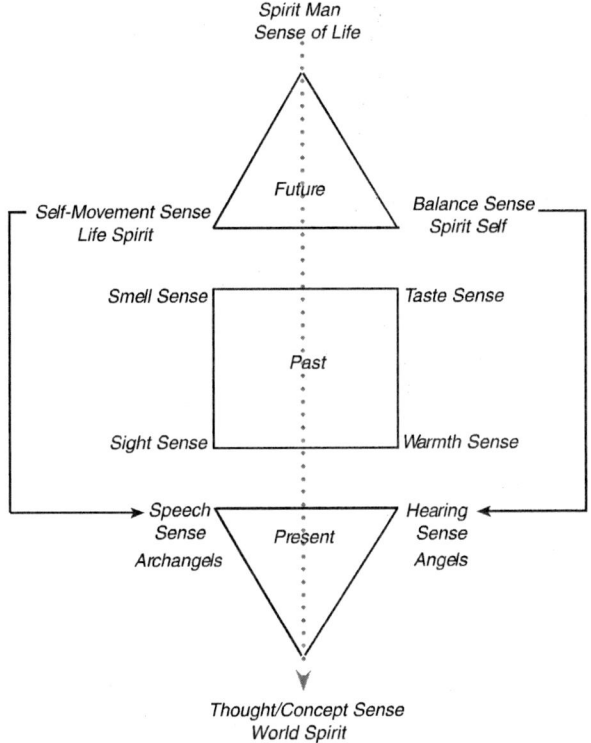

Currents Building the Physical Body

In the third and fourth lecture of the 1909 cycle, Rudolf Steiner speaks about the physical body. The physical body is the sum total of the senses. This body of senses was developed in the earliest stage of the evolution of the Earth—the Old Saturn stage. That stage was a planetary sphere of nothing but warmth. Warmth is intensive movement, intensive will, enthusiasm. The warmth was sacrificed by the Thrones; in this warmth, the Hierarchy of the Archai could live and develop their individuality. Gradually they built their own individual bodies consisting of warmth. Formative forces from the zodiac were imprinted into these bodies by higher spiritual beings. Here the seed was laid down for our special physical body with its twelvefold structure (for greater detail, see *An Outline of Esoteric Science*).

During the Old Sun stage—the second stage of evolution—light was added to the warmth of Old Saturn. It was light, together with its companion: air. Space was one-dimensional, linear as light is, as we can read in Ernst Marti's little book *The Four Ethers*. The Archangels went through a development of egohood in the Old Sun stage. By doing this, they developed the seed of the etheric body.

The third planetary stage was Old Moon. In this stage, the water element was added. Space was two-dimensional, like the surface of water or a plant leaf. Old Moon looked like spinach soup, as Steiner puts it: watery and with the beginning of the plant kingdom. We have to imagine this Old Moon plant kingdom, however, as clouds of green substance, floating in the atmosphere around the Old Moon planet, which only consisted of warmth, air, and water. The Angels now developed their individuality, preparing the astral body or inner soul life. This complex structure of astral, etheric, and physical bodies was offered to the human being in the fourth evolutionary stage: Earth. On Earth, space is three-dimensional, and the solid element is added to evolution. Now we have the four elements: warmth, light/air, water, and earth. In the Earth stage of evolution, the human being needs to develop an individuality, an ego. It is only the element of solid matter that can bring the human being self-consciousness. The free, independent human ego can only be developed during life in three-dimensional physical space on earth in a three-dimensional physical body. In this light, it is remarkable that astronauts during their long-term stay in outer space experience a deep longing and love for planet Earth. It is as if they experience that being without the Earth's gravity disconnects them from the roots of humanity.

The three-dimensional structural physical body is built up spiritually by currents. From in front streams the current of the *sentient body*, from behind the current of the *sentient soul*. The inner soul expresses itself in the face and the front side of the body. The sense organs themselves are built into the physical body by the objective outer world. As Goethe wrote, "The eye was built by the light, for the light." The eye is built according to the physical laws of the light; like a camera, it has lens, diaphragm, and a receptive medium sensitive to light at the back. That is the apparatus. The (sentient) soul makes use of this apparatus and connects itself with interest to the outside world. Plato speaks about two spiritual hands coming out of the eyes, reaching for the object. Rudolf Steiner calls this the will. Language knows the difference between the words *seeing* and *looking*.

In a similar way, the ear is built by sound from outside. The ear is like a microphone with a receptive membrane. Here, too, the sentient soul can be active in the listening process, revealing the difference between hearing and listening.

The front and back of the body show this outer and inner aspect of the senses. The sentient body, which is part of the astral body (see Rudolf Steiner, *Theosophy*), streams from the front and creates the sense organs with all that is connected to this system. The nervous system is the carrier of the astral body. The sentient soul streams from behind towards the front, passing through the senses, connecting with the outside world.

When a teacher wants to get an impression of the children's bodily condition (how they move, breathe, etc.), she had better stand at the back of the classroom and observe the children from behind. From the front, she will meet the faces of the children that will show more their inner soul life as the sentient soul streams out.

The vertical position of the human being is a result of the working of the Ego. In the early phase of earth evolution, it was the World Ego that created and prepared this vertical position of the human body. The current of the Ego streams through the body from top to bottom; as Rudolf Steiner's verse for children says, "From head to toes I am an image of God." (See Steiner, *Prayers for Parents and Children*.)

From the feet, the current of the astral body streams upward. Rudolf Steiner explains (*Karmic Relationships* II, 14) that at night when we fall asleep, the astral body spirals out of the physical body through the head. In the morning when we wake up, it penetrates the body through the toes and fingertips and it moves through the body during the day until it has reached the head and leaves the body again. Doing this, the astral body travels in a spiral movement: from below up, front to back (sentient body) and back to front (sentient soul).

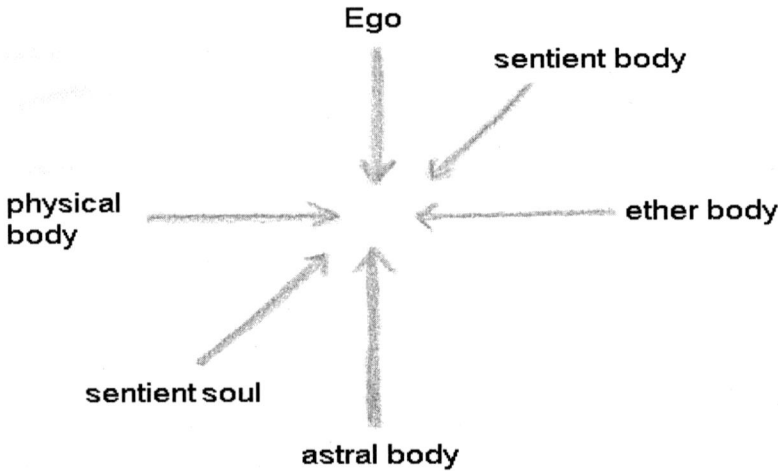

Diagram of Currents by Rudolf Steiner — 1909

The current that belongs to the physical body streams from left to right. The current of the etheric body streams from right to left. The left side of our body is stiffer than the right. The right side of the body is the more etheric, more flexible side. This is archetypal for every human being, even those who are left dominant.

Rudolf Steiner relates the structure of the human body to the structure of the earth itself. The left side of the body is built up by the same forces that have built up the northern hemisphere, with all its land masses and continents. This is the most physical side. The right side of the body is built up by the same forces that have built up the southern hemisphere with the largest portions of the Pacific, Atlantic, and Indian oceans. Our vertical midline can be compared with the earth's equator.

The East, from which the sun rises up to the zenith, is connected with the stream of the Ego that lifts us into the vertical. As mentioned before, it was the World Ego that prepared the vertical position of the human body, the World Ego that had His domicile on the Sun. In this context, it is very remarkable that churches, cathedrals, temples, and synagogues are oriented towards the East. Even the word "to orient" means looking toward the East. Old medieval maps had the East on top and not the North as we have now. Of course, these spiritual laws and insights were known in olden times, in the religious mystery centers all over the world. In anthroposophy, they are made accessible for our modern intellectual consciousness.

Since the human body is in an upright position, the forces of the Ego organization can penetrate the blood, because the flow of the blood is vertical. This is in contrast to the direction of the blood in all animals. In the animal kingdom, the blood stream is horizontal, so the individual forces of an Ego organization cannot penetrate it. The animals share their Ego as group soul.

In the human being, the Ego organization starts to work into the other supersensible bodies and transforms them. The first transformation that will take place will be of the astral body. Therefore we see the three currents that have to do with the astral forces of the soul: astral body, sentient body, and sentient soul. If we picture this as a diagram, we will find that these three astral elements will move as a spiral; from below up, front to back, and back to front; the Ego will be the spine of this spiralling movement. From folk dancing, we know the dance around the maypole in all kinds of variations. This maypole dancing is an outer archetypal picture of what is happening spiritually when the astral body with its three aspects moves through the physical and life bodies during the day, having the Ego as a spine.  One can really see this maypole as a picture of how the human spine was created by the spiritual currents building up the human body.

Rudolf Steiner pointed out that the form of every single organ can be explained by analyzing how all the different currents are moving in relation to one another. He says that the heart is formed by the different currents in a perfect balance. From embryology, we learn that the blood is already circulating before the heart is fully developed and able to pump it. In the different developmental stages of the heart chambers, we can see how the supersensible currents gradually build the septum. (See König, *Embryology and World Evolution*.)

In the embryo, the intestines are built spirally, with clockwise and counterclockwise movements of the astral body. The small tube that will become the intestine is curved around two centers, spiraling in a counterclockwise direction (from the onlooker's point of view; for the embryo itself, it would be clockwise).

The eye and the brain are constructed by similar currents, according to Rudolf Steiner. Both are organs protected and isolated in a bony cave. In the eye, however, the current of the sentient body, coming from the front, has pushed the brain matter towards the back of the organ. This became the retina. A watery, transparent glass organ was created instead of the brain matter. This is how the eye was built.

The forces of the Ego organization also transform the currents of the etheric and physical bodies. Through this activity, the *intellectual soul* and *consciousness soul* are developed. The intellectual soul is that part of our inner life that creates an inner picture of what is perceived by the senses. Judgment is affected by the intellectual soul. This can be an intellectual picture but also an inner feeling. The German term for this part of the soul is *Verstandes-Gemütsseele*, the soul that contains intellect and feelings. The intellectual soul can never be objectively connected with the sense impressions, for this soul element cannot pour itself into the outer world. It is dammed up by the skull. In the intellectual soul, we can make mistakes. We cannot make mistakes in the sentient soul. The grey matter of the brain is formed by and is a vessel for the consciousness soul.

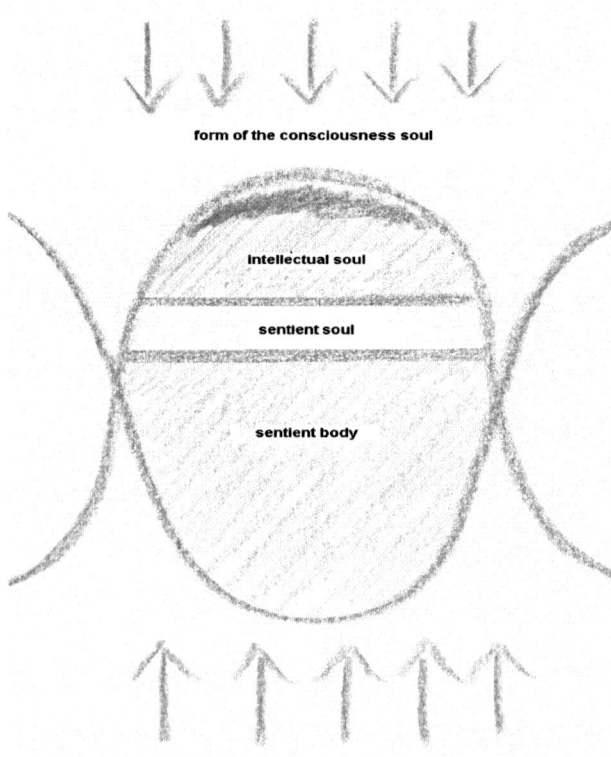

Currents Forming the Nervous System and Brain

In this second diagram, Rudolf Steiner gives a picture of the whole structure of the nervous system. The primitive sympathetic nervous system, which we share with the lower animal forms like the starfish and jellyfish, is down in the belly. Here we are totally connected with the outer world; no inner picture is produced. Could this be connected with the solar plexus? This is the sentient body.

The sentient soul pours itself out into the world through the senses and is also connected with the creation of the bodily forms that support the inner life. Therefore, the spine and the part of the nervous system located in it are formed by the sentient soul. The intellectual soul is higher up in the brain behind the forehead. The consciousness soul is connected with the forms and activities of the cortex.

Movement Patterns in the Human Being

Certain patterns of movement are determined by the structure of the human body. The limbs that are used for locomotion connect themselves with gravity, with the earth's surface. In relation to the hip, where the leg is connected with the torso, the feet will always walk with a slight inward swing. Although one is aware of walking in a straight line, the feet will always swing inward; that is, the right foot moves counterclockwise, and the left foot moves clockwise.

When the human being moves on four limbs, like a baby crawling, the movement of the arms will be similar to that of the legs. As soon as the human being is standing upright, hands and arms have the ability to move opposite to the movement patterns of the feet. The arms are lifted out of gravity as they are no longer needed for locomotion. They can be used for other gestures: for using tools, for playing, for doing work, and for expressing one's feelings. The hands move to underline the expression of our inner life when we speak. In eurythmy, we can see the hands do the most spiritual gestures we know. Here, the internal movements of the speech organs are made visible. In eurythmy, the audible becomes visible.

Stretching and Lifting

We already mentioned the lifting out of gravity to come into uprightness and its effect on the movement pattern of the hands. Audrey McAllen made a small diagram to show the archetypal movements of the feet and hands on left and right sides of the body.

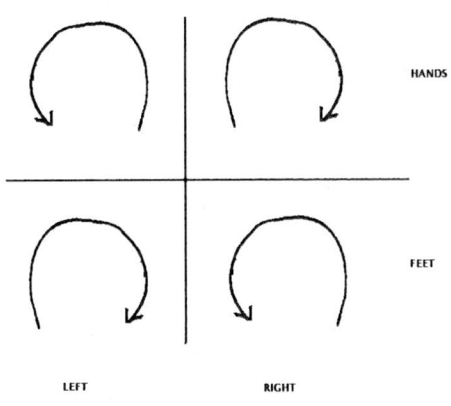

Archetypal Movement Patterns of Hands and Feet

Audrey named all movements that connect with gravity *stretching movements*. The legs and feet are connecting with the earth's surface and gravity. We need stretching movements for locomotion. These movement patterns are caused by the relation between the bones and joints of hips, legs, and feet. Although we are walking a straight line, the hips will move in a lemniscate pattern and the feet will make inward movements in relation to the upper leg and hip. Animals and small children crawling use these inward turning movement gestures in all four members. It cannot be done otherwise.

The human being standing upright has arms and hands freed from the activity of locomotion. The movement patterns of the arms and hands can therefore be in patterns counter to those of the legs and feet. It is the higher Ego (via the senses of balance and self-movement) that is lifting the human being into the vertical. The movement patterns for arms and hands Audrey McAllen named *lifting movements*. Those readers familiar with the Extra Lesson exercises will immediately recognize in the above diagram the patterns of movement used in the Threefold Spiral, Ball Twirling, and Wool Winding exercises.

The stretching movement system is that part of our movement system that responds to the outer sense impressions. When the alarm clock rings in the morning, one awakens, and the first movement reaction is to stretch. When one is tired but still wants to continue working or reading, one will lean back and stretch the muscles of the back, arms, and legs. Even yawning is stretching the muscles. Also, in cases when we need to use force, we use stretching movements, for through these stretching movements we enter into, experience, and create a relationship with gravity.

The child's movement development in the first year, with all the immature movement patterns, could be seen as a lengthy development of the stretching movement system. The astral body (sentient body) is incarnating and penetrating the physical body and is at work in this movement system, together with the sentient soul that is reacting from within to the outer sense impressions. When the child tries to stand up, the ego forces of the child lift the body out of the pull of gravity. A second system of muscles needs to come into action and needs to be practiced. From that time on, the subtle interplay between stretching and lifting movements takes place. Too strong sensory input from the environment or too early lifting into the vertical with the help of artificial aids (including well-meaning adults holding the infant under the arms so it can put weight on its feet) will create excess stimulus of the stretching system of the young child, together with a weakening of the lifting system.

We will recognize these archetypal movements when we observe activities such as cleaning the blackboard or washing windows. When doing this, one will move in lemniscate (figure eight) patterns. Whipping cream will be in a lifting movement pattern. In polishing the furniture or car with wax or stirring a heavy dough, however, we need to use more energy. Then we cannot use the lifting movements of the arms and hands. We need to go into gravity and use the stretching movement system of the arms with patterns similar to the archetypal movements of feet and legs. So in the arms, we see the possibility of using both stretching and lifting movements.

Even when we look at the subtle movements of fingers and thumbs, we will recognize the movement pattern shown above. The right thumb will, at a certain stage of movement development, take over the task of the left hand. The child will be able to use thumb and fingers in opposition. The archetypal movement of the thumbs is similar to that of the opposite hand. This pattern is used in Extra Lesson exercises such as Wool Winding, Ball Twirling, and Thumb Twirling.

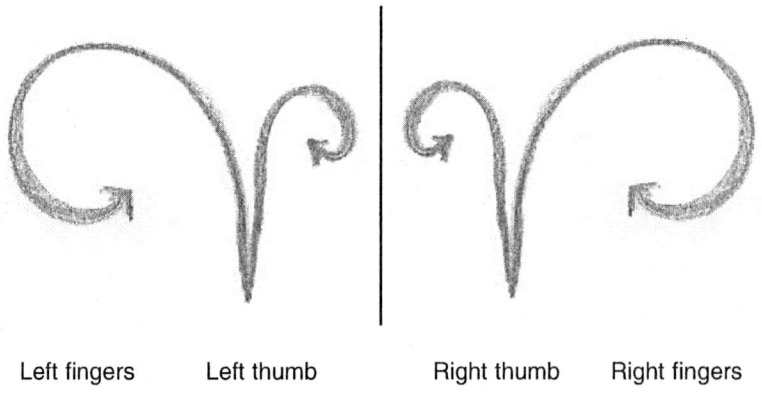

Left fingers   Left thumb   Right thumb   Right fingers

Currents in the Earth

The earth itself—like the human being—also has currents of Ego, astral, etheric, and physical bodies. We can think of the polestar, Polaris, as a stable anchor above the earth's North Pole, similar to the Southern Cross that moves around the point where the South Pole is located. This immediately gives us the key where to picture the current of the earth's Ego and the current of the earth's astral body. The North Pole with the icecap is like the skull of the earth with a fontanel. Indeed the bottom of the ocean under the North Pole ice is shaped like a deep funnel. Antarctica is the soil for the Earth being to stand on with its feet.

The West—the right side of this Earth being—is the current of the etheric body; the East is the left side—the current of the physical body. This is a mirroring of the picture of the currents in the human being—as in a flat mirror at an angle of 45°. We then look at the earth as astronauts do, from an onlooker's point of view.

In the currents of the oceans, we discover spiralling movements. The ocean currents are caused by the rotation of the earth. The earth's equator is 24,800 mi (40.000 km) long. This means that in 24 hours the earth is rotating at a speed of 1033 mph (1667 km/h). Near the two poles, this rotation speed is much slower. In the Northern Hemisphere, the currents in the oceans spiral clockwise, as in the Sargasso Sea in the middle of the North Atlantic Ocean, where the Gulf Stream originates. In the Southern Hemisphere, the ocean currents move counterclockwise.

Similar spiral patterns are visible in the movements of the air. High and low pressure areas move in clockwise and counterclockwise spiralling motions. In the Northern Hemisphere, the highs move clockwise while the lows move counterclockwise. Hurricanes are extreme low pressure areas caused by the high temperature of the ocean water in tropical zones. The warmed air rises and starts rotating counterclockwise. At high altitudes, the air spirals out into the periphery in a clockwise direction. The geometrical form is a vortex. (Note that for tropical cyclones in the southern hemisphere, these movement directions are reversed. This is because the winds swirl clockwise south of the equator.) The earth's rotation eastward makes hurricanes move westward. Farther north, the jet stream transports them toward the east. In the center of a hurricane, there is no wind at all but clear sky with clear weather. This center is called the eye of the hurricane. Note that the words *eye* and *I* sound alike in English. Like the previously mentioned maypole dance, the hurricane gives us an image of the interplay between the astral body and the Ego spiraling in and out.

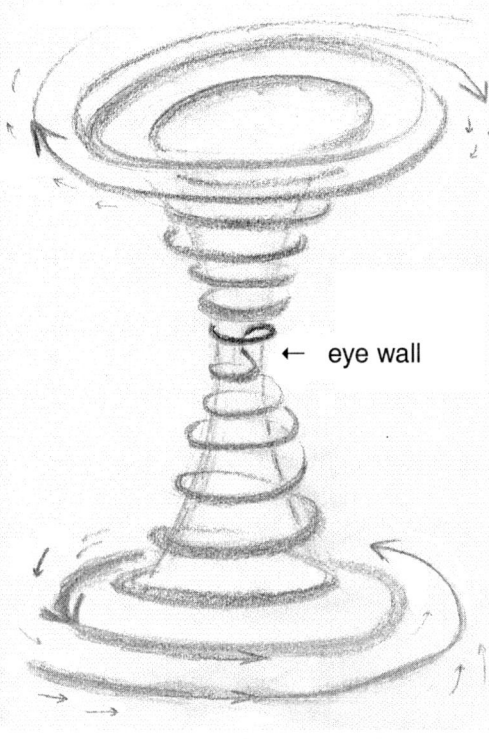

Theodor Schwenck's book *Sensitive Chaos* and John Wilkes' book *Flow Forms: The Rhythmic Power of Water* have beautiful illustrations and diagrams showing the creative principles in nature and in the movements of air and water.

In the last part of the 1909 lectures described at the beginning of this chapter, Rudolf Steiner speaks about the development of speech and memory in relation to the migration of human beings. He points out that it was necessary for people to migrate from ancient Lemuria into Atlantis to develop the speech organs. In ancient Atlantis the human being learned speech. The next stage was to develop the ability to understand the ideas within the spoken words. Therefore another migration toward the east was needed. All world mythology tells the story of this migration led by a great initiate (Noah, Manu, Utnapishtim, Deucalion). In the post-atlantean cultural epochs, we see the movement from the east toward the west (from India to Persia to Egypt-Babylon to Greece and Rome). The human soul needed to develop the ability to hold a pure concept; therefore, this cultural wandering toward the west was necessary.

In the "Psychosophy" lectures of 1910 (*A Psychology of Body, Soul, and Spirit* Part II), Rudolf Steiner is speaking of the currents in relation to time rather than space. The basic impulse of time is related to the movement of the sun, the moon, and the stars. Each day begins when the sun rises in the east and ends when the sun sets in the west. The movement of the sun is the earth's clockwork. East and west, although they are spatial directions, also carry a quality of time. One cannot really find a fixed spot on the earth that marks east and west, in contrast to north and south that are fixed at the geographical poles.

With the beginning of each day, new impulses come from the east with the rising sun, from the land of the future called Shambhala. In the west where the sun and stars set, time finds its ending, in the land of the past called Kamaloca—the land of the dead.

When we look at historical events from this perspective, we may ask: Why did Alexander the Great have the inner drive to go to the east? Was he only looking for the Ancient Mysteries, or was he looking for new impulses? Why did Henry the Navigator send out his knights to find Prester John in eastern realms? Why did Christopher Columbus have a hard time keeping the crew of his three vessels heading west? Were they afraid of going to the land of the dead?

Another aspect Rudolf Steiner mentions at the end of these lectures is the direction of writing. We write from left to right, from above to below, and even in the single letters we emphasize these writing directions. This is all connected with the development of the intellectual soul, the effect of the Ego working against the current of the ether body. The Arabic and Hebrew writing from right to left, which is also the direction we work in when doing arithmetic, is connected with the development of the consciousness soul, the effect of the Ego working against the current of the physical body. This is interesting to consider when one is working with students who are having problems in reading and writing.

Chapter 3

Right-angled Triangle and Threefold Spiral Exercises

In the last chapter we looked at the supersensible currents that build up the human body and the body of the earth itself. The reader who is familiar with the Extra Lesson exercises will have recognized the movement patterns in several exercises, such as the Threefold Spiral, Wool Winding, and Ball Twirling. You can also see the movement patterns in the beanbag exercises by Mary Nash-Wortham and Jean Hunt (see *Take Time*). Jean Hunt, who is a therapeutic eurythmist, developed these exercises out of the rod exercises given by Rudolf Steiner to the first eurythmy teachers in the Stuttgart Waldorf School. These rod exercises were given for pedagogical eurythmy, although they are often used also in therapeutic eurythmy. In her work with children, Jean Hunt found that many children nowadays simply cannot orient themselves in space and lack body awareness. She looked for a way to make the children more skillful and worked out these beanbag exercises as a series to perform before doing the eurythmy rod exercises.

When my first grade class began in 1999 (my third cycle), the children appeared to be more awake intellectually than I had experienced in previous years. They were also very awkward in catching a ball and jumping rope. They had a hard time with the first of the beanbag exercises of simple throwing and catching. After six weeks of practice on the whole series of exercises, the children were more skillful and centered.

I. Right-angled Triangle Exercise

Audrey McAllen developed the Right-angled Triangle exercise for children 12 years old and above. This exercise is meant to harmonize the child's movement patterns. With the Handedness Assessment, the educational support—or remedial—teacher may have noticed problems the child has with movement directions, dominance or choice of limbs, chaotic tracing patterns and restlessness, and unrhythmical breathing. How does the Right-angled Triangle exercise help? Let us look at the exercise in relation to different aspects of the human being, such as threefoldness and fourfoldness.

Muscles, Skeleton and Nervous System (Structural Body)

Sitting down on the floor for this exercise, moving the feet above the level of the hips, will drive the conscious and sensory activity towards the legs, feet, arms, and eyes. One will start to experience the muscles of the upper leg, lower back, and belly. Breathing is strongly affected because this is a strenuous, fatiguing exercise. The rhythmical movement of the spinal fluid is influenced in several ways: The rhythm of the breathing is influenced and the breathing is deepened by the movements and pauses. The rhythmical movements of the ribs are transferred to the spinal column. Moving while sitting on the sacrum also affects the rhythmic flow of the spinal fluid. This spinal fluid will circulate up and down the spine, up into the skull and around the brain, and thus stimulate the activity of the nervous system. Working with the breathing is most important in any healing process. This applies to medical therapies, art therapy, movement therapy, and also education. One of the main goals of a spiritual approach to education is to teach children to breathe properly. By nature, breathing is connected with the metabolic system. Through education, it needs to be brought into connection with the nerve-sense system (see Rudolf Steiner, *Foundations of Human Experience* lecture 1). We will discuss this further when we deal with the Copper Ball exercise.

For the Right-angled Triangle exercise, we have the child sit on the floor in front of the chart with the right triangle. Once a 13-year-old boy asked me why on earth he was doing this exercise. I explained:

> First your legs will do the movement exercise and then the legs will teach your arms and eyes the movements. Then your arms will teach your eyes how to move. And at the end your one eye has to do the whole movement sequence on its own. The eye will learn all possible movements there are: from left to right, up, down, and diagonal. It will trace straight lines but will move in circular patterns at the same time. We have these possibilities in writing and reading. When you are reading your eyes move around the letters and lines and imitate the movements in a very subtle way. This is how your eyes are able to perceive the letter forms. In this exercise, we are practicing the flexibility of your eyes.

He accepted this explanation. The exercise moves according to one of the basic principles of Waldorf education: going from the limbs—through the rhythmic system—into the head. Here we find the aspect of threefoldness.

Threefold Picture

Each of the four charts has a right-angled triangle drawn on it, which needs to be traced in a specific sequence. In a lecture cycle called *The Mystery of the Universe* (also published as *Man: Hieroglyph of the Universe*), Rudolf Steiner speaks about the significance of the vertical, horizontal, and diagonal line. When we draw or see a vertical line, in the soul this immediately calls on the thinking activity. Thinking occurs in the coordination between the left and right sides of the body. The horizontal line calls on our feeling life. The middle system of the feeling life lives between the head and the trunk. The diagonal, which in two-dimensional space represents going into the third dimension, gives a picture of going into the distance. This element immediately calls on our will forces. Thus, in every triangle chart that we give the child to trace, we call on thinking, feeling, and willing activities. Rudolf Kutzli's book *Creative Form Drawing* perfectly describes the effect of the use of vertical, horizontal, and diagonal lines in the graphic arts and form drawing.

Fourfold Picture

The right-angled triangle relates to the Pythagorean Theorem. The Greek philosopher and mathematician Pythagoras (ca. 560–480 BC) traveled to Egypt and Babylon and was initiated into the Egyptian and Babylonian mysteries where he learned about the sacred mathematics of the universe. Pythagoras brought this knowledge to Europe, settling in Crotone, a Greek colony in southern Italy. Plato was the first to mention this mystery wisdom of the geometric solids—the so-called five Platonic solids—in his *Timaeus*. The basic root of the Pythagorean Theorem is the picture of the three Egyptian gods: Osiris, Isis, and Horus.[1] These three names were used for the squares constructed on the three sides of the right-angled triangle. The complete construction of the Pythagorean Theorem gives a visual picture of the fourfold human being. The square on the vertical is Osiris, the physical body. The square on the horizontal is Isis, the etheric body; the square on the hypotenuse is Horus, the astral body (the soul). The three together enclose the triangle, which is like a cup into which the Ego is able to incarnate. This picture—the fourfold human being—we carry as historical memory in our subconscious, brought to us by the forces of heredity. Sometimes we see it appear in drawings by kindergarten children. They often draw their houses with the chimney slanting out from the roof (see McAllen, *Reading Children's Drawings*). One may find two symmetrical chimneys on the roof, as a picture of the symmetrical developmental stage they are in. At the same time, this gives the image of the three squares constructed around the triangle. Taken together with the square in the lower part of the house, these three squares around the right triangle are an expression of this subconscious memory of the Pythagorean Theorem.

We see the memory of the Pythagorean Theorem pop up in the Middle Ages, when Henry the Navigator had the inspiration to combine the square sail of the northern Europeans with the triangular sail of the Arabs. This combination led the sailor's gaze toward the horizon. This was the beginning of the Age of Exploration and the Renaissance.

When we look at the set of four charts for the exercise as a unity, we will discover the directions of the spiritual currents building up the human body as described in chapter 2. Moving our limbs (see diagram opposite for exercise A), tracing the first arrow down, will activate the current of the Ego. Moving from right to left will activate the current of the etheric

Countermovements Generated in the Right-angled Triangle Exercises

body. Diagonals activate the sentient body and sentient soul. Likewise, the movements following all other arrows in the exercise will activate the connected currents.

The effect will be in the sense of self-movement as the astral body makes the countermovement (see chapter 2 and Steiner's 1909 lectures). We can picture what will happen in the astral body when we make a drawing of the countermovements on the first chart of this Right-angled Triangle exercise for right handers. On the first chart A, we move down with arrow #1. The astral body will make the countermovement, which is upwards. Then we move arrow #2, which is from right to left, and the astral body will move from left to right. The diagonal #3 goes up to the right, and the astral body will go down to the left. As we continue, we see that the astral body is moving in a continuous spiraling clockwise direction.

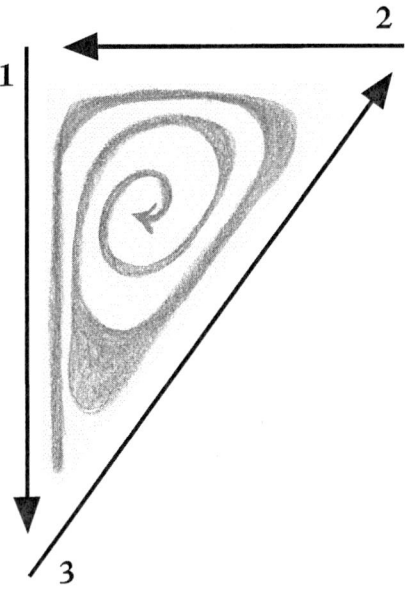

When we draw this for all four charts (the version for the right side), we will discover that, hidden behind this set of four Pythagorean triangles, there is a continuous clockwise spiralling of the astral body. Doing the exercise, one moves one's physical limbs in a certain sequence according to the given patterns. The result is that the supersensible astral body starts spiraling in the correct archetypal direction—that is, clockwise. The correct movement direction of the astral body as a whole—and for the right side of the body specifically—is clockwise. Clockwise astral countermovements to the counterclockwise physical movements make us aware of our physical movement by means of the sense of self-movement.

We can see an illustration of these archetypal movement patterns in the movements of the sun and moon around the earth. Sun and moon both rise in the east and set in the west after a clockwise journey around the earth's sphere (seen from the Northern Hemisphere). Yet we know that it is the earth itself that is turning in a counterclockwise direction from west towards the east. Sun and moon make visible the countermovement of what is really happening.

In this teaching exercise, we need to pause after every movement. What is the importance of this pause? We have learned that, whenever we make a physical movement, the astral body through the sense of self-movement is making the countermovement, and we have seen how this is taken up in this exercise. The Ego organization, however, needs to be able to find the proper movement sequence in the physical and astral body. The Ego will imprint these healthy movement patterns into the etheric body. The etheric body stores our habit patterns and memory. During the pause, the astral body is given time to relax and complete its countermovement, and the Ego organization can imprint this into the memory system of the etheric body. Here this new habit pattern will become active during sleep and will start building up new and healthy movement patterns for use during waking hours.

Making pauses is something very important in education in general. After saying the morning verse, the class teacher will keep her class quiet and wait for a little while so that the words of the verse have time to "fly out of the window" and are imprinted in the children's memory. In our modern times, we hardly take time to rest and digest what we have experienced. We rush from one event to the next. Young children during the years from birth till seven especially suffer from restlessness. In Waldorf education, we need to be aware of how things are imprinted into the etheric bodies of the children. Restlessness and chaos will often have already affected the children's etheric life forces in an unhealthy way. Calmness and pauses will cure the restlessness and heal the children. In kindergarten and in the lower grades, this principle is especially important. After the change of teeth—from seven till fourteen—teachers educate the etheric bodies of the children. This is done by teaching them good habits by repetition, restfulness, and grace in movement. The best educators of the etheric body are the arts and religion. The danger even in Waldorf schools is that teachers in the primary school already focus on the astral body that will be awakened too early by our modern civilization.

The Picture of the Currents

Those who have studied the diagrams Rudolf Steiner gave in the 1909 lectures will have found those currents in the Right-angled Triangle exercise. Every current is used twice. In chart A, we find the Ego current, the etheric current, and the current of the sentient body. Tracing one arrow of the exercise will activate the particular current. We can compare this exercise with the sevenfold rod exercise Rudolf Steiner gave to the first eurythmists of the Stuttgart Waldorf School. This exercise activates the different currents of the six directions in three-dimensional space. It harmonizes the structure of the physical body. The Right-angled Triangle exercise does the same in two-dimensional space. It is important to notice that reading and writing are always connected with the two-dimensional space of the paper. The experience of three-dimensional space needs to become translated into the two-dimensional. In writing or reading letters or numbers, students often have trouble dealing with the diagonal line, which is the line of perspective going backward and forward, the line of will. This line in the letter forms will become mirrored. Trouble with curved lines, for instance in the number 5 or the letter D, shows us the same mirroring difficulty. The curved line can be seen as a diagonal will line.

The Archetypal Picture

In the Right-angled Triangle exercise, we have the children move the Pythagorean right triangle, which is an archetypal picture of the total of the bodies of the human being, rooted in the ancient mysteries. Behind this picture, which the child will perceive through the eyes, are hidden the supersensible currents that build up the child's structural physical body. The child moves the physical body, and through these movements, the astral body is taught to move correctly.

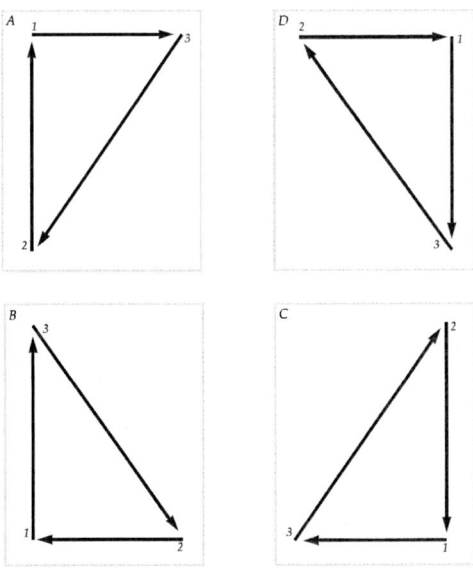

Right-angled Triangle Exercise
for a Left-sided Student

The sides of the triangles in the charts are in the ratio of 3:4:5. Why are the measurements of the charts in the book that precise? This ratio is the principle of the Egyptian twelve-knot rope, a tool that was used in agriculture and architecture for constructing right angles. It nearly equals the ratio of the triangle based on $\sqrt{1} - \sqrt{2} - \sqrt{3}$, which fits inside a cube.

The Right-angled Triangle exercise, as my German colleague Uta Stolz once expressed it, is a 20-minute meditation on the structural physical body (see chapter 2) and its movement system. Just tracing the lines of the following figures will give you the complete picture of this structural physical movement

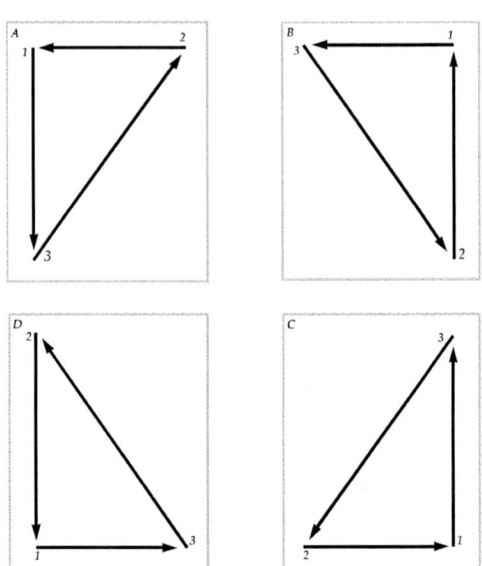

Right-angled Triangle Exercise
for a Right-sided Student

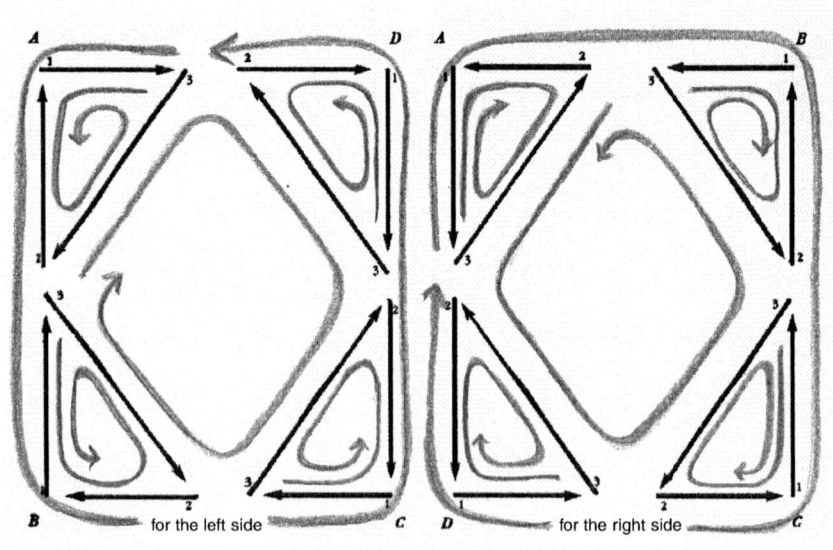

Overview of the Countermovements

system on the left and right sides of the body. In the vertical lines that form rectangles, one will discover the stretching movements of both sides of the body. Tracing the directions of movement of the diagonal lines will give one a picture of the lifting movements, clockwise on the right side, counterclockwise on the left side. Tracing the diagonals of the combined left and right charts will show one the lemniscate movement, which is an archetypal picture of the movements of the astral body. In their simplicity, all eight charts of the exercise form a unity, a complete archetypal picture of the architecture of the structural human body.

Colors

Is there something to say about the colors chosen? In the choice of colors, Audrey tried to find an archetypal wholeness as well. Looking at the complete set of charts, one will find that the arrows on top and on the left of a chart are blue; the arrows on the right and the bottom are carmine red. They are the archetypal colors for the left and the right eye and connected with the Eye Color Affinity (see chapter 6). For the two triangles where we have blue and red on the horizontal and vertical lines, Audrey chose yellow for the diagonal line. Blue, red and yellow give a threefold picture of the soul forces of thinking, willing, and feeling.

The other two charts of the set of four have either two blue arrows or two red arrows on the horizontal and vertical lines. Here the diagonal lines have the complementary colors—orange with the blue lines and green with the red lines. In this way, every single chart was constructed as a unity within the complete exercise.

Age

This exercise is for children (and adults) from twelve years up. Children in sixth grade, when they are twelve, will start to experience their bony system in a new way. Their limbs will start growing, the first sign that puberty is coming. They will experience the weight of their arms and legs and of their whole physical system. Their condition has changed from the state of the eleven-year-old fifth grader who lived more in the muscle system of the body, like the ancient Greek—and still had grace of movement and beauty of bodily appearance.

Compared to a fifth grader, the sixth grader is more physical, like the ancient Romans. The Waldorf curriculum addresses this new developmental stage of soul by introducing natural science, mechanics, and geometry. The right angle is also connected with the Roman culture.

One can think of the way the Roman army was drawn up in battle-array. In the Americas, we find the memory of this culture in the typical city architecture with right-angled patterns of streets and blocks.

The Right-angled Triangle exercise is built on archetypal pictures of the fourfold and threefold human organization. With the physical movements done in this exercise, the astral currents in the movement system of the body are harmonized. Dominance or symmetry can be strengthened; the breathing system will be rhythmically activated. The activities of the lower (bodily) senses will become integrated in the subconscious, where they can support the day-wake soul life in a healthy way. For adults, the Right-angled Triangle exercise has appeared to be a great help when one is suffering from jetlag after a long plane flight.

II. Threefold Spiral Exercise

In younger children, the bodily movement system is not mature enough to manage the Right-angled Triangle exercise. For strengthening the development of dominance, the educational support or remedial teacher can use the Dominance Form (*The Extra Lesson* 130) or "Snail Trail" as colleagues call the exercise. This exercise has the same movement sequence as the Right-angled Triangle exercise with the horizontal, vertical, and diagonal lines in the different directions and even loops to be traced.

For harmonizing the movement of the astral body through the physical and life bodies, one can use the Threefold Spiral exercise. Here we have a chart on the floor with a large red clockwise spiral. This spiral is the picture of how the astral body moves through the physical and life bodies during the day. The child traces the red spiral with the feet and right hand following the archetypal movement directions. In the left hand, which rests on the left thigh, the child holds a copper ball, a crystal, or a precious stone of some weight.

In contrast to the Right-angled Triangle exercise, in the Threefold Spiral, the archetypal spiral of the astral body is made visible. The young child will move limbs and the whole physical body according to the archetypal movement patterns. The effect on the astral body in the sense of self-movement is similar to that in the Right-angled Triangle exercise: the astral body will start spiraling in the correct direction, mirroring the physical movements on an astral level (see concave mirroring in chapter 9).

Why does the left hand not take part in the movement exercise but only hold an object? To find the answer, one can think of another exercise: the Ball Twirling exercise (*Extra Lesson* 125). This exercise is built on the same principles as the Threefold Spiral and harmonizes the astral body to spiral correctly through the physical and life bodies. Here, too, we move only three of our limbs: two hands and either one or the other foot. We need one foot to stand on. Through this foot we connect ourselves with gravity. The Threefold Spiral has this same picture.

The Ego needs to connect with gravity—with the physical element The Ego has an affinity for the physical body (see Steiner, *Discussions with Teachers* lecture 5), while the astral body has an affinity for the etheric body. The Ego current from above connects with the physical current from the left. The current of the astral body, coming from below, connects with the etheric current from the right (see diagram of currents, chapter 2, p. 22). The left side of the body is less flexible than the right side, even with lefthanders. In this Threefold Spiral exercise, an archetypal picture of movement and spiritual architecture of the body is offered to the child.

The Threefold Spiral has proved to be very helpful for children who have problems with falling asleep, nightmares, and bed wetting. Also restlessness and nervousness can be relieved. The class teacher can also use it as a single exercise in the classroom or as homework after instruction with one of the parents present during the exercise to see it done correctly.

In several cases where children needed to bang and rock their heads to fall asleep, this exercise appeared to be a cure. One can feel that, through this exercise, the astral bodies of the children learned how to penetrate and leave their physical bodies in a proper way. For young children also, this Threefold Spiral exercise can be a great help after a long journey by airplane.

As Rudolf Steiner explains in *Karmic Relationships* (v. 2, lecture 14, June 22, 1924), the astral body starts to penetrate the physical body at the moment of awakening through the finger tips and the toes. The nervous system and the brain only mirror this, and day-wake consciousness begins. During the day the astral body is spiraling up towards the head. At about 6 pm the astral body will arrive in the head, the area of the eyes. Maybe that is why Leonardo da Vinci painted his portraits at this hour of the day. The inner light of the eyes of his models was the best around that time. In the outer world the light of the sun is the best around about 6 pm to make landscape photographs (7 pm in summer).

When we fall asleep, the astral body leaves the head and spreads out into the astral world during the night. This archetypal rhythmical breathing process is taught to the astral body of the individual child through this exercise.

---

1 Daniel van Bemmelen, *Het eerste Goetheanum*, Uitgeverij Vrij Geestesleven, Zeist, The Netherlands 1979

Chapter 4

Two Painting Exercises

The art of painting addresses the soul. What we perceive as outer colors is connected with the feeling life of our soul. Through the use of colors in the exercises, the soul becomes active, especially when one is using watercolor paint mixed with water on dampened paper. Work with color engages the astral body, and the astral body works into the etheric life processes and the physical body. In painting, the working goes from an inner soul movement toward movement in the life and physical processes.

The following two exercises are connected with the movement system of the human body and therefore with the Right-angled Triangle and the Threefold Spiral exercises. Other painting exercises that we will cover later more strongly address the inner element of the soul life in a moral sense.

I. Blue-Red Spiral Exercise

Looking at shape and form, one can easily see a resemblance between the Right-angled Triangle and Threefold Spiral exercises and the two painting exercises: Blue-Red Perspective and Blue-Red Spiral. One will recognize the archetypal spiral form in the Blue-Red Spiral painting exercise for younger children and the archetypal combination of vertical, horizontal, and diagonal lines in the Blue-Red Perspective exercise for older children. Having studied the background of the Right-angled Triangle exercise, one can already start to suppose that hidden behind the straight lines of the Blue-Red Perspective exercise there will be a spiral movement archetypal to the movement of the astral body, and so there is.

The use of the two colors blue and red leaps to the eyes. They are the archetypal representatives of the two soul forces of antipathy and sympathy, which are important forces in the formation of the body of the child during the first seven years. The force of antipathy forms the bones, skeleton, and the nervous system; the force of sympathy connects itself with the blood and the metabolic system. However, in the first seven years of the child's life these forces of sympathy work in strong connection with the formative (antipathy) forces from the head down. After the change of teeth, the formative forces of antipathy and sympathy will be partly freed from their bodily functioning and will begin to play a role in the life of soul as the forces of thinking and willing. We will go deeper into this subject in chapter 6 on the Eye Color Affinity.

As mentioned before: in working with all exercises, one should pay careful attention to the student's breathing. The Blue-Red Spiral exercise starts with covering the paper with one wash of paint, working from left to right in long strokes. This simple technique does not address the student's artistic qualities; that is not the intention. Rudolf Steiner gave the advice to certain Dornach artists, who wanted to develop an anthroposophical painting therapy, to just paint in long strokes of one color. This advice was a very drastic one to these artistic individuals. It was as drastic as Rudolf Steiner's advice to Lory Maier-Smits, who wanted to develop a new form of art in movement and dance. Rudolf Steiner told her to start writing and drawing with her foot. Lory Maier-Smits did this and later became the first eurythmist.

This painting technique helps to teach the eye to control the hand movements. In Rudolf Steiner's words: "the eye should lovingly follow the hand." This is what we need to teach our students nowadays—proper eye-hand coordination.

The technique of painting long strokes also addresses the rhythm of the breathing system. There is no nervous brushing to and fro across the paper. The eyes watch the movements of the hand and brush; the hand and arm move quietly from left to right, and the rib cage expands and contracts in time with that motion. This will harmonize the dynamic of the astral body and bring the astral body into a better connection with the etheric body of life forces.

Because he is sitting down while painting, the student will start to experience the weight of his arm and sometimes will start complaining about some muscle aching. This is all part of the exercise and therefore important for the teacher to notice. It is a sign that the student starts experiencing unknown and unused parts of his physical body. Have him relax the arm for a few seconds and gently encourage him to continue.

Then we add the shape of the spiral to the background color. Always use the clockwise spiral for right-handed as well as for left-handed children. With the blue spirals, one always starts from the periphery, going clockwise towards the center. Blue is the color of the periphery. The red spirals always start in the middle. Red is the color that concentrates in a center and has a centripetal movement. Thus one paints the red spiral going counterclockwise towards the periphery. In the end, both blue and red spirals will be the same shape. Because of this alternation, at the end of the sequence, both left-handed and right-handed children will have done similar movement patterns. The technique of painting the spiral by holding the brush with the fingertips without turning it, forces the student to turn the wrist and forearm, lift the arm, turn back, and then relax the ulna and radius. The snail that walks on a broad path into its snail shell, could be an imagination for the young child.

In addition to the movement experience for the child, this exercise also strongly affects the breathing system through the arm movements. The radius and ulna need to move and alternate, a rhythmic alternation of stretching and lifting movements.

One can observe how the two principles of astral body and Ego are involved: in the movement of turning the forearm and lifting the brush the astral body will find time to complete the countermovement to the actual physical movement. The Ego will imprint the healthy movement gestures into the etheric body.

I advise class teachers to use these exercises also for a whole class. In first and second grades, it may be appropriate to do this daily for three weeks during Advent. On the fifth day of each week, one can then have the children choose to make the spiral painting they liked the most. Also, when pen and ink are introduced, this painting exercise can help children to concentrate on their arm, hand, and posture. It does not take too much time from the Main Lesson if one is able to organize and instruct the children to prepare quickly and clean up quickly. In my experience, the exercise also influences the artistic painting lessons in a positive way. In addition to practicing the painting technique, the use of the colors blue and red calls on the activity of the inner soul life and creativity in the students.

II. Blue-Red Perspective Exercise

Much of the background information needed to understand this exercise was commonly known when Audrey McAllen did her teacher training but was almost lost in the 1970s during the great expansion of Waldorf education. I once asked Audrey, "How do you know that the astral body moves in a spiral?" Her answer was, "Everybody knows!" But I didn't, and neither did my young colleagues. We were of the generation that entered Waldorf education in the seventies. That was before John Wilkes and Theodore Schwenck had published their research, and very few of Steiner's lectures were available in translation at that time.

To understand this Blue-Red Perspective exercise, one needs to comprehend the difference between a physical movement exercise and a painting exercise, especially when done on dampened paper with watercolor paint mixed with water. When doing movement exercises, the Ego and astral body need to penetrate the physical mechanical system of the body. The body needs to be lifted out of gravity. One will experience weight. The movement activity is in accordance with the laws of mechanics. As Rudolf Steiner said to the teachers in *Education for Adolescence* (see also *Deeper Insights into Education* lectures 2 & 3), there is no difference between lifting an arm or a leg and hoisting with block and tackle; the same physical and mechanical laws are involved. The supersensible organization of the human being is connecting itself with theses laws, as if it were plunging into them. In movement, the Ego organization connects itself with the physical forces that are at work on the earth (see Steiner, *Education for Special Needs*). This applies to all physical activities such as walking, jogging, gymnastics, sports, and all other movement activities: the Ego penetrates the physical elements of the body and the earth. It is like magic; the soul-spirit is able to move something physical—the will of the human psyche is able to move a physical limb.

With this painting technique, one uses color and water. Although we need to move our arm and hand to move the paintbrush, this is not the main activity. The most important element in painting is the working of the elements of color and water. The soul will connect itself with the life forces of the body. With color and water, we have the astral element and the etheric element. As a result of this activity, there will also be an effect from the etheric body of life forces onto the physical body. In painting exercises, the imprinting sequence is: astral—etheric—physical. We have an effect from the inner life onto the life forces and the physical body. This is an important perspective.

Currents

The movement directions of the Blue-Red Perspective exercise are connected with the currents that build up the structural physical body, as described by Rudolf Steiner in the 1909 lectures. But to understand this clearly, one needs to translate these movements from the astral into the physical (remember: in painting, we work from the soul—from the astral). With this exercise, we work in the opposite direction from the activity of the Right-angled Triangle exercise. In the Right-angled Triangle exercise, we start with the physical movements and the healthy spiraling movement of the astral body is hidden behind them. In the Blue-Red Perspective exercise, we are painting the objective healthy astral activity.

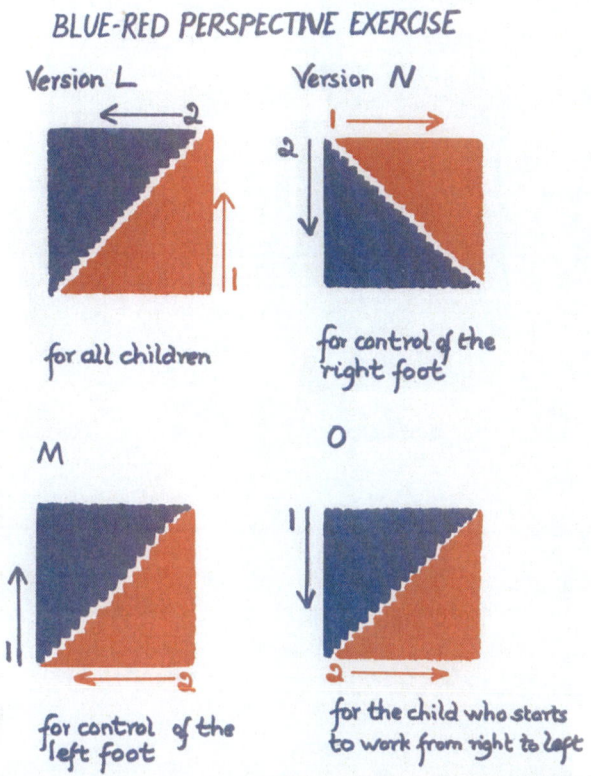

Illustration from 1976 edition of *The Extra Lesson*

With version L of this exercise (for all children, see *The Extra Lesson* 167–168), we find that the first brushstroke travels up from the bottom. It is the direction of the astral countermovement to a physical movement from above down. This corresponds with the current of the Ego. (Note that in the two-dimensional space on paper, the movement toward you corresponds with the movement from above to below in three-dimensional space.) The second brushstroke from right to left is the astral countermovement of the physical current, the physical body. In other words, we are painting the Ego current and the physical body current.

Gradually a third line—a diagonal that will look like a staircase between the red and blue brush strokes—will appear from the top right to bottom left. This represents the countermovement of the current of the sentient soul.

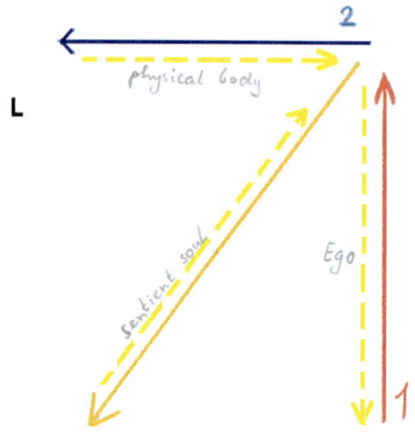

To summarize: this first painting exercise (version L) activates the Ego current to connect with the physical body, and it activates the sentient soul to go out into the sense perceptible world. This L version is the painted version of chart D of the Right-angled Triangle exercise.

Having explored version L of the exercise, one can easily find what is happening in the other three versions.

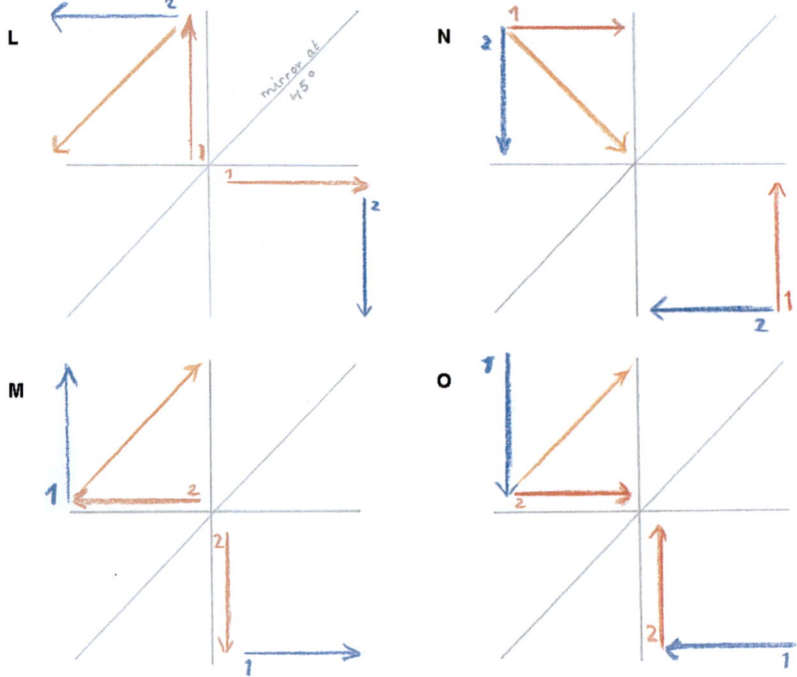

Overview of the Blue-Red Perspective Exercise

In the N version (for control of the right foot), one will recognize the currents of the etheric body, astral body, and the sentient soul. The etheric current is on the right side of the structural physical body; therefore this N version helps to control the right foot. The astral body has an affinity for the current of the etheric body and enters the right side of the structural body.

The M version (for control of the left foot) activates the currents of the Ego and physical body, together with the current of the sentient body coming from the outside world toward the sense organization. This is the left side of the structural physical body.

In the last version, O (for the child who persists in starting his work from right to left), one can find the currents of astral body, etheric body, and sentient body. This is similar to chart B of the Right-angled Triangle exercise.

To get an overview of all four painting exercises, we can also use a mirror held vertically at 45°. In the mirror, the physical currents corresponding to the painting directions will be shown. I encourage the reader to make drawings and diagrams of these currents over and over again in order to really penetrate the somewhat mysterious, geometrical—but on the other hand very practical—backgrounds.

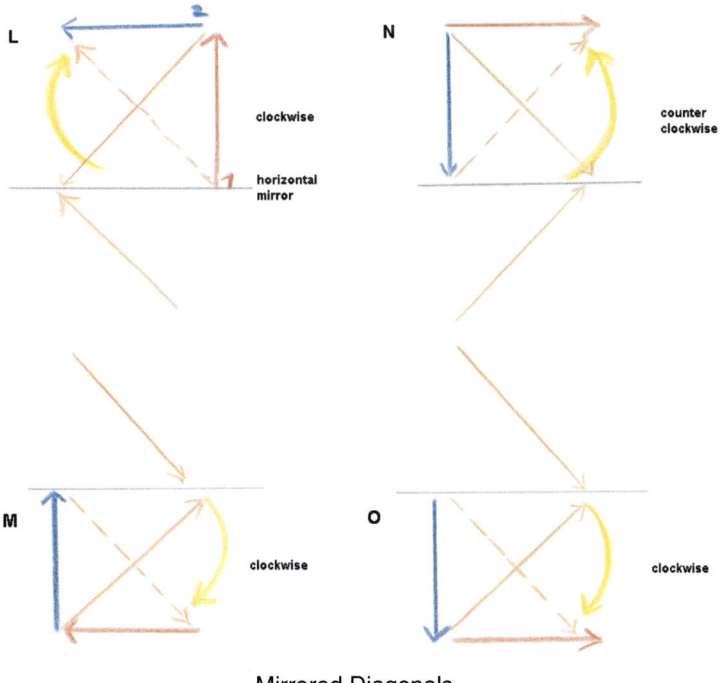

Mirrored Diagonals

Audrey McAllen once explained the working of this exercise to me, saying, "You have to look at these currents as planes of movement." As with other things, this puzzled me for years. I came to the thought that these planes of movement she was talking about create vortices when they meet, when they run into each other. The picture is similar to what happens when two streams of water, two rivers, meet. We already have met these spiral movements in the ocean currents and hurricane discussed earlier.

How can we find out what vortex is created by each of the versions of this Blue-Red Perspective painting? One needs to visualize the two surfaces running into one another. Imagining the arrows in the painting of version L are planes of movement, one can try to see that the plane of the first current (#1), which goes upward, is pushed to the left by the second current (#2). This will produce a vortex moving in a counterclockwise direction. Continuing the exercise, the brush strokes become smaller, like the whirl in a vortex. In a vortex, at a certain point the movement direction is reversed. What went counterclockwise now will turn clockwise.

The painted astral movement direction of version L will also be reversed into a clockwise spiraling physical movement. This is the movement

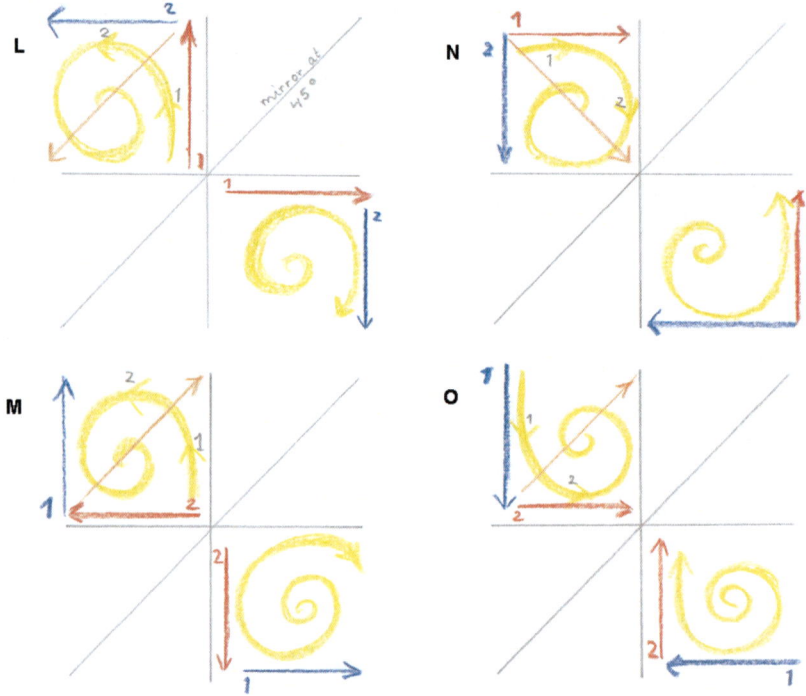

Overview of Vortex Movements

direction of the astral body in the physical body, like the movement we have met in the Threefold Spiral exercise and the Blue-Red spiral painting for the younger child (*The Extra Lesson* 127–128 & 161–164).

Currents and Vortices

Likewise, one will find vortices moving in the physical in a clockwise direction with versions M and O. In version N, for controlling the right foot, however, one will find that the plane of current #1, which moves from left to right, is pushed down by the plane of current #2. This will produce a vortex moving in a clockwise direction. In the physical, this will produce a counterclockwise spiraling movement, which is the archetypal movement pattern for the right foot (see chapter 2).

The reader will have noticed that the mirroring at a 45° angle does not work for the diagonal line. In the mirror all the diagonal lines run in the same direction. For mirroring the diagonal, we take the original painting directions and mirror them at a horizontal line. If we compare the mirrored diagonal to the original, we see that the diagonal of version N makes a 45° counterclockwise swing. This gives us the same picture of the currents as our description above: a counterclockwise movement for control of the right foot, a clockwise movement that corresponds to the archetypal movement pattren for the right foot and of the astral body as a unity spiraling through the physical body.

I confess that this mirroring puzzled me for years. Being an elementary school teacher, I needed stacks of paper to draw diagrams over and over again. Speaking to an audience about this matter, I need to make the diagrams (p. 49) anew each time to be sure I have the concept correct.

From the Astral Body into the Etheric Body

Once one has found the currents of the physical structural body in these painting exercises, one needs to go back to the starting point: painting exercises work from the astral level onto the etheric body. How can one picture this element?

Thinking of the etheric element as the watery element with its two-dimensional character—which one can observe in the leaves of plants and in the mirroring surface of a lake or a stream—one can picture the following: imagine the effect of the movements of sun, moon, and planets on the growth of plants. Although the plant kingdom represents the etheric world, plants and trees grow in *spirals*. Also, one can find the

Planetary Movement Patterns (after Kranich)

effect of the formative forces from the specific planets on the form of flowers. The geocentric apparent orbit of Mercury, for instance, is pictured in the arrangement of the six petals of the lily (see Kranich, *Planetary influences upon plants*). The five petals of the rose are likewise formed by the forces of Venus.

It is easier to imagine the two-dimensional surface of a lake. The wind will blow and small waves will appear on the lake's surface. This is the picture of how the astral/soul element affects the etheric.

Interpenetrating Triangles

Rudolf Steiner gave the six-pointed star as a meditation on the forces of the astral body (see *Farbenerkenntnis*). Geometrically, it is the figure of the hexagram; one can imagine that these are two vortices interpenetrating one another. The spiritual element penetrates the physical.

Audrey McAllen used this idea for two exercises: the form drawing of the Interpenetrating Triangles and the Triangle Rod exercise. The latter is a movement exercise based on indications Rudolf Steiner gave in a lecture for the general anthroposophical gathering right after the Christmas Conference of 1923–24. He spoke about mystery centers in medieval times and mentioned the Hebrew mysteries where the consciousness soul was prepared ("Occult Schools in the 18th and First Half of the 19th Centuries"). The exercise leads one to experience the weight of the bony system. One can imagine Moses standing in this position at the Red Sea (Exodus 14:16–31). This exercise was also taken up by eurythmists, but was definitely not given as an exercise exclusive to eurythmy. We also see it in Bothmer Gymnastics and Spatial Dynamics.

What one has here as a movement exercise is also found in the form drawing exercise of the Interpenetrating Triangles (*The Extra Lesson* 154–155). In a lecture for Dutch Extra Lesson teachers (November 22, 1989) Audrey McAllen gave the following meditative thoughts for the teacher to inwardly support the student who is doing this form drawing exercise.

1. The top triangle penetrates the lower:

When we incarnate, Lucifer darkens the light. All we bring from the past, all our astrality, is darkened by Lucifer. But there is also light ascending from the earth, because the earth has become the body of the Resurrected One.

2. The lower triangle penetrates the upper:

The world is cold without the heart of the human being. Warmth must penetrate the coldness of the outer sense world. The warmth coming from the earth must penetrate into that coldness.

3. The two triangles interpenetrate one another—the upper takes 3 steps down; the lower one takes 2 steps up:

   The human being finds the world and the world sees itself in him.

One can have these thoughts in mind as a feeling when doing this exercise with the student.

Chapter 5

Copper Ball and
Moving Straight Line and Lemniscate Exercises

A wonderful and most effective exercise for the whole educational process of incarnation is the Copper Ball exercise, a must for all children and adults from 10 years on.

How did Audrey come to this exercise? She was working with a boy and one day asked him to raise his arms above his head. He could not do this in a standing position, so she asked him to sit down on a chair and try it—but the boy could not manage it in a sitting position either. Then she asked him to lie down on the floor and try to move his arms above his head. Now he could manage it, but he still found it difficult. Then she developed an exercise for him to do in a horizontal position to learn to move his arms from the sides of his body to the position above his head—the Copper Ball exercise. Every teacher who has experienced this exercise will observe how it harmonizes the breathing system. The arms move from the sides of the trunk to a position on the floor above the head. This movement opens and closes the rib cage. Children will start to breathe deeply; they sigh or start yawning.

The Importance of the Breathing Process for Education

As Rudolf Steiner points out in the first lecture for the Waldorf teachers in Stuttgart (*Foundations of Human Experience*), education is teaching the children to breathe and sleep properly. The breathing process is the rhythmical link between the soul-spirit of the human being and the physical-life body. Breathing in the young child is already connected with the metabolic functions of the body. In education, breathing needs to be connected with the functioning of the nerve-sense system. Deepened breathing will affect the circulation of the spinal fluid into the cranium. The brain and the rest of the nervous system will be stimulated. In my opinion, the rhythm of breathing helps to form the fine inner structures of the brain and nervous system and even plays a role in integrating the early childhood movement patterns and neurological reflexes. It is the breathing that makes it possible for the child to incarnate into its bodily organization.

In a therapeutic sense, one needs to take Rudolf Steiner's words about the importance of the breathing literally. As already mentioned, the teacher should try to carefully observe the breathing rhythm of the children she is teaching. Observing children doing a simple movement exercise such as Wool Winding will help the teacher focus more on the breathing. Of course one focuses on the movements which need to be done correctly, but at the same time one will learn to experience how movement, when it becomes harmonious, affects the rhythmic system. In our modern times, most children have shallow breathing. Only the upper torso will be involved when they do not breathe properly. Lots of static air stays back in the lungs.

In addition to oxygen, the other main component of air is nitrogen. Air consists of 21% oxygen and 78% nitrogen. In 1923 Rudolf Steiner points out to the Stuttgart teachers (*Deeper Insights into Education* lectures 2 & 3) that both oxygen and nitrogen come into connection with the carbon in the human body. The carbon dioxide compound produced supports the thinking process in the head. A subtle effervescing carbon dioxide ascends from the lungs into the skull. Whenever there is an incomplete connection between oxygen and carbon, caused by shallow breathing, the dissolved carbon inside the head will react with hydrogen. Then methane (CH_4) is produced. This will make the head drowsy and obstruct thinking. One often can observe this situation in phlegmatic children sitting in the classroom with their mouths closed.

The nitrogen component of air (N) is important for the organs and for movement, for bringing the will into the body. It will also find a connection with the carbon inside the human body forming hydrocyanic acid (HCN and HCNO). Further chemical reactions, between cyanide and the potassium inside the human body give a dilute potassium cyanide (KCN). This poisons the body, but it is kept in a *status nascendi* (state of coming into being), which means that the moment the cyanide comes into being, it is destroyed by the bile (see also, Steiner, *Lectures for Workers* at the Goetheanum, October 10, 1923). The very instant that the body is poisoned by the cyanide, which is prevented by the bile, the spirit-will of the human being can take hold of the body and use it as an instrument of the will. This is the magic process by which the spirit can work into the physical, as Rudolf Steiner said in both the above mentioned 1909 lectures and in 1923 (*Deeper Insights into Education*). Without these refined metabolic processes of production and the dissolving of chemical combinations, the human being would not be able to even raise an arm. In this general way Rudolf Steiner explains these processes to the teachers. I am convinced that for an audience of chemists and medical doctors, he would have spoken much more in detail. It makes clear to us, however, the mediating function of the rhythmic system between head (thinking) and metabolic processes (willing)—hence the importance of healthy breathing.

These indications are often taken figuratively by class teachers in the sense that the teaching should be arranged in a rhythmical way. And, of course, there needs to be alternation between listening and working activities, between musical and plastic activities. Joy and laughter need to be alternated with "weeping," as Rudolf Steiner said (*Balance in Teaching* lecture 4). Knowing how to use this soul breathing in daily teaching makes the profession of teaching into an art, similar to that of an actor or musician. For the educational support teachers and the therapists, the focus should be more on the bodily aspects of breathing. For instance, raising the arms up expands the rib cage, deepening the breath.

Another aspect important for grade teachers and educational support teachers is what Rudolf Steiner says in *Balance in Teaching* in 1920. In the breathing system, two opposite streams of sensory information meet—the visual and the auditory. Visual input comes in via the head where the visual sense organs are located. Auditory input enters via the nervous system of limbs and trunk. This is confirmed by the research of the French otorhinolaryngologist, Dr. Alfred Tomatis (see www.tomatis.com). In fact, Rudolf Steiner points out that what in mainstream science are called motor nerves going from the center to the periphery play an important role in auditory perception. The middle ear with hammer, anvil, and stirrup is constructed like a miniature limb—upper leg, knee, and lower leg. The eardrum is like the sole of a little foot, listening to the eternal sound of gravity (*Faculty Meetings with Rudolf Steiner* December 5, 1922).

Processing sensory information within the nervous system and brain is first a physical (electrochemical) process. This process needs to be mediated by the Ego in order to be taken into the soul life. In the breathing of the middle system, as the second level, sensory information is connected with the feeling life of the soul. Thus, in the breathing life of the soul, comprehension of perceptions takes place. In this way, auditory and visual input are interlinked. On a third level, the memory becomes involved. Visual memory is imprinted in the metabolic system of the limbs. Auditory memory is imprinted in the metabolic processes of the head (*Balance in Teaching* lecture 3). Again, we see that the rhythmical element of breathing and heartbeat is a healing element, both educationally and medically (*Deeper Insights into Education*).

Lifting and Stretching Movements

Focusing on the arm movements in the Copper Ball exercise, one will recognize the rhythmic alternation of stretching and lifting movements—the alternating movements of the radius and ulna. The principle of rhythmical alternation between lifting and stretching movements is basic to the Extra Lesson exercises. The early movements of the young child are mainly stretching movements. The newborn baby has its arms and legs curled up. What a joy it is when it can raise its head. Arms and legs will stretch out when the head is lifted, caused by the tonic labyrinthine reflex (TLR). In the other early childhood movement patterns, one will also recognize that the movements of the head very strongly influence the movements of the limbs. Turning the head left or right or moving the head up or down will cause extension or flexion of limbs. The asymmetrical tonic neck reflex (ATNR) divides the body into left and right sides. The head will turn to one side of the body. On that side of the body the limbs will extend while on the other side they will flex. The tonic labyrinthine reflex (TLR) divides the body into front and back. The symmetrical tonic neck reflex (STNR) divides the body into above and below. Here we see the three-dimensional aspects of the physical body itself: above-below (STNR), front-back (TLR), left-right (ATNR). The spirit-soul of the incarnating human being must integrate these physical elements and transform the body into a suitable instrument for his or her life on earth.

In the stretching of muscles, we see the incarnating process of the astral body. This stretching will activate the metabolic system in the muscles, the breathing, and the nervous system. Then, in the lifting out of gravity, we see the forces of the spiritual Ego.

As adults, we are familiar with the stretching movements from common experience. If we are tired and there is still work to do, we will lean back in the chair, stretch our arms and legs out, and take a deep breath. This will energize the nervous system and keep us alert. We make the same gesture every morning when waking up. We make very subtle stretching movements before sitting up in a vertical position. These are all stretching movements connected with the astral body. They help to establish the connection between inner soul and outer sense world. It is through the stretching movements that we plunge into the sense world and connect ourselves with gravity. The Ego lifts us out of gravity into the vertical and teaches us to keep our distance from the outer sense world, to filter out what is not essential to us.

Increasing numbers of children nowadays do not connect with their physical life body in a healthy way because they do not stretch themselves into their bodies. To them, the physical-life body is a heavy burden, difficult to move and lift. Other children are not able to breathe healthily between the stretching and lifting aspects. They are overwhelmed by too much sensory input and do not pause as their Ego moment of rest (see p. 38).

The life of a contemporary newborn child is influenced by an immense amount of sense impressions to digest. Vacuum cleaners, ringing telephones, coffee machines, refrigerators, radio and television sets, traffic noise and so on all have an enormous impact on the delicate sense organs of the newborn child, which are open to every sense impression. The Ego is not yet able to filter and select from this overwhelming barrage of sense impressions. This overstimulating of the sense organism has a deep effect on the movement system of the child.

I once observed a mother with a one-year-old in a stroller waiting at the pedestrian traffic light. The child was facing forward. A huge truck passed by, and the child reacted in fear. It blinked its eyes, moved head, arms, and legs and started to cry. These are gestures of fear arising out of startle reactions (Moro reflex). This kind of stretching reaction will be imprinted into the movement system of the child. Lots of children I have worked with showed in their movement system the stretching element predominating over the lifting element. When catching beanbags, they grabbed them (sometimes even overhand) instead of receiving them in a more relaxed way. Doing the Rod Rolling exercise, they turned their palms down avoiding the use of the untrained lifting muscle system, not using the interplay between the ulna and radius.

Lifting movements—such as lifting oneself into a vertical position—are full Ego activity. Through the body, the Ego connects itself with the mechanical forces in movement (*Foundations of Human Experience*, lecture 12) and the terrestrial forces like the forces of gravity and those forces produced by the earth's rotation (*Education for Special Needs*, lecture 3). For the young child, it will take about half a year to be able to sit upright and over a year or more to independently lift its body into a vertical position and stand upright. In our modern culture, one can see the habit of carrying even newborn babies in an upright position or putting them in upright strollers far too early. These habits interfere very strongly with the child's forces of will to get hold of his own body in a proper way. Early stretching movement patterns can become fixed in the muscles and in the nervous system , and the cartilage of the skeleton may not at that point be hardened sufficiently, making the child more prone to injury. One can even have the thought that this excess tension might interfere with the child's ability to connect with his own karma or destiny. This is what teachers and school doctors should take more and more seriously into consideration as a hindering element for the contemporary schoolchild.

The importance of the Copper Ball exercise is that it helps to harmonize the rhythmical interplay between lifting and stretching movements. When overstretched, the movement system needs to learn to relax. It can also happen that the child does not really stretch into its movement system. This can also be caused by too many overwhelming sense impressions, resulting in a kind of withdrawal from the world. If there is too little of this stretching element in the movements, by doing the Copper Ball exercise, the child will learn how to really stretch into the muscle system.

The lifting system is invited to come into action too. The weight of the arm and hand holding the copper ball needs to be lifted up and slowly put back on the floor. It is not only the arms that are involved in this movement exercise. The soft woolen ball between the feet activates the entire body from head to toe. Subtle movements of the feet will show this; often the child will drop the woolen ball between the toes. This experience confirms what Karl König states in his book *The First Three Years* (chapter 1) that the whole of the movement system is a functional unity in which the different parts do not move independently of each other. Every movement is taken up by the whole of the movement system. Also the muscles that are at rest play an active role in the movements. This is an important statement, which we will cover more deeply in chapter 9 on the mirroring system.

Movement Sequence

One of the principles of the Extra Lesson exercises is that there is always a sequential repetition of the child's movement development. The first part of the Copper Ball exercise is done with one arm and hand while the eyes watch the moving hand with the copper ball. This is the repetition of the early stage when, in the cradle, the young child develops the first eye-hand coordination. In this exercise, the head needs to be turned and lifted a little. When one arm is in the position on the floor above the head the total gesture resembles the early movement pattern of the ATNR (see p. 58). The movements are alternating between left and right sides of the body. One can observe the inactive parts of the body—for instance, the legs and feet where the opposite foot extends ever so slightly (see König *The First Three Years* chapter 1). Later, when the small child tries to move forward, one will recognize the cross lateral movement stage in which the muscles on one side of the body contract and the muscular system on the other side of the body expands. This is the movement pattern of reptiles and fish. Their movement is held back to an instinctual level, as during evolution they could not develop the complete human patterns that are a fuller expression of the spirit, such as motivation.

In the second part of the exercise, both arms move symmetrically and simultaneously. The eyes are closed. The movement sequence is a repetition of the symmetrical stage of development (3–5 years). The student will be fully stretched out when the arms are above the head. The breathing will become even deeper as the rib cage is opened fully. Close observation will show that at a certain moment the student will take a deep breath or sigh deeply. This shows the effect of the exercise on the deep breathing, which eventually will come into a rhythm of breathing to heart rate of 1 to 4. Through this effect on the breathing, there will also be an effect on the brain, either directly from the breathing rhythm and its effect on the rhythm of the spinal fluid or through the nervous system that is registering the movements through the sense of self-movement. We can picture that it is only through functioning that the bodily organs are completed. By using the body, the spirit-soul is completing and improving the body's structure. That is how we can understand the forming of myelin around the nerves, which differentiates and forms the subtle nervous system.

In the third and last stage of the exercise, both hands move simultaneously in opposite directions. This is a repetition of the stage in movement when laterality is developed (5–7 years). The eyes are still closed, so coordination of the arms and hands needs to be processed through the sense of balance and the sense of self-movement. The movement pattern of the muscles will activate the crossed muscles on the chest and back that rotate the upper torso. These movements will have a unifying effect on the two brain hemispheres and stimulate the functioning of the corpus callosum.

Eyes Closed

The eye is connected with the sense of balance and the sense of self-movement. Through the eye, it is always possible to consciously control one's movements and balance. To focus on the perception through the bodily senses, the eyes need to be closed. That is why we have the eyes closed during the last two parts of the exercise. Research by H. A. Witkin, published in his article "Personality Through Perception," showed the competition between the sense of sight and the sense of balance.

Often students will show their hidden early movement patterns during these last two stages of the exercise. One can observe students putting their head to one side, showing the insufficiently integrated pattern of the ATNR. Others will show difficulty in lifting their arms and lose track of their coordination. I have observed numerous children who start making faces, showing the great inner pain or grief they carry in the subconscious area of their souls. Often they produce soft sounds of consonants like "pff," "hhh," or "sss," or press their lips in a tight mmm-gesture, showing the great stress they are under. They often also made slight extra movements that showed there was a problem in the movement system they were dealing with during the exercise. The students were mostly unaware that I could observe this. Observing this way requires the teacher to be restrained and respectful towards the individuality of the student. These moments are most sacred and intimate.

Audrey McAllen has described how she had some students do the exercise with two bags of sugar to help them experience the weight of the body. I once worked with a twelve-year-old seventh grade boy who was not able to do the arm movements of the Copper Ball exercise slowly. While moving very fast, he kept beating his arms on the floor with every movement and moved very unrhythmically. He complained that his arms hurt. I suggested he slow down his movements, but he did not do so. After two months of making no comments on his behavior, I suggested he perform the exercise with two teacups. We filled both cups with water, which he had to balance on his hands. Now he needed to slow down his arm movements because he was spilling lots of water on the floor and on his pants. It made him breathe in and out far more deeply than he ever had done before. After a couple of weeks, the harmonizing effect on the breathing rhythm was noticeable, and his behavior in the classroom also improved.

The Copper Ball exercise is performed lying on the floor. This horizontal position tones down the day-wake consciousness a little. A vertical standing position requires full day-wake consciousness; sitting is the dreaming position, best for meditating. The horizontal position is the position for sleeping. Having the eyes closed, one could easily excarnate and fall asleep. However, this is prevented by the soft woolen ball that needs to be kept between the feet. This ball activates the presence of the consciousness deeply into the area of the will.

Supersensible Currents

The horizontal position during this exercise can be seen as a two-dimensional picture of the human being standing upright. Now compare this with the 1909 diagram of supersensible currents working in the structural physical body (p. 22). The soft woolen ball between the feet pulls deep down into the body the supersensible current of the Ego that streams

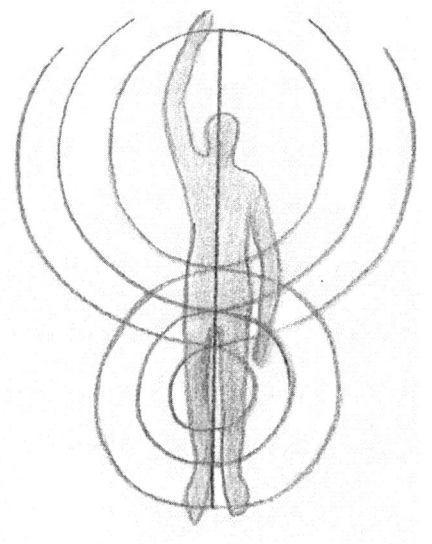
from the head down to the feet. As mentioned above, the woolen ball between the feet prevents the student from falling asleep. It also calls on the legs to be active but still, as mentioned by Karl König (*The First Three Years*). The arm movements have an effect on the whole muscular system of trunk and legs. The rhythmic alternation between stretching and lifting movements invite both the astral body and Ego to connect with the movement system of the physical-life body. Breathing is activated and deepened, which will have an effect on the nervous system, as discussed previously. The sensory organism is activated including the balance system and system of body awareness.

The astral body will penetrate its physical component, the nervous system. It will start to move in spiraling patterns inside the body, through the nerves and into the brain.

I once had the experience of working with a thirty-year-young lady. (The Extra Lesson exercises have no age limit. They can be of value for adults too.) While doing the second part of the Copper Ball exercise with eyes closed, she suddenly said: "You know what this makes me think of? Leonardo da Vinci. You know, the picture of the human being in the square and circle. That is what I am doing right now!" Then I realized she linked the exercise to Leonardo's drawing of the *Vitruvian Man*, the anatomy of the human being according to the ideal principles of the golden ratio—and she was right. The Copper Ball exercise makes students move the archetypal principles behind the physical body. It is a movement exercise for inner spiritual memory of the mathematics of the universe that created the human form.

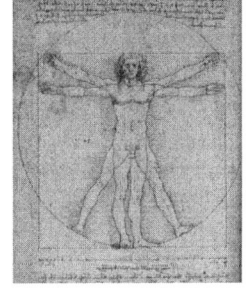

In the gesture of the complete human figure lying on the floor, one can imagine and recognize another Extra Lesson exercise: the Flower Rod form drawing (*Extra Lesson* 52). A straight line is drawn by the Ego working from the head down into the feet. The two arms that move from above the head to the sides of the body are represented by the opening lemniscate form around this straight line. The crossing of lines in the middle of the Flower Rod form drawing represents the processing inside the rhythmical system. Where the lemniscate lines touch the midline in the lower part of the drawing, one will have an impression of how the visual sense impressions are imprinted in the area of memory that are carried by the etheric body in the metabolic system.

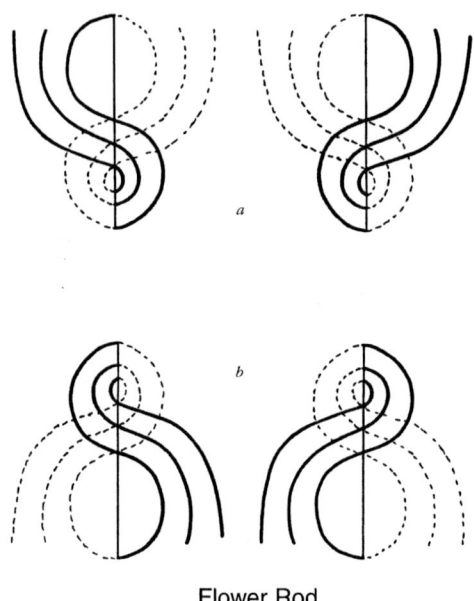

Flower Rod

To repeat: one can keep in mind all the different indications Rudolf Steiner gave about the sensory process. The nervous system receives the outer sense impression. The senses vibrate, as it were. They move like limbs imitating the movements of the outer sense world. The processing of these outer impressions by the nervous system has nothing to do with the inner soul life. However, the nervous system tunes down the outer vibrations of the sense impressions. Then these are mirrored by the middle system. It is the rhythmic system that connects the sensory impressions with the feeling life of the soul. Likewise, the brain does not carry the memory. Memory is imprinted into the etheric realm of the metabolic system. The brain only plays the role—an important one—of bringing the outer impressions and the inner memory pictures into daywake consciousness. Rudolf Steiner gave these indications to the future Waldorf teachers to be in lecture 10 of *Foundations of Human Experience* (1919). He worked this out differently in *Balance in Teaching* (1920).

Watching a student perform the Copper Ball exercise, one can picture the 1909 diagram or the drawing of the Flower Rod and form an idea of the currents that run through the structural body of that student. The Ego can lose control; the soft woolen ball will drop. Immediately one can "observe" the astral body spiralling from below upwards through the body.

The Moving Straight Line and Lemniscate

The Copper Ball exercise *always* needs to be followed by the form drawing exercise of the Moving Straight Line and Lemniscate (*Extra Lesson* 147). The Copper Ball exercise produces a kind of excarnating mood. Following this mood, the day-wake Ego needs to get hold of the body. The correct, healthy movement patterns need to be imprinted into the movement system.

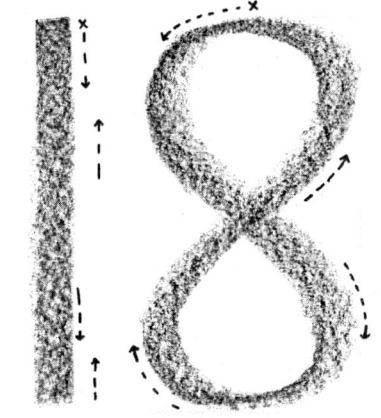

As an adult, one can try to experience the difference between drawing two very large vertical lemniscates simultaneously with both hands and then the Moving Straight Line and Lemniscate. With the first of these drawings, we experience that one can do this easily without even paying attention to the hands and paper. The Moving Straight Line and Lemniscate, however, calls on the conscious activity of the eyes controlling the movements of the hands as they draw the exercise. Because the form drawing is not symmetrical, the two eyes need to work together and watch both hands, alternating between the one that is drawing the straight line and the one drawing the lemniscate. This calls on the conscious will activity of the Ego.

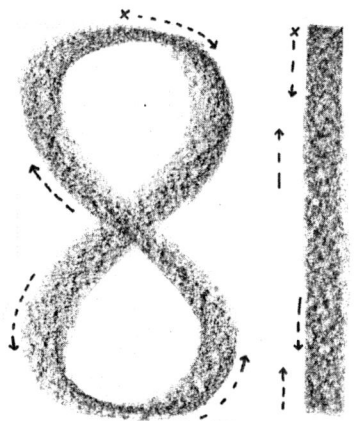

From *The Extra Lesson*, page 148

A rhythmical movement much like that of rowing a boat develops and harmonizes the breathing. The student leans forward then backward rhythmically, activating the rhythmical flow of the spinal fluid and the alternation between stretching and lifting movements.

Archetypal Form

For the first day teaching first grade, Rudolf Steiner indicated that the teacher should have the children draw the archetypal forms of the straight line and the curved line (*Practical Advice to Teachers* lecture 4). These are the basic linear forms in form drawing and geometry. In the Moving Straight Line and Lemniscate exercise, we can see these archetypal forms. The straight line is an image of the Ego, and the lemniscate is an archetypal image of the astral body penetrating into the physical-life body. The eyes take in these archetypal images, while the arms and hands experience the archetypal movement patterns in these forms. In drawing the line and lemniscate, the student needs to make stretching movements and lifting movements. In the lemniscate, one will recognize the clockwise and counterclockwise movement patterns for the left and right arms in stretching and lifting. The student has to really stretch out toward the top of the paper where the movement of the lemniscate goes inward bringing the hand into gravity. That is the correct stretching movement. At the bottom of the paper the lemniscates will move in the archetypal counterdirection into levity.

This is another principle of the Extra Lesson exercises: they are multisensory experiences. The sense of self-movement will teach a student the archetypal movement directions. The sense of sight gives the archetypal images of Ego and astral body—line and lemniscate. Remember the Egyptian pharaoh carrying the crook and the straight flail, showing he was king in the heavens and on earth. The student's day-wake experiences are taken into sleep life by the soul. During sleep, the individual can reach into the world of the archetypes, where higher hierarchical beings can help to restore and refresh the physical-life body. True pedagogy takes into account the spiritual and moral 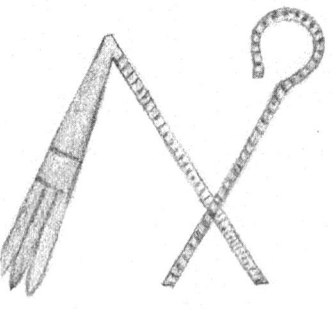 experiences in sleep. What the soul of the child experiences during the day will influence sleep life. Audrey McAllen covers this in her book *Sleep: An Unobserved Element in Education*.

Currents

The movement direction the student chooses for the exercise will give the teacher an indication of whether the currents of the astral body moving through the physical-life body are correct or reversed. This can appear incorrect on just one side of the body. When the Ego organization is not able to anchor properly within the physical structure, the astral body can go out of control. Over-stimulated senses cause reactions in the stretching movement system; too little movement experience in the first seven years causes too little lifting experience. In the astral body, which uses the nervous system as its vessel to penetrate the physical body, this over stimulation prevents it from making the countermovements to physical movements. In other words, the astral body is penetrating too deeply into the physical. A healthy breathing relationship between the physical-life body and the astral body (in the sense of self-movement) is not possible.

Besides reversals in movement directions, a student may also push too strongly when forming the line and lemniscate. Sometimes even the paper that is taped to the table will be pulled off or damaged. This shows us the strong pushing force of the astral body. It could be the sentient soul strongly pushing from inside out (that is, from back to front), or it could be the sentient body element strongly pushing from outside in (that is, from front to back), exerting itself onto the paper.

Standing behind the student who is doing the Moving Straight Line and Lemniscate, we can see how the movements of the two hands influence one another. The left hand drawing the line will often take over the lemniscate movements of the right hand or vice versa. This copying of movements can either be symmetrical or asymmetrical. In the latter case, the one hand shows the tendency to move in the same pattern and direction as the other, as the feet do in downhill skiing. Another way of showing an irregular movement pattern is when the student starts with one hand at the top of the form and the other hand at the bottom. The movement pattern will not be symmetrical, but similar to the movement pattern of the hands when walking. This indicates that the movement development is far behind the normal schedule. With right-handed students, the left side will copy. Often their left side is stiffened. Left-handed students, in most cases, will have difficulty with controlling the movements of the right hand. Their right side will often be too weak from insufficient exercise in the second third (the symmetrical developmental stage, 3–5 years) of the first seven years. Doing this exercise on a regular basis will correct the supersensible movement system. I encourage class teachers to practice this exercise with the whole class, from second grade on. One can practice daily for two or three weeks or once a week for a longer period of time. Children will be very helpful in setting up the room. The teacher should not be afraid of wasting time. A better incarnated class will be fresh and awake for the academic work.

This is the third principle of Extra Lesson exercises: they bring about self-correction. With most exercises, the teacher does not interfere when the student uses incorrect movement patterns. The Extra Lesson exercises are educating the spirit inside the physical body. The supersensible organization of the student will gradually recognize the archetypal patterns of the movements in the exercises and will imprint these into the bodily organization. The exercises integrate the students' movements into the universal earth movements.

Ideally the student will recognize the correct archetypal movement pattern. Sometimes the student does not. In a conversation, Liane Collot d'Herbois (see chapter 7 below) suggested that in such cases one can use the sense of sight as a help. Prepare two similar collections of 4–5 inch (10–12 cm) squares of colored silk (up to a hundred different colors if possible). Have the student choose some colors. Then let him from memory pick the same colored pieces from the other collection and then compare what he finds. Give him the chance to correct if necessary. Repeat this for some weeks. By taking the detour through the sense of sight (sense of color), we can help the sense of self-movement. (Note that visual memory is in the metabolic system of the limbs as discussed previously.)

Colors

The Extra Lesson teacher can take note of the colors of the block crayon colors the student uses for the Moving Straight Line and Lemniscate. The sequence of colors can give an impression of how the exercises are helping the student's process of incarnation. One can take the reversed version of Rudolf Steiner's color diagram (chapter 7, p. 89) as an archetypal picture. Of course, one hopes for a correct use of the archetypal colors blue and red as an indication the soul-spirit of the student is able to manage the structural physical body and to perceive outer sense impressions objectively without interference caused by immature development of the structural body of nervous system, muscles, and skeleton. More information about this can be found in chapter 6 on Eye Color Affinity.

Thumb Twirling Exercise

To relax the fingers at the end of each part of the Moving Straight Line and Lemniscate exercise, one can use the Thumb Twirling exercise (*The Extra Lesson* 147–149). Close observation of the movements of thumb and fingers will show that the right thumb is moving according to the movement direction of the left arm—counterclockwise. The right fingers tend to want to move in a slightly clockwise direction. The pattern for the left hand mirrors the movements of the right thumb and fingers (see chapter 2). The same archetypal movement patterns will be found in the Ball Twirling and Wool Winding exercises.

Chapter 6

Eye Color Affinity
Blue Moon and Red Sun Drawing

Ernst Lehrs worked for eleven years as a science teacher in the upper grades of the young Stuttgart Waldorf School, where he began as a teacher some time after finishing his academic training as an electrical engineer. In his book *Man or Matter*, he wrote about his research on Goethean science, as inspired by Rudolf Steiner. In this book Audrey McAllen found Lehrs' description that the eyes have different modes of seeing and that the right eye has an affinity for red, the left an affinity for blue. That gave her the idea of developing the Eye Color Affinity drawing.

The Eye Color Affinity exercise (Blue Moon and Red Sun) is a help to the educational support or Extra Lesson teacher for diagnosing how freely the student is living in his own inner relationship to space. It shows whether the child's will forces are held in the habit patterns and organic activities of the body or whether he is free to use his will. Is he "asleep" and living passively in what he has imitated and inherited as gestures, will-activities, and thought patterns from his parents and his close environment? Is the student able to be free and awake in his sense perceptions and thinking? Is the student able to properly experience his body in relationship to three-dimensional space, and is he able to visualize this inwardly?

This drawing of the Blue Moon and Red Sun can become a living language telling the Extra Lesson teacher the effect of the remedial work. The drawing of the Blue Moon and Red Sun has strong archetypal value and it reveals a person's constitutional and structural development. After long experience, one will be able read these archetypal drawings. As a beginning teacher, however, one should not jump to conclusions too soon. The teacher needs to take the student's drawings, together with her other observations, into the meditative life for a time before trying to interpret them.

The teacher asks the student to draw a blue moon and a red sun. (The instruction needs to be given in this specific order, because in reading and writing we start from the left. If the teacher says the reverse—Draw me a red sun and a blue moon—she is suggesting the red sun should be on the left.) We make sure the student has a set of about 24 colored wax crayons:

dark blue, ultramarine, pale blue, turquoise blue, viridian green, dark green, pale green, olive green, carmine red, vermilion red, orange, pale orange, golden yellow, light yellow, dark brown, pale brown, brown ochre, yellow ochre, blue violet, red violet or purple (magenta), rose pink, gray, white, and black. This same range of colors is needed for the Person-House-Tree drawing. (See McAllen, *The Extra Lesson* 75 and *Reading Children's Drawings*.)

To understand the Eye Color Affinity drawing, we need to look at several different aspects:

- construction and functioning of the eye on a physical and soul-spiritual level
- the archetypal quality of the colors blue and red
- the archetypal character of the moon and sun forms.

The Eye

In the second lecture of *Foundations of Human Experience*, Rudolf Steiner speaks about the forces of antipathy and sympathy. These are the two primary soul forces that build up the human body before birth and during childhood. We bring the forces of antipathy with us from the spiritual world. As Rudolf Steiner said, the nervous system is formed by the forces we bring into this life as a result of our previous incarnation. These antipathy forces work formatively—from the head down—to build up the nervous system, the brain, and the whole skeletal system. These same forces of antipathy will gradually metamorphose into the capacity for drawing and writing and into the soul ability for thinking and memory.

In contrast, the forces of sympathy come towards us from the future and work in the blood system—from below upward. They play a role in the functioning of the metabolic-limb system and enable us to develop our will. This is the newly formed part of our body—not connected with the forces from previous incarnations, but carrying the seed for the future, the time after death. During the first seven years of development, these forces of sympathy serve the forces of antipathy and work from the head down. They are strongly connected with the functioning of the sense organs—as the inner interest towards the world—and with the forces of imitation. They are the basis for the young child's unconditional loving devotion to everyone and everything in the outer sense world. Their inner mood is: The world is good. These two forces—from the past (antipathy) and from the future (sympathy)—are the basic forces for our soul life after the change of teeth in our present earthly life.

For the human eye to have objective sense perception, the forces of antipathy and sympathy need to be in perfect balance. The retina and the optic nerve that goes from the eye to the brain are the representatives of the forces of antipathy in the eye. The blood vessels and muscles that enable the eye to move are the representatives of the forces of sympathy.

Rudolf Steiner speaks of the eye as a "selfless" organ (*Foundations of Human Experience* lecture 8). Inside the human eye there is a balance between antipathy and sympathy. The eye is the king of the senses. It is the eye's special task to enable perceptions of the outer world to enter into our soul as objectively as possible. In cases of illness—for instance, a fever—the changed metabolic processes in the blood and the high temperature caused by the illness may influence sense perception significantly and we may become delirious and hallucinate.

Inside the eye, the constant interplay between blood and nerves plays an important role in the process of visual perception. When light comes into the eye, the retina and optic nerve are affected. The nerves transport the visual sense impression of light, darkness, and color towards the brain. Also the blood in the small blood vessels of the choroid will be affected so that the light upon the eye simultaneously arouses activity in the blood. Metabolic activity in the eye itself is influenced. Sensory activity always goes together with metabolic processes.

From a psychological (soul) point of view, we could say: in the process of perception, the soul forces of antipathy and sympathy work in a constant, alternating rhythm. They collaborate in a rhythmical breathing: antipathy—sympathy, breathing in—breathing out. In the inner life of the human soul live ideas. As a reaction to the outer sense impressions, the soul produces images. These inner pictures are created by means of the forces of antipathy. These images are our individualized ideas. Through the forces of sympathy, the soul directs the sense perception to an interest in the outer world. The sympathy forces work in the sense organs when the soul is motivated to make a connection between its inner world and the outer sense world. These sympathy forces enable us to look or listen actively—with interest, instead of seeing and hearing passively. This is a will activity of the soul.

The picture of the physiological and psychological functioning of the eye can easily be seen in the light of what Rudolf Steiner says in the Berlin 1909 lectures, when he speaks about the supersensible currents of the sentient body and sentient soul. In describing the sense of sight, he explains that in the eye the inner astral forces (the current of the sentient soul) connect with outer astral forces. The latter can be seen as the current of the sentient body, which has an objective connection with the outer light; it can also be said that these outer astral forces are the forces of the world astral body, the Cosmic Soul (see Liane Collot d'Herbois, *Colour*). The meeting of inner and outer astral forces gives us the sense impression of color through the eye. This means that in this sense perception there is not only the light that touched our retina but also always an active response from the inner human organization toward the outer world. The sense of sight gives us the ability to become aware of the color of an object—for example, a rose. Through the sense of sight, we are not able to penetrate deeply into the inner being of this object, the rose. We can only perceive its surface. However, the rose itself will express its (soul) quality to the outside world by means of its colored surface.

Another important aspect is the fact that most living creatures, except the very simple forms of life, have two eyes. In fact, all the senses have this left and right symmetry in the body: two ears to hear, two hands to touch, two sets of sense organs for balance. According to spiritual research by Rudolf Steiner and mainstream research by Alfred Tomatis, these left and right sense organs have different tasks. Alfred Tomatis (www.tomatis.com) observed the different length of the nerves from the left and right ear to the brain hemispheres. The left and right sensory organs sense the outer world differently because of the different functions of the two brain hemispheres. The right brain hemisphere gives us a global overview connected with feeling, while the left hemisphere has a more intellectual analyzing quality. In the nose, the left nostril and the right nostril have different tasks in the activity of smelling.

In the neurological and movement development of the human being, we recognize the symmetrical stage: age 3–5. After this stage, laterality and dominance will be developed. The left and right sides of the movement sensory system will develop their different tasks simultaneously, yet independently. The difference between the two brain hemispheres is related to these left and right side activities.

The body's asymmetry enables the human being to be self-conscious while sensing the outer world. It is the necessary condition for the development of the day-wake Ego activity so that one does will not "fall asleep" in the outer world of sense experiences. One will not plunge into the sense world with too much sympathy like the animals do.

Ernst Lehrs wrote in his book *Man or Matter* that the left eye perceives the visual picture and is active in surveying space and form. The right eye perceives movement and details. It was Ernst Lehrs who connected Goethe's color theory with the functions of the left and right eye and with their affinity for the color blue or red.

These archetypal colors blue and red lead us back to the soul forces of antipathy and sympathy. Antipathy and sympathy work differently as body building forces and as soul forces in the left and right side of the body (Steiner 1910 lectures). On the left, we find the forces of antipathy being more active and, on the right, the forces of sympathy. Rudolf Steiner indicates (*Faculty Meetings with Rudolf Steiner* May 15, 1923) that the left side of the body is formed by the forces from the last incarnation, the past. The right side is formed during the time between death and rebirth and belongs to the future. We need to learn to incarnate into this new right side.

Antipathy and sympathy work in the first seven years mainly in the vertical directions, furthering the development of the nervous system and blood system. The antipathy forces (or plastic-architectonic forces) work from the head down. The sympathy forces (or musical-speech forces) work through the sense organs (the imitation of the outer world) in service to the antipathy forces (*Balance in Teaching* lecture 2). After the change of teeth at the end of kindergarten, these two forces will become active in the realm of the soul. Then they will become active in the horizontal plane between left and right, between past and future. In children's Eye Color Affinity drawings, one sometimes will find the moon and sun being drawn vertically above one another. This could indicate that the vertical midline is still present. It certainly is a sign of a continuing young stage of development.

The Archetypal Quality of the Colors Blue and Red

There is a simple experiment. Cut two equal-sized circles or squares out of colored paper, one ultramarine blue, the other carmine red. Then stick these on a larger white sheet of paper. Look at the two for some time in a relaxed way and compare them. The red shape will appear to be larger than the blue one.

In psychology it is known that blue and red have different effects on people—a different impact.[1] These insights are used in architecture and advertising. The modern advertising industry is well aware of the effect of the combination of blue and red (see below, p. 75).

As another example: experiments have shown that introducing red telephones in office buildings makes employees use the telephone for a shorter time. The red elephone gives the impression of action and that time flies. The same result was found with doors of cloakrooms painted red. Even blind people seem to react to the different colors with which rooms are decorated. Being in a red room makes their blood pressure go up a little and their heart beat faster, even though they do not have the visual experience.

Maria Montessori, another 20th century education reformer, was a theosophist. For many of her teaching materials, she used the archetypal colors blue and red. When a third color was needed, she used green.

In children's drawings at the end of kindergarten, one often finds the two archetypal colors blue and red in combination: a person with a blue jacket and red trousers or two people, one in red and the other in blue. The house may be colored with a red roof and blue walls. This combination shows us that the soul forces are working in the body.

In nature, blue is the color that goes into the depths of perspective. It is the color of distant mountains and the vast blue dome of the sky above us. Of all colors, the cobalt blue of the sky stays visible the longest. Other colors will fluctuate and disappear. In the visual arts, one can also find blue and red in their archetypal form. Raphael's Sistine Madonna wears a blue veil over a red dress, as in numerous other Madonna paintings. This choice of colors expresses the inner harmony of soul of the Holy Virgin. Her inner life is the perfect balance between antipathy and sympathy: no passion or pride, no hate, only objective balance. Because of this, she was able to become the mother of Jesus.

The medieval cathedrals in Europe, such as the ones in Reims and Chartres, have rose windows in the left and right transepts. These rose windows give different color impressions. In both windows, pieces of glass in blue, red, and yellow were used; however, the left rose window gives a bluish impression while the right window appears red.

In the Oberufer Shepherds Play, often performed by Waldorf school teachers as a Christmas gift to the children, the costume of Mother Mary is also in the archetypal colors of blue over red. These colors are reversed in the costume of the Father God in the Oberufer Paradise Play: red over blue. The colors of this costume represent the wrathful character of his being and also the importance of heredity in the development of the Jewish people. In old paintings, we will find this same combination of colors.

There is a similar reversal of color in the fresco of *The Last Supper* by Leonardo da Vinci (at Santa Maria delle Grazie, Milan). In the center of the fresco is the Christ Being dressed in blue over red. On the left next to him is Saint John, wearing red over blue. Saint John is the representative of the human being in earth's future evolution. He is considered to be the author of one of the Gospels and the book of Revelation. He symbolizes the new creative force of the Logos, the Word that will flow through the generations.

Rose Windows in the Cathedral at Chartres

The sequence of reversals of this color combination reveals the stages of human evolution. The Father God—Jahwe or Jehovah—is the creator of the world and humanity. With Adam and Eve the stream of heredity began. In the middle of earth evolution, there is the historical event when the Christ Being, the Logos himself, becomes a man. Future humanity is represented by Saint John. New forces are brought to life in him by the Christ Being himself, forces that will work into the far future of humankind: the new forces of the resurrected Logos. Blue-red reversals could be an image of the development of human consciousness. In chapter 7 (Qualities of Color) we include Rudolf Steiner's meditation on the staff of Mercury (caduceus). In this chapter we combine the caduceus with the signs of the moon and sun. This can give us an idea of how the reversed eye-color-affinity is connected with different states of consciousness, the development from a past dreamy consciousness towards a transcendental consciousness in the far future.

In our times, in the lower heredity body where the consciousness is asleep, the eye-color-affinity is reversed. In the day-wake consciousness, where the senses objectively can connect with the outer world, the eye-color-affinity should be correct. In transcendental consciousness, which humankind will develop in future times, the eye-color-affinity will be reversed. This is a mirroring sequence (see chapter 9 on imprinting and mirroring).

From 1906 till 1915 in Stuttgart, the medical doctor Felix Peipers did research developing a colored light therapy. Rudolf Steiner suggested that Peipers start his experiments with a blue and red therapy.[2] In a lecture published in *Colour* (Feb. 21, 1923), Steiner spoke about the activating influence on

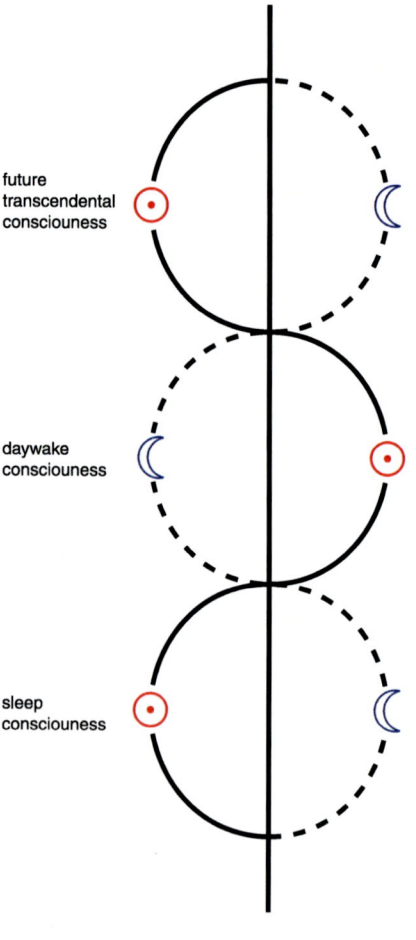

future transcendental consciouness

daywake consciouness

sleep consciouness

the blood and the metabolic system of the red colored clouds and rising sun at dawn. Rudolf Steiner regularly visited the clinic in Arlesheim, Switzerland where Klara Müller was a patient suffering from irregularity of the heart rhythm. Rudolf Steiner and Dr. Ita Wegman examined her, and Rudolf Steiner said that her heart was in good health but the etheric body was not penetrating the physical body sufficiently. That could be corrected by practicing a meditation with the following words:

> Cornflower—blue, Rose—red:
> They are the world's words
> For water and fire.

Through Ita Wegman, director of the Arlesheim clinic, Rudolf Steiner added the instruction, as reported by Klara Müller: "I had to imagine the blue as flying away from me. The red, however, I had to imagine as a large flat surface coming towards me."[3]

The reversed eye-color-affinity (left eye red, right eye blue) in a child's drawings shows the teacher that the student is more or less asleep in his sense perceptions, hindered by bodily difficulties. The objective sense perception is hindered by bodily developmental or organic problems. Those will influence the child's experience of his body in relation to three-dimensional space and his ability to visualize outer sense impressions inwardly. Audrey McAllen wrote that often these children's forces are held back in the habit patterns and organic activities of the body. They are asleep in what they have imitated and inherited from their environment.

Students will sometimes use different shades of blue or red, even violet or yellow, to draw the moon and sun, even though the instruction was given to them clearly. Chapters 7 and 8 will go more deeply into these phenomena. The use of yellow for the sun indicates that the forces of sympathy are still working from the head (*Balance in Teaching* lecture 2). This is a color combination that belongs to the age of the kindergarten child.

Blue and red are counter-colors. Green and red are complementary colors. Blue and red are connected with the outer aspect of the astral body—with the total system of the senses, while the color combination of green and red is connected with the inner aspect of the astral body—the constitutional processes of the body (see also chapter 7).

The Archetypal Character of the Moon and Sun Forms
In anthroposophy, the moon and the sun are not thought of only in an astronomical and physical sense. They are—as are the other planets and

stars—physical representatives of spiritual identities and forces. In *An Outline of Esoteric Science*, Rudolf Steiner describes the development of the earth's evolution and explains that higher spiritual beings were connected with this evolutionary process. Originally, the sun, moon, and earth were a unity. One stage of its development went too fast, so certain beings had to separate the sun from the earth and form a new planet to live on. From there, they could influence the earth's evolution in a different way—from without. Then the evolution process went too slowly. Other beings needed to separate, and the moon was created as their domain. From that time, a harmonic balance between the forces of sun and moon was created, and the further development of the earth became possible. The earth was placed in the balanced center between forces that speeded up evolution (the sun) and those that hardened and slowed down the evolutionary processes (the moon). It is the balance between the twofold archetypal opponents: antipathy—sympathy, nerve—blood, past—future, cosmos—earth.

In religious architectural traditions, moon and sun have also a symbolic connotation. Sun and Moon were used in the old Yoga tradition. Lama Anagarika Govinda, in his book *The Way of the White Clouds*, relates the landscape of the Tibetan Highland to the forces of the Kundalini in the human being. Govinda is describing the relationship between the landscape around Mount Kailas in the Himalayas and the architecture of Indian temples.

> A glance at the map [in his book] which shows the position of Kailas (the "Jewel of the Snows") on the highest elevation of the Tibetan highland and its relation to the river systems of the Indo-Tibetan region give an immediate explanation of how Kailas forms the spine of the "Roof of the World," as the Tibetan plateau is called. Radiating from it, like the spokes from the hub of a wheel, a number of mighty rivers take their course towards the east, the west, the northwest and the south. These rivers are: the Brahmaputra, the Indus, the Sutlej and the Karnali. These rivers have their source in the Kaila-Manasarovar region which forms the highest tier of the Tibetan plane.
>
> The mountain stands so completely isolated in the center of the Trans-Himalayan range that it is possible to circumambulate it within two or three days: and its shape is so regular as if it were the dome of a gigantic temple, rising above a number of equally architectural forms of bastions and temple-shaped mountains which form its base.

And as every Indian temple has its sacred water-tank, so at the southern foot of Kailas are two sacred lakes: Manasarovar and Rakas Tal of which the former is shaped like the sun and represents the forces of light, while the other is curved like the crescent moon and represents the hidden forces of the night, which—as long as they are not recognized in their true nature and directed into their proper channels—appear as the demonic powers of darkness. These ideas are also expressed in the names of the two lakes. *Manas* in Sanskrit means "mind" or "consciousness": the seat of the forces of cognition, of light and finally of enlightenment. *Rakas* or more correctly, *Rakshas*, means demon, so that *Rakastal* means "Lake of the Demons."

The solar and lunar symbolism of the sacred lakes is illustrated in Tibetan pictures by showing the sun-disk in the sky above the circular shape of Manasarovar and the waning moon above the crescent shaped Rakastal.

These sun and moon symbols are used in every Tibetan scroll-painting (*thang-ka*) in which the Buddha, deities, or saints are depicted. Sun and moon signify the two streams or currents of psychic energy, which move upward to the right and to the left of the central channel or "meridian nerve" of the spinal column. In Yogic meditation these two currents are integrated in the centre channel and rise through it from one psychic center or level of consciousness to the other until the integrated stream reaches the highest multi-dimensional level of an enlightened consciousness. As Mount Kailas corresponds to the spinal column, it represents the axis of the spiritual universe, rising through innumerable world-planes (indicated by the actual horizontal stratification of the mountain, which is as regular and distinct as that of an Indian temple), from the human to the highest divine level, while the two lakes are looked upon as the reservoirs of the two streams of psychic energy.

Comparable to the Indian temple architecture, the two obelisks at the entrance of the Egyptian temples can be thought of as moon and sun symbols. The ancient temple of Solomon in Jerusalem also had two pillars at the entrance named Boaz and Jachim. Rudolf Steiner speaks of these in the lecture cycle on the Golden Legend.[4] The medieval cathedrals have their two towers; the Chartres cathedral even has a moon and sun symbol on top of the spires.

Rudolf Steiner speaks of the forces of moon and sun in quite different ways. In the karma lectures, he speaks about their forces in relation to the forming of individual destiny—karma. The moon holds the results of previous lives, the past. When incarnating, one passes the moon sphere and picks up a package of old karma. The moon gives the individual talents, faculties, and temperament. This is incorporated in the etheric and physical bodies and in the deep subconscious soul life.

The sun brings new impulses for the future. Its forces work in will, in deeds, creating seeds for future incarnations. Events and people one will meet in the present life are brought to us from the past by the moon as old karma. This old karma has the element of necessity. From the sun, we receive freedom to act, to freely form new karma for the future. Moon and sun are like two gates of the spiritual world through which the past and the future work into the present life.[5]

In a lecture entitled "The Cosmic Origin of the Human Form"[6], Rudolf Steiner speaks about the forces of moon and sun creating the paired human eyes. Moon and sun guide the incarnating individual from the spiritual world towards the new birth. At a certain point, the individual loses the cosmic consciousness and goes through a phase of darkness. The individual dives down through a tiny aperture into the embryo after conception. At that stage, the forces of moon and sun unite. The pupil of the eye is the image of the tiny aperture. Human eyes were the united sun-and-moon; then they turned inside out. Rudolf Steiner tells us that we must get used to the "turning inside out." If we do not, we gain no real idea of how the physical world surrounding us is related to the spiritual world.

One can become strongly conscious of the fact that, because of these deep spiritual and symbolic connotations in color and form, the Eye Color Affinity drawing has great archetypal significance. These drawings show the Extra Lesson teacher the projection of the forces of moon and sun at work in the child's deep subconscious. Is the individuality able to keep balance between the forces of antipathy and sympathy, between left and right, above and below, front and back? Can it keep its free position in the middle? In *The Extra Lesson*, Audrey McAllen writes:

> Experience has shown that this gives an indication as to the relationship between the newly freed ether body and the development of the soul forces in the breathing and circulation. When the colors are correctly placed on the paper, the soul is able to live freely in their functioning. When the colors are reversed, then the soul is too deeply engaged in the bodily functions which then in turn condition behavior and learning ability.

Form Phenomena

Children often draw different shapes for the blue moon and red sun. Ideally one would like them to draw a full moon and a sun of the same size next to that, two equal-sized colored circles like the two pupils of the eyes. This gives the impression of a perfect balance. However, there can be many variations in size, placement, and form.

Small compressed forms often indicate too strong an impact of the senses along with predominating intellectuality influencing the life forces. Generally, when the shape of the moon is small and compressed, the ether body is shrivelled and too strongly connected with the physical body, causing a certain dryness.[7] A large thickly drawn sun can indicate too strong astral forces working as lower will forces in the blood system. Sometimes the shape of the sun does not even fit on the paper. Often this is combined with an overly strong watery element in the constitution.

There can be cases where the shape of the moon is drawn like a kidney. Here we see the connection between the organs and the senses; eyes and kidneys have a specific connection. The kidney shape can indicate that the soul is still engaged in bodily processes.

When a child draws only the contours of the moon and sun, this may indicate that the soul forces are held back in the bodily organization—that the soul has not been able to free itself from the bodily processes. Audrey McAllen described this way of drawing as being done by children and adults she worked with who have developmental disabilities (e.g., Down's syndrome). I often have seen this type of drawing done by normal school children. In most cases, this was an indication that the soul forces of the child were called upon too early by the environment—too early a call on the intellect or awakening of the astral body by, for instance, an adult with a hysterical constitution.

When the shapes of moon and sun are drawn at the very top of the paper (sometimes the sun can be a half circle in the corner), this may indicate that the child is not yet fully incarnated into his body. It is a picture we normally find in drawings by children of kindergarten age.

If the moon and sun are placed far to left and right or just on one side of the midline, we can assume there is a midline problem. Sometimes the children who keep drawing their moon and sun in extreme corners are in need of psychological help.

Sometimes a child draws the moon with a nightcap added to it, with moon craters, or adds faces personifying moon and sun in a childish way. Gradually this will disappear. It could indicate the formative forces building up the body during sleep are very much influenced or disturbed by our modern lifestyle, by sense impressions that are too strong during the day. Over time, various Extra Lesson teachers have seen strange shapes in the drawing of the moon that made them think space exploration on the moon and penetration into the planetary cosmos were harming to the sleep life of the children. We had the impression that the children were not really able to meet the archetypal cosmic formative forces during sleep because of outer disturbances.

A child can draw the sun with rays in chevron patterns. We have seen this more and more in the last decade. It can be done very clearly, almost like a flower motif or a crown. Sometimes the coloring is in scratches around the sun, and looking closely, one can distinguish a chevron motif (you might need to use a magnifying glass). From experience, we can tell that these children subconsciously are experiencing the pressure of the cranial pulse on the bones of the skull and membranes around the brain, caused by a bone structure problem. There might have been an accident or technical interference during the birth delivery (for example, vacuum extraction) or premature breaking of the membranes to start the birth process. These children often also have this motif in their Person-House-Tree pictures, drawn as a crown or a hat on the figure of the person (McAllen, *Reading Children's Drawings*). A child can even draw a person with flames burning on top of the head or a Native American headdress. These motifs will disappear when exercises from *The Extra Lesson* have harmonized the breathing, but in most cases help with cranial osteopathy is needed.

Esoteric History

In the esoteric history of religion and mystery wisdom, people were always conscious of the two main streams that are at work in earth evolution and in the human being. Ancient initiates were aware that there was one stream descending from the heavens toward the earth, from the past to the present, from the prenatal world—the stream of antipathy—that brings the world and the human being into existence; and another stream ascending from the earth toward the heavens, coming from the future into the present—the force of sympathy.

The Ancient Indian Mysteries spoke of the Kundalini, consisting of two currents of energy along the spine; one is female—connected with the moon, the other male—connected with the sun. In the Jewish tradition, Kabbalists describe the forces of the Sephiroth tree, a symbol which shows the spiritual scholar how to keep balance between the two forces here called Boaz and Jachim, after the two pillars of the temple of Solomon. In Ancient Egypt there were two obelisks at the entrance of the temples.

Rosicrucian and Freemasonry traditions also knew these forces that Rudolf Steiner later depicted in the red window of the Goetheanum, where on the left side the human being descends toward the earth and on the right side ascends toward the spiritual world. The balance between the two forces is created with the help of the archangel Michael in the middle window. Rudolf Steiner sometimes spoke of these opposing forces as antipathy and sympathy, in other contexts as Lucifer and Ahriman. (See Appendix B, Audrey McAllen's lecture "Intrusion of the Adversarial Powers.")

The Eye Color Affinity drawing can become a living language that the teacher can use to evaluate the educational support lessons. It is the Extra Lesson teacher's thermometer. It can help the teacher to build up a spiritual, creative, meditative picture of the student. One can have the student draw the Eye Color Affinity regularly at the end of a lesson.

Once a student asked me: "What is this drawing for?" I promised to explain this to him at the end of our last term working together, and he remembered this on the last day. I took all the moon and sun drawings from the file and put them in chronological order on the floor in front of him. He saw the series of different pictures, the shape getting more harmonious and balanced. His only comment was, "Oh, now I see." He did not need any explanation, and he understood what it was all about.

---

1 F.W. Zeylmans van Emmichoven, *De Werking van Kleuren op het Gevoel*. Utrecht: W. de Haan, 1923.

2 F. Peipers, *Farbentherapie*, Beiträge zur Rudolf Steiner Gesamtausgabe Vol. 97, Dornach 1987.

3 J.E. Zeylmans van Emmichoven, *Who was Ita Wegman? A Documentation*, Vol. I 1876–1925. Spring Valley, NY: Mercury, 1990.

4 Rudolf Steiner, *The Temple Legend*. London: Rudolf Steiner Press, 1997. (GA 93) Lectures 11, 12, and 13 given in Berlin May 15, 22, and 29, 1905.

5 Rudolf Steiner, *Karmic Relationships: Esoteric Studies*, Vol. 6

6 Rudolf Steiner, "The Cosmic Origin of the Human Form." (GA 214) Lecture given in Oxford August 22, 1922.

7 Rudolf Steiner, *The Balance in the World and Man: Lucifer and Ahriman*. (GA 158) Three lectures given in Dornach, November 1914.

Chapter 7

The Qualities of the Colors

In the previous chapter the two archetypal colors blue and red were discussed. In this chapter we will try to broaden the color theme and develop an understanding for the qualities of the different colors in relation to the Extra Lesson exercises and diagnosis. To begin with, we need to bring back to mind the 1909 diagram of supersensible currents building up the human physical body.

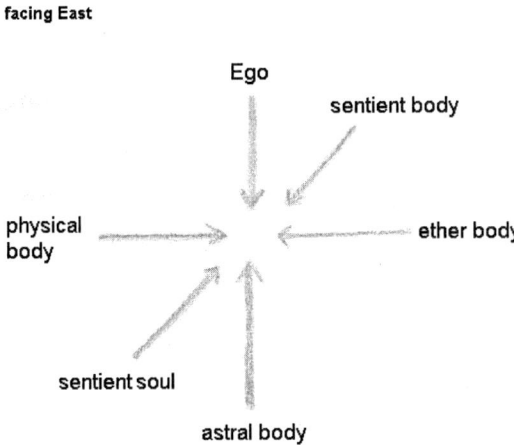

In color, we enter the realm of the soul. Through color, the feeling life of soul can easily find access to the outer world. We have the world of our feeling as an inner rainbow. Color in the outside world and the feeling life of our inner world are two sides of one glove. Rudolf Steiner points out that in the process of perceiving color, the astral forces of the individual meet the astral forces of the world. When these forces meet, the human being perceives color (Steiner 1909 lectures). In the previous chapter about the two archetypal colors of blue and red, we learned about the objective forces of antipathy and sympathy. In the whole rainbow scale of colors, one will find all the different qualities of the soul.

Liane Collot d'Herbois has made an intensive study of the colors in the atmosphere (*Colour*). She is regarded as one of the most important anthroposophical researchers in the field of color and painting. She lived in

Holland for the last long period of her life. I had the opportunity to visit several times and have conversations with her. One day I was able to take Audrey McAllen to visit Liane for tea, and we had a fruitful discussion. Basic to Liane's work was Goethe's color theory, together with what Rudolf Steiner added to it. As Margarethe Hauschka wrote in the preface to Liane Collot's book *Colour*:

> Newton considers only the physical plan. Goethe moves into contemplation of the world of the etheric forces (formative forces). His work mirrors the laws of the world of life. Rudolf Steiner rises to the level of color as expressing what lives in the soul. He penetrates into those worlds, where beyond space and time the creative forces of the soul and spirit reign.

Liane Collot was also an extremely good observer of colors in the atmosphere. She lived in and with color. Her observations were not from the paint box but from actual nature, the interplay between light and air. Goethe had already pointed out that the different colors are created because veils of darkness move around the light. Unseen light and invisible darkness together create the world of color. Color reveals itself in the sense world as a moving interval between the unseen creative activities of light and darkness.

The total blackness of the outer cosmos and the invisible sunlight is described by US astronaut Eugene Cernan in a reflection on his flight in orbit[1]:

> You look out of the window and you're looking back across blackness of space a quarter of a million miles away, looking back at the most beautiful star in the heavens. You're not close enough to any other planet to see anything but a star, but you can look back on the Earth and see from pole to pole and across oceans and continents, and you can watch it turn and see there are no strings holding it up, and it's moving in a blackness that is almost beyond conception.
>
> The Earth is surrounded by blackness though you're looking through sunlight. There is only light if the sunlight has something to shine on. When the sun shines through space it's black. All because the light doesn't strike anything, so all you see is black.
>
> What are you looking at? What are you looking through? You can call it the universe, but it's the infinity of space and the infinity of time.

In space and on the moon, one cannot see a colored sky like we see from the earth. On the moon, the heavens are incredibly black. There is no surrounding atmosphere to diffuse the light. The light of the sun is unbearably bright and intense, yet invisible. Its rays shine unfiltered onto the moon's surface where they are reflected. Astronauts report that moon dust, blown around by the engines of the landing craft or the wheels of a moon buggy, creates an interplay of the colors rose pink and green. Of all colors, this rose pink (magenta) is the closest to the color Rudolf Steiner named peach blossom. Black, white, green, and peach blossom Steiner calls "image colors" or "picture colors" (*Colour*). These four colors possess, according to Steiner, a spiritual character. They hardly display any movement.

When the light is clouded by a first veil of darkness, the color green is created. To be more exact, this is viridian green or emerald green. If you look at the edge of a window pane or into a white bathtub filled with water, you will see this color. The color pink—magenta—is created by the first light that shines through the misty darkness of the morning clouds. This color is the closest to the color Rudolf Steiner called peach blossom.

The other colors that one can observe in the earth atmosphere were called "gleam colors" or "luster colors" by Steiner. Liane Collot d'Herbois describes how the different colors in the atmosphere become visible in their relation between light and darkness. It looks as if there are two types of darkness: the darkness of the universe behind the sky above us (darkness behind light) and the darkness of the atmosphere we look through at the colors of a sunset (darkness in front of light). The totality of darkness moves like a spiral around a center of light—a spine of light. Light moves in one straight direction. In the earth atmosphere with its small particles of moisture and dust, the colors become visible to our eyes.

Darkness spiraling around the light
by Liane Collot d"Herbois

Because of her observation of the movement and dynamics of the different colors, Collot could describe the characteristics and movement of every single color. She could show how each color is created in relation to light and darkness. Being an artist, she painted according to these laws of light and darkness.

In addition to her artistic work, Collot worked for a long time with Dr. Ita Wegman. She learned to make painting a therapy, as a support for the medical therapies for many diseases. Her findings and indications were published in *Light, Darkness, and Colour in Painting Therapy*. In her book, *Fundamentals of Artistic Therapy*, Margarethe Hauschka based the chapter about colors on Collot's indications. Collot could translate the laws of the macrocosm—in this case the laws of the movement of light and darkness in connection with color (the astral body and ether body of the earth)—into the microcosm (the astral body and the ether body of the human being).

Describing the twofold human organism, Rudolf Steiner says that to the spirit the blood system is opaque. The blood and the metabolic system dam up the spirit inside the body. The nerves are as transparent to the spirit as glass is to light. The spirit and soul can run through the physical body via the nervous system. Here the soul-spirit is inside the bodily element. In *Colour* (lecture of December 5th, 1920), Rudolf Steiner speaks of the polarity of light and darkness in relation to the human being. This lecture was fundamental to the work of Liane Collot d'Herbois; it was translated into English especially for her. Based on these indications, Liane Collot describes the polarity of light and darkness in relation to the soul forces of thinking and willing:

> Thinking enlightens. The inner light is the great bearer of our consciousness. From this conscious human element the powers of antipathy shine: they form, lead to an end, create distance, analyze and are causing death. By the processes of thinking well-defined images are created. Thinking has as a characteristic that it always reviews the past. If it shows an event straight away, it will break it down and let it transfer into the past. Thinking tries to create a whole, an isolated in itself resting world, in which the ego itself appears as subject and object. This creative deed conquers the quality of understanding and observation and raises thinking beyond the past contemplating and analyzing.
>
> Willing in contrary arises from an unconscious area that we experience as darkness. Thinking is centered in the head and willing is centered in the metabolic system, where the impulse toward movement, toward the future, arises through the exchange of nutrients. All willing has a character of germinating; it starts in darkness, unshaped, chaotic, like a seed falling into the soil. That is how an impulse that is fed in the element of our will develops to manifest itself in a future appearance.

Where thinking lightens in the inner self we can experience darkness as something moving from the periphery, enclosing, developing and bearing. We can sense to a certain extent the secret of the creative will, which we don't understand, by means of the mediating and breathing area of feeling that weaves itself between thinking and willing and in doing so creates movement and life. Feeling passes off in a dreamy way. It leads towards a subjective area. We can say with certainty "I feel," but we don't feel what the other feels. Feeling sways between sympathy and antipathy, in which experience works immediately, where mood follows mood, coloring our perceptions. Feeling mediates between the activities of the radiating, weightless thinking and condensing willing. Like colors arising as intervals between the actually invisible light and the actually invisible darkness in the perceivable world, we have an inward rainbow, arising between light and inward darkness and which has been formed from the movement of mind and the state of mind. We are involved in this when we are dealing with colors.[2]

If we compare the diagram Rudolf Steiner gave in *Colour* with the earlier 1909 diagram, we need to mirror the color diagram and put the light at the top. The white light comes from above. In this way it corresponds with the 1909 diagram, with the Ego current running from top to bottom (see *A Psychology of Body, Soul, and Spirit*). The aspect of mirroring will be covered in chapter 9. This is a concave mirroring of Steiner's diagram.

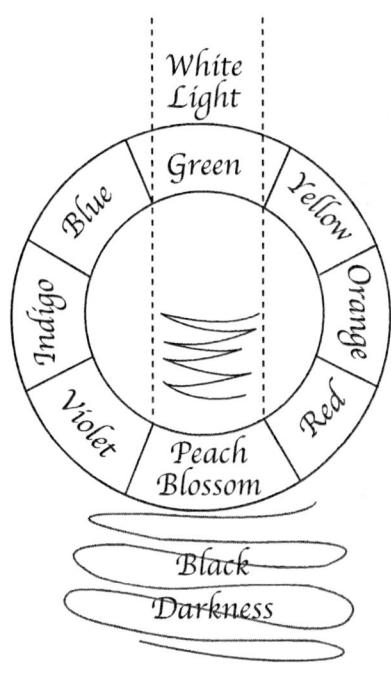

Concave color diagram (see *Reading Children's Drawings* 59

Another diagram (meditation on the Caduceus[3]) confirms what we have found. In this meditation diagram, Rudolf Steiner relates certain colors with corresponding levels of consciousness. Day-wake consciousness appears at the bottom of the diagram with the color green. In a human being standing in front of us, the center of the day-wake consciousness is located in the head. So this diagram too, when inverted, could be a picture of the human being.

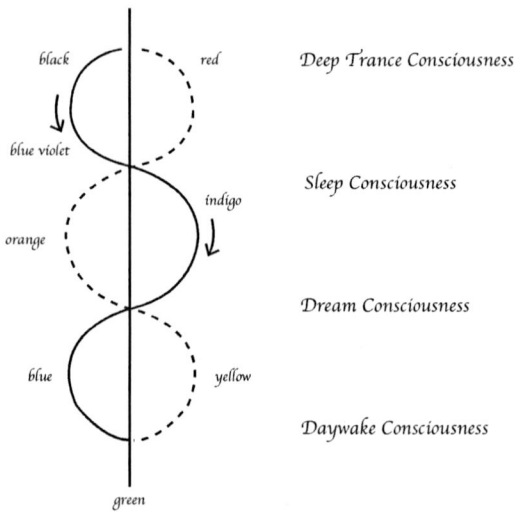

Caduceus diagram by Rudolf Steiner
Reading Children's Drawings, p. 60

Liane Collot d'Herbois published a drawing of the movement of colors called The Big Diagram (*Colour* 80–81). This was made from her observation of the color movements in the sky. To use the diagram as a map, one needs to transfer it from above the head to under the feet, which means one needs to mirror it. We see the light in the center and the darkness moving around this center. Liane Collot drew the space created by the light as two interpenetrating circular shapes. The shape created is like that of the two interpenetrating cupolas of Rudolf Steiner's First Goetheanum building (see chapter 12). If we want to connect this diagram with Steiner's 1909 diagram, we just need to turn it 45° clockwise. By doing this, we are making the human being the center of the diagram. In other words, we move from observation of outer color into the inner soul aspect of the world of color. Now we see that the colors appear on the diagonal of sentient body and sentient soul currents, the two currents in the structure of the human being that are active in perception. More interesting is Steiner's remark (second 1909 lecture): "At the limit of the outward and inward astral influences color arises." We can see that Collot's work and that of Audrey McAllen meet and correspond with Rudolf Steiner's indications.

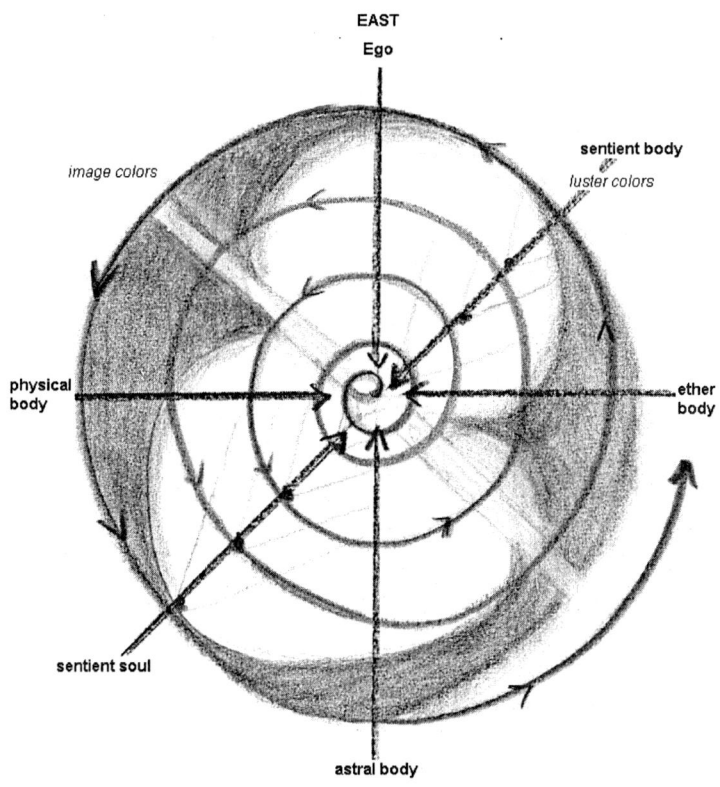

The Big Diagram Mirrored

Colors That Appear in Front of the Light

Darkness that moves in front of the light is the darkness we look through in the direction of the sun. The beauty of a sunset is created by the air and moisture in the atmosphere that darkens the intense light of the sun. Colors in front of the light appear as magenta to yellow-green. They are connected with the forces of the will in the inner microcosm of the human being. The will forces have their physical representation in the limbs and the metabolic system.

Magenta appears when the first light softly and gently penetrates the darkness. Magenta is the color that is most closely connected with the life forces of the ether body. The astral body connects itself with the forces of life. The color magenta, therefore, has a therapeutic effect. It is the favorite color of small children. A company like Mattel makes use of this and sells Barbie dolls in pink wrapping.

Carmine red then appears as a warm glow. It is connected with the blood flow and the metabolism. Darkness decreases and a slow movement ensues.

Vermilion is much more dynamic than carmine. In the vermilion there is a visible fight between light and darkness with a lot of movement. This color was used by the native peoples in South America to paint their bodies. In the human being it is like blood that has been brought into feverish movement, perhaps by nervousness in the soul that arouses too much movement in the blood circulation. The gall processes could also be involved here. Rudolf Steiner called this vermilion red "the wrath of the gods."

Orange is a color that brings about balance; it is a constant fluctuation of veils of darkness that rise against the light and then fall back again. When orange appears in the Person-House-Tree drawing (around the sun, in the house, or in the clothing of the person), the student's soul often is too engaged in the processes of the etheric body. Orange in the human being is connected to the processes of the liver. The liver plays a role in changing food into bodily substances and in cleansing the blood. The liver also helps to break down the heredity body given to a child at birth and to build up the new individual body during the first seven years.

Yellow arises in an overpowering light. It shapes and conquers the darkness. Yellow is connected to the human being through the forces of sympathy at work in the senses and in the thinking. Just as red belongs to the will in the blood, yellow belongs to the will in the senses and in thinking. Therefore, yellow is the color we can see in connection with imitation during the kindergarten age. Small children are completely open to the sense-perceptible world around them. They want to imitate what they perceive through their senses. That is how they learn to stand, walk, and talk.

Cobalt and ultramarine blue in combination with yellow is a favorite combination which we often find in drawings by a kindergarten child. We can also see this combination in the flame of a candle. The Egyptians, too, had a preference for this yellow and blue combination, as seen on the mask of Tutankhamen's sarcophagus. The Yellow Sun in the Blue Sky exercise addresses this color combination. Doing this exercise brings a new impulse to the formative forces of the child.

After the age of seven, the use of too much yellow may indicate that the soul of the child is living too much into the sense world (passion). If this passion is turned inward, it will become egoism or pride. The intense connection of the young child (birth to seven) with the world, which manifests through imitation, is no longer healthy at a later age.

Yellow Green arises when a single veil of darkness goes across the light. This veil of darkness is as if split up by the intense light into little fragments that then disperse. In Grimms' fairy tale "Snow White," the stepmother turns yellow and green with jealousy. This is the soul gesture belonging to yellow green. It is the very strong luciferic element in the sympathy forces of sense activity and thinking.

Green is in the center of all colors. It is not to be looked at as a mix of yellow and blue. That is just thinking of colors from the paint box; only by mixing paints can one produce green synthetically. In nature, green has an identity of its own. As said before, green is the first appearance of light in the atmosphere. Viridian green is the color through which the Ego incarnates into the human being. It is connected with the formation of the spine (Steiner, *Occult Physiology*). Margarete Kirchner-Bockholt formulated another aspect of the green as follows: "Green is the color of the Christ, when green appears in what is alive. The sprouting and budding green in spring is the color of Christ. Otherwise green is the dead image of life. Green, if it is not mirrored in the living, becomes the dead image of thinking...."[4]

The sprouting and budding green in spring surely is an Easter experience for the Northern Hemisphere. In the Southern Hemisphere, for example in Brazil, people have a totally different experience of the forces of spring—and not just because their spring is in September.

When we see green, especially viridian (blue-green) used excessively and in strange places in a child's drawing—for example, in the triangle or square of the house, in the tree trunk, in an unusual way in the person—then it is possible that processes that are connected with the awake, intellectual thinking have too great an influence in the soul of the child. The soul of the child then is too much engaged in the physical body. The child may have become too intellectual or may be influenced by too much intellectuality in his environment. This use of green can also indicate that the child needs to consciously control his movements and that the lower senses are not sufficiently integrated. An excess of the earth color "sap-green" (a Stockmar and Winsor & Newton paint color—the spring green of young leaves or grass), however, can point to rampant (or overpowering) life forces (see Earth Colors, 100–101).

On one of my visits to Liane Collot d'Herbois, she gave me an indication on how to use viridian green for a healing painting exercise. This exercise (published in *The Extra Lesson* 172 and *Learning Difficulties* 124–125) helps to strengthen the activity of the Ego in the sense of sight and the eyes.

Colors Behind the Light

When darkness is lit up because light shines in front of it—like the total darkness of the cosmos that we see as blue sky—that darkness appears as different colors from turquoise to violet (U.S. purple). Collot calls these "the colors behind the light." We can observe this when we look at a distant mountain range with light shining from behind us toward the mountains. The mountains appear to us in various shades of blue. An actor looks into the darkness of the theatre and sees a blue sheen around the stage lights that are shining into his face. The different colors behind the light are connected in the soul of the human being with the formative forces of antipathy. These antipathy forces have their physical representation in the nervous system.

Turquoise is especially noticeable in the sky when it is cold. It is the first and lightest blue color that appears behind the light. Turquoise is the coldest of the different shades of blue. This is in contrast to the cobalt. According to Collot, turquoise is the most unyielding color amongst the colors, except for green. Turquoise is so clear that one cannot observe any movement in it. This color in the human being represents those antipathy forces that give form to the cerebral cortex and the nerves. Prussian blue is a type of turquoise.

Cobalt has already been mentioned as a color that holds much more warmth. The firmament over the Mediterranean Sea and also the cornflower in the golden cornfield is cobalt. Cobalt always weaves in the distance. There it forms a hollow space, like the dome of the sky. In the human being, cobalt is present in the hollow spaces and concave organs: the cranium, the lungs, and the bladder. The inside of the bladder is actually cobalt blue.

Ultramarine blue has more or less the same quality as the cobalt. It actually is a form of cobalt, but the ultramarine is only visible in a very damp atmosphere, like one that hangs over a peat bog. The word ultramarine comes from *ultra mare*, meaning "from across the sea." Is it the color of the sea reflecting the cobalt of the sky above it? Children like both cobalt and ultramarine. In contrast to turquoise and Prussian blue, cobalt and ultramarine have a warm character.

Indigo appears in the sky on melancholy days when the sun is not visible, also in the clouds of an approaching thunderstorm. One can observe this color in a mussel shell. It is a color that calls up isolation and loneliness. It is remarkable that present day western people so often dress in this color—blue jeans! In the human organism, the skin separates, by creating the boundary between outer and inner world. One can connect indigo

Colors behind the light

Colors in front of the light

paintings by Erica Eikenboom

Colors behind and in front of the light

Concave and convex color movements

paintings by Erica Eikenboom

with the process of skin forming. The skeletal bones are separated from the rest of the inner organization by a "skin" that covers the bones. Thus we can say of the skeleton that it is the three-dimensional outer world that we carry within us. Formation of the tubular bones is also connected with this color. In our modern times we see more and more frequently that youngsters grow taller than the generations before them. Because of this, the experience of gravity is changing, which will influence the soul life of present and future human beings. In this way, indigo is the color of the developing consciousness soul.

It is not good to use this color when children are too young. It calls on too many forces that they cannot digest. It is understood that Liane Collot d'Herbois here means the use of indigo in *painting* (not in drawing, see Considerations, p. 105). Those of us who have ever painted with indigo will have experienced what effect this painted color has.

Violet (blue-violet, purple in the U.S.) appears as the final color behind the light. It is the final color before we have arrived at absolute darkness. It is a color that can appear on a hot summer evening. (In California, the sky can be a beautiful cobalt violet.) A haze of violet lies over the earth, because violet can be very transparent. It is mysterious and tranquil. In the human being, violet seems to belong to old age. It is the color that carries us over the threshold at the end of our life. Violet does not really belong to the young child, more to the elderly human being. When blue-violet is used in excess in a child's drawings, it can be a sign that the soul is too strongly engaged in its own processes, in the processes of the astral body itself. Through this, the soul is being pressed strongly into the physical body. This can be caused by an early call on the child's responsibility, by asking the young child to choose what he would like all the time, or not offering the child enough room to develop his own will by an overprotective environment.

Earth Colors

In addition to the bright colors in the atmosphere, there are colors formed when light penetrates the darkness insufficiently. There, the so-called earth colors come into being. Clear yellow can very quickly become like an ochre brown when the atmosphere becomes more dense and heavy. One can see this when the sky is polluted. Orange and vermilion can become raw umber and burnt Sienna. Carmine and magenta become brown madder or *caput mortuum*. It is notable that these colors often carry a geographical name: raw or burnt Sienna, raw or burnt Umber (Umbria), Venetian Red, Naples Yellow, but also Prussian Blue, Delft Blue, Windsor

Blue and Antwerp Blue. Prussian blue is the earth equivalent of turquoise and has the same hard and immovable quality as turquoise. In Waldorf schools Prussian blue tends to be used too often in painting, because, when mixed with yellow, this blue creates the color green. Instead of this, we can let the children use other kinds of green. They love to experience this. Read Rudolf Steiner's indications for the first painting lesson in first grade; he definitely used green right from the paint box (*Practical Advice to Teachers*, lecture 5).

The earth tints of green are olive green, "green earth" (green with a little gray in it), and "sap green." When these colors are used excessively in children's drawings, it can mean that the life forces or the processes that are connected with the etheric are too much in the foreground and thus form a blockage in the child's consciousness.

The different tints of brown that are used reflect the way the processes of the lymph organization are experienced. When this color appears too often, one can get the impression that the astral body and the ego are not able to penetrate and shine through the processes of the etheric sufficiently. The breathing can be shallow. Old heredity forces and possibly old and unresolved karma, which is carried around in the lymph system of the human being, could be an obstacle in such a situation. The darker the brown, the further we are distanced from the light, the more strongly this element plays a part and is stuck.

Children rarely use *grey*. It is not really a color that belongs to the realm of the soul but is created when one is working with the spiritual qualities of light and darkness—as in charcoal drawings. In the atmosphere we do not find grey except in the rain clouds. White clouds consist of ice crystals; that is why they reflect the light so brilliantly. Light cannot penetrate clouds made of water drops because this liquid water is denser matter. Grey clouds predict rainy weather. With this in mind, we can understand that when children use grey it shows that the organism is not sufficiently transparent to the soul-spirit.

The use of *black* in drawing seems to lead to different and often negative reactions from today's class teachers and kindergarten teachers alike. This color often calls up connections with death, depression, and other negative soul elements. However, if we look at this color from the standpoint of light and darkness, black represents the darkness, which is not connected with the forces of death, but on the contrary, with the new buds of life and the new impulses that live in the subconscious of the will.

"In the darkness I find God's Being" says Rudolf Steiner's verse (see below, p. 100).

During a conversation with Liane Collot d'Herbois, Audrey McAllen and I asked her if she could agree with us that it is necessary to give children, even already in kindergarten, the opportunity to draw with black. Her answer was positive. "Of course, darling," Liane said, "because black represents the darkness; it has an enfolding quality like a shell, which, for instance, gives protection to a mussel. Children can have an enormous urge to express themselves with this color. So please let them do so."

Black can also indicate that the child perceives areas in his physical body that he needs to work on, which he as yet has penetrated insufficiently. Children who are new to a Waldorf School or who have just arrived in the Waldorf kindergarten often grab this color. Also children who have started a new phase of their development can do this for a while. A teacher can notice the use of this color and can observe whether the work he is doing with that child is bearing fruit. After a while the use of the black crayon will disappear. Children will then be able to apply black in the right proportions and in the right place (for instance, a black cat, crow, or chimney smoke).

In our work with the Extra Lesson we have often experienced that children when they shed the "black phase" choose the color *purpur* (red-violet). This indicates that new life forces have been brought into play. After all, purpur is the color of the royal mantle and, in the ancient mysteries, of the outer robe of the initiate. It seems that in those cases a sort of resurrection has taken place. Without the black, this resurrection would not have been made visible.

What has been written and used here of Collot's approach to color is not the complete picture of her artistic and medical work. For Liane, the world of light and darkness was never a fixed picture. The light does not need to come in vertically from above as in the diagram we use. Those who studied painting with Liane Collot report that she only corrected them by pointing out the objective laws of darkness moving in relation to the light. She would, however, always stress the thinking element: "You have to think before you paint, darling!" she used to say.[5] This shows that Collot's approach to the world of color and painting is totally in harmony with what Rudolf Steiner wrote in his *Philosophy of Freedom* (chapter 1)—that human action is grounded in thinking.

I have translated below a verse by Rudolf Steiner published in *Farbenerkenntnis* (GA 291a):

In der *Finsternis* finde ich Gottes=Sein
In *Rosenrot* fühl ich des Lebens Quell
In *Ätherblau* ruht des Geistes Sehnsucht
Im *Lebensgrün* atmet alles Lebens Atem
Im *Goldesgelb* leuchtet des Denkens Klarheit
Im *Feuers Rot* wurzelt des Willens Stärke
Im *Sonnenweiß* offenbart sich meines Wesens Kern

Weiß—Ich / Finsternis—Gott

In the *darkness* I find God's Being
In the *rose red* I feel the source of life
In the *ether blue* rests the Spirit's desire
In *life green* everything breathes life's breath
In *golden yellow* shines thinking's clarity
In *fire red* roots the strength of will
In *sun white* the core of my being is revealed

White—Ego / Darkness—God

Counter-colors—Complementary Colors

For painting the small cupola of the first Goetheanum, the Dutch painter Miss J. M. Bruinier was given the task of painting the left side in counter-colors to those on the right side. She did not understand the term "counter-color," and she asked Rudolf Steiner whether he meant complementary colors, such as red as the opposite of green. Rudolf Steiner replied: "No, surely you will have noticed that I have not used green at all in the small cupola. In the large cupola the colors have been taken from the day spectrum. The basis for the small cupola is to be the colors of the night spectrum."[6]

The small cupola was painted with pictures of the history of humankind. It was supposed to be an imagination of spirit recollection, as it was later called in the Foundation Stone Meditation. These paintings included Indian, Persian, Egyptian, Greek, and Northern initiates, and the modern human being represented by Faust. The north side would have similar illustrations in counter-colors. The soul element in this small cupola was expressed by the use of the three soul colors—yellow, red, and blue—on a magenta ground. The red pictures on the right side were expected to be painted in the darker blue counter-color on the left. Yellow on the right would have become lighter blue on the left. Here we see expressed the astral body in its own astral element of reversal. This we find in the Eye Color Affinity—blue moon and red sun—drawing (chapter 6).

Complementary colors can be discovered in the phenomena of colored shadows. When a dark shadow in a colored light is lit by a second light source, the complementary color will appear in the shadow.

The ceiling of the large cupola was painted in the day spectrum, so green would appear in that part of the building. Wherever there is color, one can say that the astral body is active there. The complementary colors show the astral body in its connection to the organism, to the etheric body. In the large cupola, we have the inner aspect of the astral body as in the sevenfold lower human being, the trunk. In the small cupola, we have the astral body in connection to the twelvefold upper human being: the head and the nerve-sense system.

In chapter 9, the element of mirroring sequences, reflection, refraction, and reversal will be covered. It would be good for the reader to keep in mind these two different aspects of the astral body.

Diagnostic Painting of a Person in Green and Red

During a conversation, Liane Collot d'Herbois suggested that, for a diagnostic painting, one can ask a student to paint a person with just the two colors green and red. Often things only need to be done, for the insights are already given—so I started to work with this indication. To my surprise, the paintings gave me valuable information about the condition of the students with whom I was working. The shape of the person was in most cases comparable to the person in the Person-House-Tree drawing (done in the Extra Lesson assessment), showing the difficulties in the structural physical body. I went back to Liane to show her the material; she looked at it and said—to my astonishment—"These children are all healthy." This showed me she was only looking at color, not at shape. Her diagnoses considered the constitutional element, and indeed these children, in spite of their learning problems, were medically healthy. The way the student uses the colors shows his constitutional condition. The following instructions are for this exercise:

> Prepare a piece of painting paper about 12" x 18" (32 x 44 cm). Wet it thoroughly and put it vertically on a board. In order that the paper is not covered with so much water that the painted form will run, dry the paper with a sponge or with a tea towel if needed.
>
> Prepare two jars of paint mixed with some water: viridian green and carmine red. Stockmar: Blue Green and Carmine Red will do, or Winsor & Newton: Viridian Green and Rose Madder.
>
> Use 2 brushes, one for each color.
>
> Ask the child to paint just a picture of a person—a human being and nothing else—using only these two colors, green and red. Gesture with your hand across the paper from top to bottom to indicate where and what size the painted person could be. If the child asks how to do it, tell him that he can paint it any way he thinks is best.

Considerations

Collot's indication was to use the colors green and red. In Extra Lesson exercises we work with blue and red. Blue and red are connected with objective observation of the outer sense world (see Eye Color Affinity, chapter 6). The combination of green and red is related to either the inner life of the personal soul (see the the panel of the Isenheim Altarpiece in which Mary is visited by the Archangel Gabriel) or to the inner aspect of the astral body at work in the metabolism. Therefore, green and red are called "threshold colors" (see the colored windows of the Goetheanum building in Dornach).

In *drawing*—for example, in the Person-House-Tree drawing—the soul is making a statement about itself in relation to movement, perception, and feelings. This is the working of the spirit (Ego) onto the physical, the structural, aspect. In *painting*, the colors call on the soul activity to merge with them and become active. This is the working of the personal astral body on the etheric body, the constitutional aspect (see McAllen *Sleep* 62).

With this painting we ask the astral body of the child what inner picture it has of the child's bodily condition. There are two aspects to look at:

- The form of the human being the child paints is connected with the structural aspect of the physical body. Here we will find an image of the body geography, which should be threefold. Any strange structural representations in the form can be connected with structural problems. We can compare this with the Person-House-Tree drawings. Was the child able to paint the complete figure on the page; did the head fit on the paper or did the child need more space?

- The colors are connected with the constitutional aspect of the physical body. Here we look at the colors the child chose for the head, middle system, and metabolic-limb system. Did the child mix colors and produce gray? This might indicate an area where there is a problem. Did the child use so much water that the form was washed away? This could also be a structural problem, if not constitutional.

Archetypally, the color green is connected with consciousness and the color red with metabolism, will forces. It can very well be that a child uses red for the head and green for the limbs. So far we do not have a thorough understanding of this. I encourage the reader to do research and share the results with colleagues.

---

1. Loren Acton, cited in *The Home Planet*, edited by Kevin W. Kelley (Reading, MA: Addison-Wesley, 1988).
2. Liane Collot d'Herbois, "Malen in Schichten" published by the Iona Schülungsstätte für künstlerische Therapie, Germany. Translated from German into English by Ineke Rijsdijk.
3. Rudolf Steiner, *Farbenerkenntnis* (GA 291a), Dornach, Switzerland.
4. Margarete and Erich Kirchner-Bockholt, *Die Menschheitsaufgabe Rudolf Steiners und Ita Wegman*, Dornach, Switzerland, 1981.
5. Rösli Rienks-Läser, in Liane Collot d'Herbois *Erinnerungen von Freuden und Schülern*. E. Leonora Hambrecht ed. Dürnau, Germany, 2003.
6. D. van Bemmelen, *Rudolf Steiner's New Approach to Color on the Ceiling of the First Goetheanum*. Spring Valley, NY: St. George Publications, 1980.

Chapter 8

Colors in the Extra Lesson Painting Exercises

Ultramarine blue and carmine red are the main colors used in the Extra Lesson exercises, as they are objective and archetypal representatives of the soul forces of antipathy and sympathy. The blue and red eye-color-affinity directs the soul into the outer sense world. As we have seen in the last chapter there is another opposing pair in green and red. This color combination leads into the inner feeling realm of the astral body where the astral body is connected with the constitution. One could assume that the colors of national flags are rooted in subconscious knowledge of these archetypes. Think of the difference between the general impression of the Italian and French folk souls or the difference between the Hungarians and the Dutch. Italy and Hungary have green, white, and red; France and Holland have blue, white, and red. What do we think when flying the English or American flags? In Mathias Grünewald's altar painting we see the Archangel Gabriel visiting the young virgin Mary. The colors used here for the decoration of the virgin's room are green and red, indicating her inner life. She was in meditation or prayer when this happened.

Painting Technique

To begin with, it is crucial to stress the importance of the simple painting technique of having the child or student work in long strokes from left to right. The hand moves as fast as the eyes can follow. At the end of the page the arm is lifted and returned to the left. A rhythmical movement needs to be established. In some cases the educational support teacher can choose to exercise this technique just with one color suitable for the situation. Also grade teachers can decide to start the morning lesson with a simple color exercise. One could choose the colors of the day, of the rainbow, or any other appropriate color sequence. This will help the students to connect the spiritual and soul bodies with the physical and life bodies. Breathing is the connecting and healing element here. This is most suitable when children have to drive a long distance in a car to get to school. For the weeks when this exercise is used, circle activities can be skipped.

The educational support (remedial) teacher will be able to closely observe the student's breathing. In some cases, the student will complain when he starts to feel his muscles and the weight of the arm. Exhaling a deep breath or shaking the arm will relax the tension.

Audrey McAllen developed this simple painting technique in her work. However, in therapeutic painting there is a similar technique of painting in veils. This was developed by Liane Collot d'Herbois based on indications by Rudolf Steiner, probably passed over to her by Ita Wegman. Liane Collot reported to us the following history:

When Rudolf Steiner was already bedridden with his final illness, he asked his secretary to bring him paper and painting supplies. He made examples of painting in veils and asked his secretary to bring them to the Goetheanum painters and explain to them that this was a new way of painting that had to be developed. All of the painters objected and protested; no-one wanted to paint that way. Then after some time one of the painters—Fräulein Geck—came to the Schreinerei with a number of paintings she had done. Dr. Steiner saw she had not understood, so he showed her how to paint in veils. He asked her what she thought about it and she answered, "Everything you do is good!" That made Rudolf Steiner angry. "That is not the question!" he said to her. Fräulein Geck did not take up the new way of painting as he wished, but Liane Collot d'Herbois brought the technique to Bad Boll, Germany, where it became part of therapeutic painting.

Secondary Color Exercise (from age 9)

In this painting exercise, the teacher gives the student the choice of green, orange, or blue-violet (purple). One can connect the choice of color with the information given in the last chapter. Audrey McAllen gives the following suggestions as to the possible significance of the color chosen:

Orange is connected with the liver processes. We often see this color used in drawings by children in kindergarten. After the age of 9, the choice of this color indicates that the day-wake personality is still too strongly engaged in heredity carried by the ether body. Green is the color of the first appearance of light. If the child chooses green, it can indicate that the day-wake consciousness is too strongly at work inside the body. Choosing blue-violet—the last color before one enters the darkness—can indicate the day-wake personality of the soul is too strongly engaged in its own antipathy and sympathy forces.

This painting exercise helps to release the soul problem by objectively offering the related primary colors. One will recognize the archetypal elements of three-dimensional space painted in the second painting.

Only a few years ago, a color *meditation on the hexagon*, given by Rudolf Steiner, was published in *Farbenerkenntnis* (November 29, 1907). The lower members—astral body, ether body, and physical body—are represented by the triangle colored green, orange, and violet.

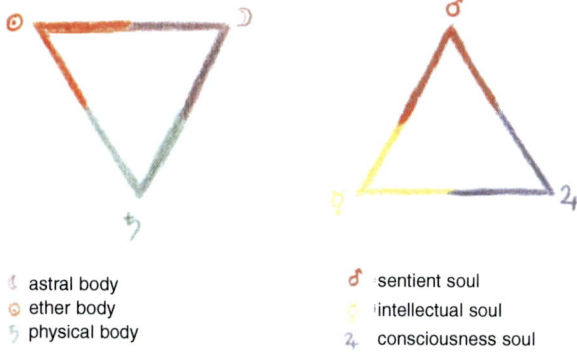

- astral body
- ether body
- physical body

- sentient soul
- intellectual soul
- consciousness soul

These members are the result of the evolutionary stages of Old Saturn, Old Sun, and Old Moon. The second triangle represents the three soul members Sentient Soul, Intellectual Soul and Consciousness Soul. This triangle with the soul colors red, yellow, and blue is connected with this present earth's evolution of Mars and Mercury stages and with the future stage called Jupiter. This publication confirms what Audrey McAllen developed as color indications for the Person-House-Tree Drawings (see *Reading Children's Drawings*).

Meditation on the Hexagon

Moral Color Exercises (from age 11)

These painting exercises were published in Audrey McAllen's *Sleep: An Unobserved Element in Education*. Audrey studied painting with Hilde Boos-Hamburger in Dornach, Switzerland. Hamburger was one of the artists working on the construction of the First Goetheanum. She also had a small class at the Friedwart Schule in Dornach. She reports that Rudolf Steiner came to visit the class; he suggested having one of the students leave geometrical forms unpainted on the paper while the rest of the sheet was covered with one solid color.[1] The geometrical form was to be colored in with another color. The student had a talent for painting but appeared to be a somewhat clairvoyant child. Rudolf Steiner advised this should be healed so that her view would become more connected with the objective world of the senses. This shows how down-to-earth Rudolf Steiner was. He did not like the ecstatic and luciferic state of mind at all. Future clairvoyance can only become healthy when it is under the guidance of the Ego, which needs first to be anchored in the objective physical world.

In *Sleep,* Audrey McAllen reports how Hilde Boos-Hamburger[1] had developed several combinations of form and color and later asked her to complete the series. The total of six paintings are done in the archetypal sequence of rainbow colors. This is the archetype of the healthy soul or astral body as offered to us by the hierarchy of the Angels (see Steiner's lecture of January 4, 1924 "The Hierarchies and the Rainbow" in *Colour*).

The first painting in vermilion red offers the soul the ability of cleansing the inner personal conflicts hindering the individuality from incarnating properly and freely. The student is able to explore different color combinations to paint a five-pointed star. The given combination gives the *soul* a picture of its condition: vermilion represents the luciferic elements of pride, desire, and passion in the blood, brought to man by the Fall. The star will eventually be colored magenta, which is the cleansed blood, the element of the Christ Being. This inner work for the soul is connected with the back to front current of the sentient soul, as we know from the 1909 diagram. This movement direction is aligned with the moral virtue of *courage* (see McAllen, *Sleep*). We could think of the courage the European sailors had when beginning to explore the New World. They had to leave the safe shores of the Old World and head west, go across the ocean.

The second painting is an objective picture of three-dimensional space given as a two-dimensional six-pointed star. It is the current of the sentient body coming from in front. Experiencing the beauty of the sense world fills us with *joy*. Orange is the background color; the star shape is pale Prussian blue, or maybe a lighter turquoise.

The third painting is an orange circle in a yellow field. The circular motif is the form similar to the apple-in-tree motif at the end of kindergarten, when the child has become ready for elementary school; the ether forces are available for learning, and the astral body starts slowly incarnating. The Grimms' fairy tale of Mother Holle says: "She went on till she came to a tree covered with apples, which called out to her, 'Oh, shake me! shake me! we apples are all ripe! So she shook the tree till the apples fell like rain, and went on shaking till they were all down, and when she had gathered them into a heap, she went on her way." Yellow represents the sympathy forces of the young child drawing the soul out into the sense world. This painting represents the astral body not yet connected with the physical and life bodies. It is the current of the astral body from below up. The virtue is *faith*.

The fourth painting is the green background with leaf motifs. Please remember all that was said about the color green in the last chapter. In this painting we have the vegetable kingdom, the world of the etheric, which carries all the wisdom from the Old Moon. In the 1909 diagram this is the current of the etheric body running from right to left. The virtue connected with the Old Moon and the world of the etheric is *wisdom*.

In the third painting we had the objective astral body ready to incarnate. Now in *the fifth painting*, we see the astral body incarnating into the physical body. The objective archetypal soul colors are blue and red. The archetypal form is now the lemniscate (which is a spiral seen from the side). In the 1909 diagram this is the current of the physical from left to right. Every human being has a similar structural physical body. That has to do with *righteousness*.

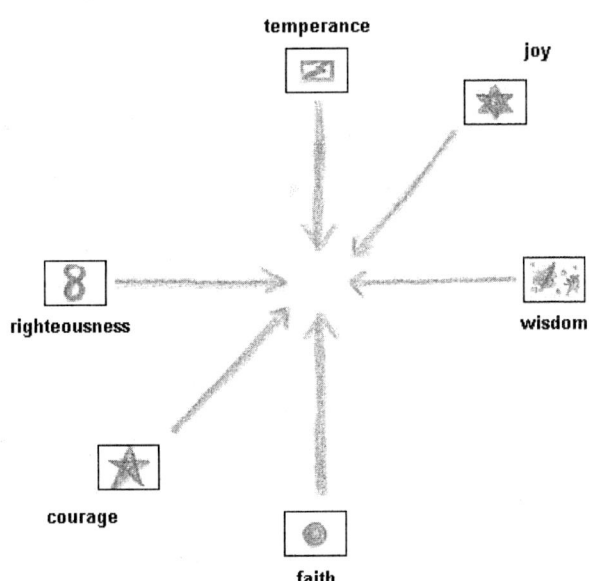

This was all a preparation for *the last painting*. Together the five currents form the cup into which the Ego incarnates. In the sixth painting we see the forces of the Ego incarnating into the total structure of the body. The square is the two-dimensional cube. For the background blue-violet is used, somewhat darkened with black paint or ink. The Ego makes use of the forces of antipathy (cobalt blue) and sympathy (yellow flash) that work from the head down in the years from birth to seven (Steiner *Balance in Teaching* lecture 2). The yellow flash of lightning represents the electric sparks that jump over the synapses of the nervous system. The spiritual will be anchored in the structural physical organization. The Ego will be able to keep all forces in balance, which is the virtue of *temperance*.

Having heard the story about Hilde Boos-Hamburger, my German colleague Ernst Westermeier asked me whether the Moral Color Exercises should help children to incarnate into their body. The reason he asked this was that he had noticed that in the Person-House-Tree drawings a number of students he worked with were drawing extra windows in the roof part of the house (the triangle). These dormer-windows indicate either that the supersensible organs (chakras or lotus flowers) are still at work organically building up the brain, the movement system, or the nervous system (Steiner1909 lectures) or that something in the soul element was hindering the process of incarnation (see introduction). I suggested he try to find out, for in our work one must have courage to follow one's intuitions and do research. It is as Rudolf Steiner once wrote to Willem Zeylmans van Emmichoven: "We must have complete confidence in the ever present help from the spiritual world. Without this nothing goes."[2] Westermeier combined a series of movement exercises with exercises for integrating early and immature movement patterns and then ended the lesson with painting. For younger children, he used the Yellow Sun in Blue Sky painting exercise. After some time working with this series of paintings, the attic windows in the drawings disappeared. The work on the structural physical body combined with help for the inner soul element led the children to make huge steps in their development.

I highly recommend not mixing paint to produce orange, green or violet. Please use paint right from the tube. Mixed colors will never have the same objective quality as manufactured paint. Mixing colors in painting is teaching the students a painting technique. Rudolf Steiner himself used manufactured colors as described by Hilde Boos-Hamburger and one can read this in his lectures.[3]

Yellow Sun in Blue Sky (from age 6)

This painting is a version of the Moral Color Exercises for younger children. The objective colors of antipathy (blue) and sympathy (yellow) for the young child are used as it is in the sixth Moral Color Exercise. The repetition of this painting exercise and establishing a harmony between the two colors will help the child to bring harmonious balance between these two soul forces. In Rudolf Steiner's color diagram given in the foregoing chapter, one can see blue and yellow active in the region of the head as colors of antipathy in the nerves and sympathy in the will to connect with the outer world through the senses and imitation.

Eventually the teacher will have the child paint extra elements besides the motif of sun and sky. One can have the child make a continuing story adding a new motif after repeating the earlier ones. It is possible to have the student write down sentences as a written version of the story. One can produce a story book with illustrations and text.

In my experience and that of colleagues all over the world, the children will chose archetypal elements from the depths of their inner soul life that show the hindrances on the path of incarnation. The Extra Lesson educational support teacher will learn to read these elements and interpret them as archetypal pictures, as described by Audrey McAllen in *Reading Children's Drawings*. Often the total sequence of images painted by the child will show the process he went though during the terms of educational support. Both the Moral Color Exercises and the Yellow Sun in the Blue Sky painting exercise show the personal soul of the student on an objective path into the structural physical body and into the outer sense world.

Moving Straight Line and Lemniscate (from age 8)

Another image of children's incarnating process can be built when the Extra Lesson educational support teacher takes note of the colors the students use for the Moving Straight Line and Lemniscate exercise. In the choice of color one will see the soul indicating where the incarnation got stuck or where it is experiencing hindrances. The color diagram as the archetypal picture of the human being can be a great help. One needs to compare the colors the student chooses with this objective color diagram. One will hope for the choice of blue and red and correct eye-color-affinity as an indication the soul forces are free from their bodily engagement, that the soul has control over the physical. Reversed eye-color-affinity will indicate that the body is still overpowering the soul. Blue and yellow as colors of the young child already show a new step in the incarnation process. One will often see combinations of green and red, shades of yellow and green, green and blue-violet, or black. From my experience, the black, after a time of successful work, will often be followed by the use of magenta, when the educational support lessons have the expected results. Magenta is the color that shows that healing forces from the heart are flowing into the etheric body. One can be happy when this color of resurrection appears.

Eye Color Affinity

When the child chooses to draw a blue moon and a yellow sun, the child is taking the archetypal colors of antipathy and sympathy that are strongly connected with the head: the formative forces of the cranium and the sympathy forces at work in the senses. Audrey McAllen named this yellow-blue combination the *kindergarten colors*. These appear in most of the drawings children make at kindergarten age. In the school age child, the choice of yellow and blue gives one the indication the young developmental stage is not yet entirely overcome.

When the soul is too strongly engaged in the forces of heredity, orange will be taken or added to the sun. Nervous overstimulation of the senses will make a child choose vermilion.

There is also the possibility of a magenta or violet moon with a yellow sun. I came to an idea of the meaning of this during a eurythmy performance. The group performed Rudolf Steiner's "The Twelve Moods" (see *Verses and Meditations*). The representatives of the moon and the sun were costumed in violet and white respectively. I realized that, in this setting, moon and sun together with the planets were connected with the inner aspect of the astral body, with the bodily processes, and thus could not be in blue and red. When the color combination of yellow and magenta (or yellow and blue-violet) appears in the Eye Color Affinity, Moving Straight Line and Lemniscate, or in the drawing of the Person-House-Tree (such as a person in a magenta dress with a yellow pram, or with yellow and magenta ribbons in the person's hair, or yellow and red or blue-violet windows in the house), the student will be living more in the ether processes of his constitutional body. Objective perception of the sense world may possibly be washed away by ether forces that are too strong. Memory problems may be the result.

---

1. Hilde Boos-Hamburger, *Gespräche mit Rudolf Steiner über Mahlerei*, Basel 1961.
2. The complete verse is published in *Willem Zeylmans van Emmichoven: An Inspiration for Anthroposophy*, by Emmanuel Zeylmans van Emmichoven, p. 206.
3. Rudolf Steiner, *The Spiritual Ground of Education* (the Oxford course) lecture of August 16, 1922, and *Practical Advice to Teachers*.

Chapter 9

Mirroring and the Imprinting Process

A most difficult and complex chapter within anthroposophy as a whole and the Extra Lesson concept in particular is the understanding of the supersensible processes of perception and memory. In fact it has always been a deep philosophical question how the outer world can be taken into the inner life of the human being. Rudolf Steiner deals with this topic in his *Philosophy of Freedom* in a fresh and humorous way. When he lectured at the annual gathering of the Theosophical Society in 1909, the organization of the human senses and the physical body were the first subject he covered. A year later, in November 1910, he spoke there about the activities of the soul and the inner processing of perception. He spoke about the spiritual aspects the following year, in December 1911. These three lecture cycles, as he said himself, gave the fundamentals of the anthroposophical picture of the human being. In preparation for opening the first Waldorf School in 1919, Rudolf Steiner referred to these lectures. I assume he knew, or expected, that the new teachers were familiar with their content.

In concerning ourselves with learning difficulties and dyslexia, as teachers we are obliged to occupy ourselves with how sense impressions are processed in the body, soul, and spirit. Here, as in the description of the different exercises, one needs to approach the matter from several different angles—from the bodily, soul, and spiritual aspects and from the twofold, threefold, and fourfold pictures of the human being.

The anthroposophical medical doctor and curative educator Walter Holtzapfel published two chapters on dyslexia.[1] I highly recommend this reading material as a starter. Audrey McAllen published an article "The Mirroring Process in Relation to Two- and Three-dimensional Space" (*Learning Difficulties*) with diagrams on the mirroring process. This chapter will give background information on this matter as related to the Extra Lesson.

Twofold Picture

The twofold picture of the human being is of the head in contrast to the rest of his organism. On the one side the human being is a being of perception; on the other side he is a being of action, deeds. The twofold picture Rudolf Steiner gave in the first lecture of *Study of Man* is of the soul-spiritual element in contrast to the physical and life bodies. The twofoldness expresses itself in the bodily structure of nerves—blood, upper man—lower man. In the soul it expresses itself as the soul forces of antipathy in contrast to sympathy, past—future.

The human being, however, is a unity. There always needs to be a relation between the first and the second aspect of the twofold human organization (Steiner *Kingdom of Childhood* lecture 1). Think of Rudolf Steiner's picture of the fourfold organization of head and trunk in *Education for Special Needs* (lecture 5), where he says that, under normal, healthy circumstances, whenever one perceives something through the senses located in the head, this always causes vibrations in the supersensible organization of the trunk. If not, we would not have memory.

Threefold Picture

Between the two opposite poles, a third interlinking element develops. This happens mainly in the child's development in the primary school years. It is the time when the feeling life is very important. It is the realm of the rhythmic system. At the age of nine, the Ego needs to find its new anchor in the etheric body. The blood system of the metabolism and the ratio of breathing to heart rate (1:4) will be established by the end of 4th grade.

In chapter 5 (Copper Ball Exercise) we already mentioned Rudolf Steiner's point that the processing of outer sense impressions by the nervous system has nothing to do with the inner soul life itself. The nervous system receives sense impressions and tones down the outer vibrations of these impressions. The senses, as it were, vibrate together with the vibrations and movements of the outer world. The sense organs imitate the movements of the outer sense world as if they were the limbs of a small child. Sound is created by movement; color is movement of darkness around light. The auditory system of the ears and the visual system of the eyes resonate together with these outer movements. They are imitating.

These inner imitations of the outer world are mirrored by the rhythmic system. Through the rhythmic middle system, sensory impressions are connected with the inner feeling life of the soul. Breathing, which is strongly connected with the feeling life, connects with the toned-down sense impression. The toned-down sense impression is then received by the inner light of the soul.

The soul impressions are then imprinted as memory images into the etheric processes of the metabolic system. The carrier of the memory is not the brain. The brain itself plays an important role in bringing the inner memory pictures back into day-wake or thinking consciousness (Steiner *Foundations of Human Experience* lecture 10). This is the threefold picture of the process in the nervous system, rhythmic system, and metabolic system.

Fourfold Picture

Rudolf Steiner also speaks of the fourfold picture of the physical, etheric, and astral bodies and the Ego. Steiner gives different images of how these four members of the human being are arranged and work differently in head and trunk. There is the medical and therapeutic education picture as given in *Education for Special Needs*. There are other pictures given to the teachers, which resemble the ideas given in general anthroposophical lectures. The medical and therapeutic education approach is directed towards the inner, personal, karmic element that is behind every illness. This is the constitutional picture. In contrast, the teachers are engaged in the objective organization of the senses and the physical outer world (*Deeper Insights into Education*).

As an introduction to the mirroring aspects of the etheric and astral bodies, one can look at how the mineral, plant, and animal kingdoms appear to us. The physical is the mineral material of creation. In crystals, which took time to coagulate, one can discover the work of an etheric forming principle that was working from the outside creating planar forms. Even the hexagram in the structure of snowflakes shows this principle.

In plants, this forming principle works from within in the formation of leaves. The leaves of the plants and trees can be looked at as planes, as having a mainly two-dimensional character, just surface. The etheric forces working inside the plant support life, growth, and multiplication. An archetypal picture is provided by the mushroom. There is, however, another principle working from without, which creates specific forms and differentiation. Waldorf class teachers who have taught 5th grade botany will know the developmental stages within the plant kingdom. These differentiating forces come from the world of the stars and planets. There is, for instance, the influence of the sun and the seasons on the dynamic of growth and the shaping of leaves, flowers, and fruit. In biodynamic farming one also takes into account the rhythm of the moon travelling through the different signs of the zodiac.

Anthroposophical scientists have shown the influences and rhythms of the different planets on the shape of trees and flowers. Most obvious is the spiralling tendency in the way plants and trees grow. Herein one can see the starry, astral forces working from without into the etheric forces of the plant kingdom. These forces are named formative forces by Ernst Marti who described them in his book *The Four Ethers*. The formative forces are of an astral origin, from stars and planets.

In the different species of the animal kingdom, one can recognize that astral forces are incorporated into the bodily organization. The spiralling or lemniscating qualities of the astral body, with convex and concave aspects, created step by evolutionary step the vessel for an inner feeling life, which became the nervous system. Primitive animals, like an amoeba, have no nervous system; jellyfish or sea stars have a very simple nervous system that is connected with the processes of the body and a simple sensing of the environment. They are totally dependent on outer conditions. In the evolutionary development from invertebrate to vertebrate animals, the appearance of the neural tube shows the condition for a possible inner life. The animal kingdom consists of 90% invertebrate animals, which have in common that they have one or more eyes as main sensory organ; they have no ears, and they do not make vocal sounds. The other 10% is made up of the vertebrate animals that have an ear, larynx and the ability to produce sound.[2] There one can recognize that elements have been turned outside in, and a space for an inner life has been created. A similar image is found in the evolution of the lungs. The development from fish to reptile is beautifully shown by the frog, developing from the tadpole. Lungs are created by taking the element of air into the body. An inner space, a vessel for the feeling life, is created. In a diagram these outer and inner aspects of the incorporated astral body are represented in the lemniscate or the ingoing and outgoing spiral. The mammals, closest to the human being, certainly have a delicate inner feeling life. Think of dolphins or chimpanzees. The individual element of an incorporated Ego, however, is still missing. Due to the horizontal position of the spine, the current of the blood cannot incorporate an individual Ego. The group soul of the different animal species works from without, from the periphery of the earth (Steiner 1909 lectures).

Metabolic Processes

To penetrate this complex matter more deeply, one can try to build up a picture of what is happening when something from the outside world is taken into the human body, for example, food substance that one eats. Let us look at salt as a mineral food substance. Inside the mouth the salt is immediately changed because the saliva will dissolve it. The physical will be made fluid, be dissolved. This happens with everything we eat. A piece of bread will be chewed up and mixed with saliva. The substances will undergo an immediate change by the saliva, which contains not just water but also enzymes. The process of metabolism starts by digesting the starch content. In the stomach, certain acids will continue the job of destroying the total structure of the food. Inside our physical body, nothing alien is accepted. Every single outer element needs to be destroyed. If the human being is not able to do so, allergic reactions will be the result.

In the next stage, the substance will be transported from the intestines into the body by the blood. Inside the cells it will be taken into a sort of inner combustion process. The oxygen transported by the blood from the lungs will help with that. Carbon dioxide will be produced. Completely new body substances will be created. Every single cell inside the human body carries the unique genetic material of that person. Nothing can be found that remains of any outer substance eaten.

When we describe this process from the point of view of the elements, we find that the physical food substances are lifted up from the physical into the watery element. Then, with the process of combustion, the process is taken up to the airy element. The Ego, with its element of warmth, will build the individual bodily substances and imprint its unique stamp on every single cell. The sequence is from earth to water, air, and warmth. Translated into the names of the supersensible bodies, this is: physical, etheric, and astral bodies, and Ego. All is taken up by and under the direction of the Ego, which will imprint its individual hallmark.

It is obvious that the organization and functioning of the metabolic and limb system is completely different from that of the sense organization. Also the activities of the supersensible members are different. In *The Light Course* (lecture 2), Rudolf Steiner says:

You need only to think, for instance, how differently your etheric body penetrates your muscles from the way it penetrates your eyes. It is inserted into a muscle so as to blend with the functions of the muscle; not so with the eye. As the eye is very isolated, the etheric body is not inserted into the physical apparatus in the same way but remains comparatively independent. Consequently, the astral body can come into very intimate union with the portion of the etheric body that is in the eye. Inside the eye the astral body is more independent and independent in a different way from the way it is in the rest of our physical organization. Let this be the part of the physical organization in a muscle, and this the physical organization of the eye. To describe it, we must say: our astral body is inserted into both, but in a different way. It is so inserted into the muscle that it goes through the same space as the physical body part and is by no means working independently. It is only a half-truth to say that our astral body is present in our physical body. We must ask how it is in the physical body, for it is present differently in the eye and in the muscle. In the eye it is relatively independent, and yet it is there no less than it is in the muscle.

Sensory Processes

Although there is a difference in the organization, we can imagine that a sequence comparable to that of taking up food substances is taking place in the processing of sense impressions. Food substances come into our body from the outer world, and likewise one can think of the input through the senses impressions as also belonging to the outer world. In reality, they are alien to our inner life. In the first lecture of *The Apocalypse of St. John*, Rudolf Steiner gives the following information:

> Impressions from the outside world come towards us during the daytime. By means of the physical sense organs, they work upon the etheric body and the astral body, until the Ego becomes conscious of them. The astral body records what the physical body undergoes. Light comes into the eye. The light impression is transmitted to the etheric body, and the astral body and the Ego become conscious of it. This is the same for the ear and all other sense organs.

In a letter to Walter Johannes Stein he describes the process more in detail.[3] When reading Rudolf Steiner's lectures, one must always be aware of the context in which he speaks about a subject. One has to know when, where, and to whom he was speaking. The things he said to one group of people could be very different from what he said to others. Rudolf Steiner had many layers of consciousness. One usually sees Rudolf Steiner too small. Liane Collot d'Herbois reported that Ita Wegman once told her that Rudolf Steiner could complete the preparation for all his lectures for the next month in five minutes. That illustrates his kind of consciousness. In a medical lecture, Rudolf Steiner describes the perceptual process from the point of view of the inner constitutional condition.[4]

The eye is the sense organ only for perception of light and darkness and of color. When one perceives a color, the light comes into the eye and is projected onto the retina. The sense input is transmitted through the optic nerve to the visual cortex of the brain. At the same time, the life processes in the eye are affected. The blood in the eye and in the blood vessels accompanying the optical nerves is aroused; with this, after-images are produced. It is the etheric body that is the carrier of life processes. Outer etheric forces, connected with the outer sense impulses, are toned-down; inner etheric forces enliven, bring new inner life to, the toned-down outer color impression. This etheric reaction to the outer sense impulses one can call *etheric mirroring*. These are etheric reflections of the physical sense impressions.

The sequence described above took place in the physical body and the etheric body of life processes. There would, however, not be any conscious experience of the sense impression without the activity of the astral body. So another reaction—reflection—needs to take place within the astral body. This reflection one can call *astral mirroring*. In the process of perceiving color, the astral body creates the counter-color (see chapter 7) following the law of astral mirroring, which is that the astral body always makes the counter-gesture to the actual physical sense impression.[5]

Part of the astral body is connected with the etheric processes of the lower human being, of the metabolic processes and the blood. This is the inner astral body that separates, condenses, and radiates. It activates the seven processes of secretion, nourishment, growth, warmth, breathing, reproduction, and sustenance. This aspect of the astral body, in connection with the metabolism of the blood, also produces the inner complementary colors in the eye. The inner astral body can also reflect images back into the etheric body. In color we enter the color scale of the dark and light pink, the light and dark lilac, and in between them, the color Rudolf Steiner calls peach blossom—the color we do not yet perceive because we live in it and are part of it, as fish in water. These five colors complete the seven day-wake colors of the rainbow. These colors rise from the etherized earth. They will be experienced by human consciousness in the future.

The other part of the astral body is connected with the upper human being—the sense organization, the nervous system, and brain—and carries the conscious inner soul life. In evolution and in embryology, one can trace down the gradual incarnation of this aspect of the astral body. In the animal kingdom, it is when the spine is first developed—with the appearance of the fish. In the development of the human embryo, the neural tube is formed around the twenty-first day. This is a process of turning inside out. It is an aspect that shows the creation of an inner space, the bodily carrier of an inner soul life. Another reversal is the development of the lungs shown to us archetypically by the tadpole becoming a frog. An outer aspect is taken inside, like a glove being turned inside out. Other examples where one can trace the activity of the astral body are in the retina of the eye and the kidneys. Between the astral world and the physical is always this relation of reversal. The spiritual astral element is mirrored into the physical as a glove turned inside out. Likewise, the physical situation is mirrored into the astral. Rudolf Steiner gives the example of the sense of hearing: as the ear physically perceives a certain tone, the astral body inwardly will produce the rest of the scale (notes of a conversation with Walter Johannes Stein in *Farbenerkenntnis*). When Rudolf Steiner spoke to the first Waldorf teachers, he pointed to the great reversal of the tubular bones becoming the skull in the next incarnation (*Foundations of Human Experience* lecture 10).

The meditation Rudolf Steiner gave at the course published as *Education for Special Needs*—"I am in God, God is in me" (the point and periphery)—has this aspect of reversal within the astral body. Reversal is the inside becoming the outside, the outside becoming the inside, the point becoming periphery.

The total process of reflecting, refracting (etheric body and lower astral body), and reversing (upper astral body) takes place in the subconscious realms of the human organization. Under normal circumstances we are not aware that this process is taking place, just as we normally are not aware that in our eye we are creating the complementary colors.

Finally it is the Ego that takes hold of the physical outer sense impression. This is only possible when the Ego is able to firmly anchor in the structural physical body as a result of a proper first seven-year development. In the case of color perception, when the Ego is not firmly anchored in the sense organization, for instance, the complementary color can play up. It is known that young children before the age of three years perceive the complementary color of the actual physical color. This can also happen with psychotic patients if their Ego has lost connection with the concrete three-dimensional physical world and is living in the two-dimensional. These patients can be calmed down by active red colors and certainly not with the color green.

Mirroring Process in Sense of Self-Movement

With dyslexia, which is not a medical illness, one of the symptoms is the mirroring or rotation of letters. This mainly has to do with the sensory processing of movement and balance. In perceiving letter forms in reading, one needs to be very conscious of the fact that the eye as a sense organ only perceives light, darkness, and color. As far as we are dealing with light and color, we need to speak about the eye as organ of the sense of sight. On the retina there is a yellow spot where the visual information is best perceived. We can only see clearly a spot as big as the thumbnail at arm's length. To have more visual information, the eyeballs constantly have to move—jump from the one detail to another. The eye has six small muscles to accomplish this. There are tiny sensory organs that perceive the eye movements and coordinate these muscles. The sensory organs in the eye muscles are part of the sense of self-movement and of the sense of balance. It is the sense of self-movement that we use to perceive form. We perceive outer form through sensing the activity of our own physical body. The very young child is already able to perceive color and light before it is able to distinguish form. Its consciousness is still strongly connected with the life forces of the two-dimensional. The development of orientation in three-dimensional space and the coordination of the body is the foundation for perception of form.

Looking from the point of view of spiritual science at the sensory processing of movements through the sense of self-movement, we also need to take into account the mirroring of these movements in the supersensible members—the reflections, refractions, and reversals in the etheric body and outer and inner astral bodies. In eurythmy training, students learn to become inwardly conscious of these mirrored movements and integrate them into their performance. The physical movements of the muscles and joints of the body and the position of the body in space is reflected, refracted, and reversed by the sheaths of the human being's supersensible organization. One can get an idea of this when watching a eurythmy performance. This is a highly multisensory experience of sound, color, and movement, including the reversal of these movements made visible by the veils of the costumes.

Mirroring Sequence by Audrey McAllen

To picture the complete mirroring sequence in *The Extra Lesson*, Audrey McAllen suggests to just start playing and experimenting with mirrors and tablespoons (*Learning Difficulties* "The Mirroring Process"). I did so myself and also with colleagues and groups of students. Doing this for years was a big help in visualizing and building up the picture of this complex process.

When one perceives a red circle, the eye as sense organ for light and color perceives the color red. However, the sense of self-movement brings one the perception of the form of the circle (Steiner *Foundations of Human Experience* lecture 8 and *Practical Advice to Teachers* lecture 1). The eye moves rapidly around the form; inside the small eye muscles, sensory receptors register these movements. The information about the movements gives us the impression of the form. What is happening in the supersensible organization of the sense of self-movement? To picture this, we take as example the movement of the eye tracing the form of some letters and use the ALM sequence.[6]

Reflection in the Ether Body

To start with, we have a physical eye movement sensed by the sense of self-movement. The ether body will mirror this eye movement. The etheric element has the quality of a flat surface, like leaves in the plant kingdom or the surface of water. This two-dimensional space mirrors the physical in a flat way. Physical movement will be reflected in the supersensible mirrors of the etheric body. There are two possibilities of mirroring or reflection. Images may be mirrored upside down, like trees that appear upside-down when reflected in a lake. They can also be mirrored on the vertical, from left to right. We use this flat mirroring when we look at ourselves in the mirror.

Rudolf Steiner points out that the etheric body of the human being is divided into two parts (*Balance in the World and Man*). The etheric body has a left side and a right side. According to Audrey McAllen's research, the left side of the etheric body is connected with the twofold picture of the human being. Therefore the left etheric body will produce a twofold reflection: upside down—head to trunk. The right side of the human being is a representation of the threefold human being. In contrast to the left side of the etheric body, the right side of the etheric body has a threefold structure. This is physically imprinted into the structure of the lungs: the left lung has two lobes whereas the right lung has three. Therefore the reflection sequence for the right side of the etheric body is threefold: first from left to right, then upside-down into the trunk. The etheric body will produce a mirroring image in three steps: 1) left to 2) right and then 3) down.

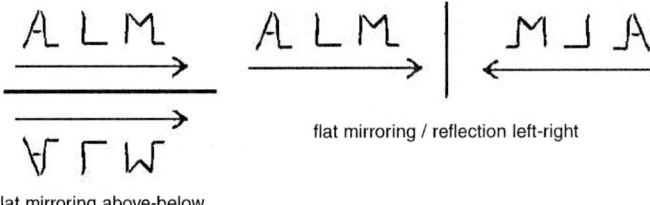

flat mirroring above-below

flat mirroring / reflection left-right

The four possibilities of flat mirroring (etheric reflection) can be put in a palindrome. Walter Holtzapfel used such a palindrome with the letters FORT in his book *Children with a Difference*. He shows the relation between the birth of the etheric body at the change of teeth and the ability of distinguishing between the different reflections of letters. The milk teeth are generally in a beautiful and harmonic symmetrical arrangement, as a picture of the pure etheric forces. The new teeth often are somewhat rotated or displaced, giving a picture of the incarnating, individual astral element at the age of six or seven.

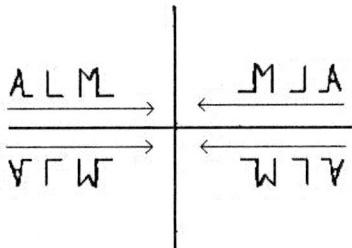

palindrome of flat mirroring in ether body

In the development of the child, one can also recognize the different stages of spatial orientation. The very small child looking at a picture book is unable to distinguish above from below. Only after the child has learned to stand upright and walk will it turn the upside-down picture book upright. This is mirroring on the horizontal midline. Likewise the kindergarten child very often will write his name in mirrored print, unaware of the difference. This is mirroring on the vertical midline, a stage of development that goes together with symmetrical movement patterns and the development of the two brain hemispheres. During these different developmental stages, physical movement patterns are imprinted into the etheric body; there they are integrated into the etheric processes. When the etheric body is freed from the physical body at the change of teeth, these imprinted patterns form the foundation of the mirroring system. This inner mirroring system is highly important for recognizing letter forms in writing and reading.

Reflection and Refraction in the Astral Body

Until now we only have dealt with reflection, the mirroring sequence in the two-dimensional element of the etheric body, the body of life processes. We need to follow the sensory impression into the inner life of soul. Therefore we also need to look at the processes within the astral body. In the astral body one needs to distinguish between the inner astral element that is connected with the metabolic processes and the outer astral body, connected with the sensory organs. The inner astral body will produce a reflected or a refracted image of the original physical movement. Audrey McAllen names this aspect *convex mirroring*. One can picture the glittering and sparkling of the sunlight in the rippling waves of a lake. The little waves curve the surface of the water. The light is reflected and sparkles around. Under the surface the rays of light are refracted and shine downward to the deep. Refraction is bending, splitting, and changing colors by making them more brilliant. This is a picture of the activity of the astral body in the metabolic system. The sense impressions, coming from the sense organs, are reflected and refracted by the convex inner astral body, which is strongly connected with the etheric body. The inner astral reflection and refraction will produce a curved mirror image, as in a distorting mirror; however, this mirror image will be similar to the flat reflection of the etheric body. Of course this is so, because this aspect of the astral body is connected with the inner processes of the etheric body. Look at the mirror images on the back side of a spoon.

In the sense of sight, the inner astral body plays a role in producing complementary colors. To make the sequence complete, yet even more complicated, we have to keep in mind that this lower part of the astral body is also in resonance with the upper astral body. If it were not so, we would have no memory.

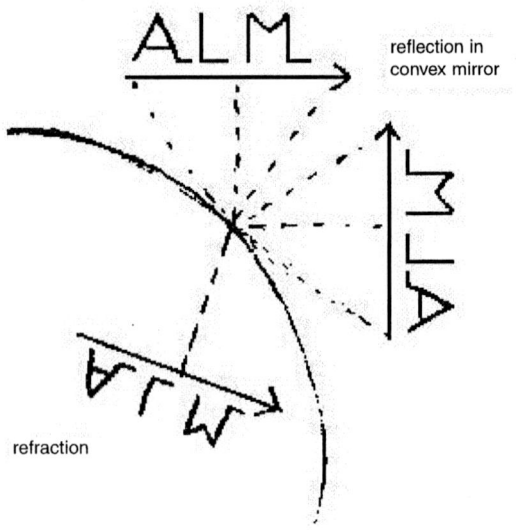

Reversal in the Astral Body

The other part of the astral body connected with the senses is always producing a counter-gesture to the physical input, a reversal. This aspect will produce a reversal of the original physical sense impression. In the sense of self-movement, when we are writing a letter or reading a word, the astral body will go in the opposite direction, in a counter-movement that is the reverse of the physical movement. The part of the astral body connected with the nervous system and the senses normally operates in this way.

To illustrate, one can write the small ALM sequence and copy the reversal of every writing movement. Think of what was described in chapter 3 on the Right-angled Triangle exercise.

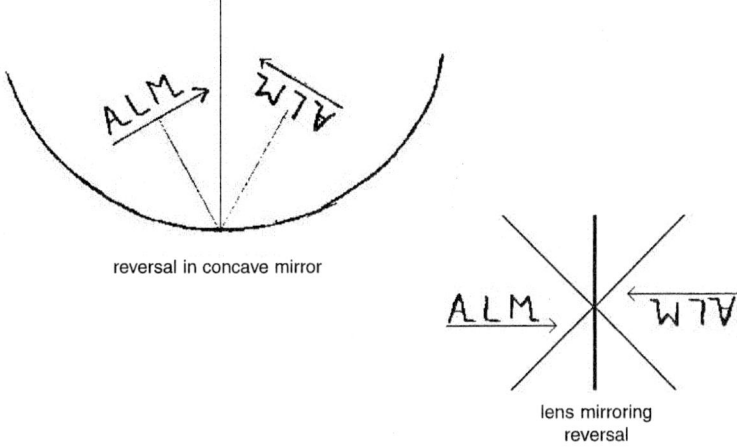

Ego Connection with the Physical

The total of the complex mirroring process gives a complete set of possibilities of mirroring images: reflections, refractions, and reversals. In the complete mirroring system the letter forms or forms of words rotate. These processes of reflection, refraction, and reversal all take place in the subconscious of the human organization. The conscious Ego needs to connect with the original physical sense experience, with what is written or printed on the page. Then the Ego can receive and reconstruct the outer impression, make it its own, and imprint this image into the memory carried by the etheric body. The Ego can only connect with the outer sense impression properly, without being disturbed by the subconscious organization, when it is properly anchored in the physical structural organization. This is a result of a proper development in the first seven years of the neurological and movement systems and senses.

Problems in reading and writing will appear when this anchoring of the Ego in the physical body has not taken place adequately because of an incomplete first-seven-years development. Then mirror images from etheric or astral levels will pop up into the consciousness, and the child will become disoriented. The child will have trouble with recognizing letters, letter sequences and words—with proper eye tracking, visual discrimination of letter forms, and analyzing words. This is all in the visual system. The auditory system also depends on the proper development of the self-movement and balance systems. The inner ear gives us the connection with gravity, the capacity of verticality, and the experience and awareness of three-dimensional space. As Karl König points out in *The First Three Years of the Child*, the sense of speech and the sense of thought have their bodily organs in the nerve organization of the sense of self-movement and sense of life. With improper development of these senses, auditory discrimination—analyzing words into sounds and sound sequences—can also be problematic.

Once again we would like to stress the fact that we concern ourselves with the mirroring process of the sense of self-movement. This brings us the perception of form, in reading and writing the perception of letters, words, and sentences. The perception of color has a quite different character. The perfect perception of color is a two-dimensional experience. The atmosphere is the real element where colors are at home. The character of the different colors gives us the idea of perspective. It is the interplay of the astral and etheric bodies. In the perception of form we find the relation of Ego and physical body—hence Steiner's indication to teach children painting in color perspective long before they are taught linear perspective. The latter is in the 7th grade curriculum (age 12–13). Rudolf Steiner advised that we practice color perspective painting to help with reading problems (*The Renewal of Education*). It is also known that Rudolf Steiner thought that education would be healthier if children did not learn to read until the age of 14. He said that, for the Waldorf method he initiated, he was compromising between the ideal and the demands of modern times.

Imprinting

Observing and studying the early movement patterns of the small child, one can understand that what appears as early physical movement patterns will be imprinted as habit patterns into the etheric body (*A Modern Art of Education*). What in mainstream science is looked at as the integrating of early movement patterns, from an anthroposophical point of view could be considered as the taking up of physical habits into the rhythmic processes of the ether body. The movement patterns of the limbs in crawling and creeping, the movement patterns recognized as related to certain neurological reflexes, and the homolateral, crosslateral, and symmetrical movement patterns all play an important role in the imprinting process from the physical into the etheric body. In this way a complete set of mirrors is imprinted into the system of the etheric body. Under certain circumstances these patterns, which work as etheric movement patterns, can pop up again on a physical level. This can happen, for instance, after an accident or the use of certain medications. This process of imprinting shows the importance of a proper first-seven-years development of the structural body, of the nervous system, and of the movement system. It is the foundation for learning skills.

In his book *The Gift of Dyslexia*, Ronald Davis describes his own experience of disorientation when confronted with signs and symbols. Children have difficulty orienting themselves in this two-dimensional realm. Davis states that they think in three-dimensional pictures and have difficulty with the two-dimensional representation. He teaches the child to consciously manipulate perception, a method he developed for himself. He says, "I am a corrected dyslexic." By inner visualization, the mind's eye needs to be consciously anchored at a point behind the skull. Davis helps the child to model the letter forms in clay and connect the names of the alphabet with them rather than with the sounds. This approach is something I would not recommend for non-English speaking students. Ronald Davis's therapeutic approach makes use of day-wake consciousness in manipulating the sense perception. We need to ask ourselves how this method works and wonder if what the child learns is a compensatory technique rather than a furthering of his development. In contrast, the Extra Lesson concept takes into account the subconscious levels of the human organization in which the supersensible Ego needs to be anchored. The results, therefore, can be transformed in later developmental phases. The development of the consciousness soul from age 35 to 42 depends on the anchoring of the Ego in the physical body. As Waldorf teachers, we need to take this seriously.

The process of perception therefore needs to be structured. As a result, the memory will be structured, because unstructured perception will give no memory images. Structuring the process of perception will help to solve memory problems, because in most cases there is no essential memory problem as such. When there are underlying memory problems, we are dealing with constitutional medical problems or special education. In spiritual scientific terms, this means that the Ego needs to connect with the physical structure and imprint the Ego experience into the rhythmical processes of the etheric body. That is where the memory is located.

Ronald Davis describes perfectly from his own observation the dyslexic situation, when letter forms appear to the perception of the child in their rotated versions. He also points to the stressful effect of the so called "trigger words." The child cannot picture the meaning of certain words inwardly with his imagination. These words arouse an inner pressure and stress; therefore the child is not able to read properly. In this picture, we can see that the astral body is interfering in the process of perception while the forces of the improperly anchored Ego are not able to control the situation. The reflected or reversed mirror images of the astral body start to pop up consciously in the soul rather than working subconsciously. The astral body is taking over, and the Ego is unable to grasp the proper physical sense impression. This observation by Ronald Davis is exactly what Audrey McAllen describes in *The Extra Lesson* and in *Learning Difficulties*:

- Physical space is three-dimensional.
- Written word is a projection of three-dimensional into two-dimensional.
- The eye traces forms of physical letters, words, sentences.
- Etheric body mirrors physical eye movements (reflection).
- Lower astral body connected with processes mirrors (refraction = complementary convex mirrored movement).
- Higher astral body mirrors physical (reversal = concave mirroring, counter-movement).
- The Ego needs to take hold of the physical impression; the whole mirroring process needs to stay in the subconscious.
- The Ego imprints the percept impression into the outer etheric body as memory.

The proper neurological and movement development of the first seven years anchors the Ego in the physical structural body. As a result, proper dominance, spatial orientation, and body awareness are established. The primitive movement patterns and midline barriers are integrated and proper mirroring leading to ease in learning can take place.

Visual and Auditory Processing and Mirroring

When teaching writing and reading, primarily two sensory aspects are involved: visual and auditory processing. In writing, children need to learn to connect the spoken word with written or printed signs. Before that they need to be able to consciously analyze spoken words into sounds and be aware that sentences are made up of single words. Then the auditory information needs to be connected with the visual.

In reading, the visual information needs to be analyzed and connected with speech. Everyone having the experience of being a first grade teacher will recognize the different stages of this educational process.

In the four lectures published as *Balance in Teaching*, Rudolf Steiner describes the contrasting processes of visual and auditory sense perception. He also tries to build the picture of how the physical sense perceptions are bridges to the inner soul life and are connected with memory.

Visual perception is processed in the eye and in the entire nervous system from the retinas to the occipital lobes connected with them. This total system is the organ for visual perception. Only in the breathing system can the feeling life of the human soul connect with the outer input from the nervous system. Understanding of what one perceives takes place in the rhythmic system. The rhythmic system is the bridge between the outer sensory organization and the inner psychological life of soul. In the body, we recognize the rhythm of heartbeat and breathing; in the soul life it is the forces of antipathy and sympathy that alternate rhythmically. Thirdly, the images created within the soul need to become imprinted as memory images into the metabolic processes of the limb system. This is where the etheric body plays its part.

Auditory perception takes place through the ear as the central organ, but also through the nerves known as motor nerves. We perceive lower tones with the nerves in the legs and abdomen, higher tones with the upper part of the body. Even the skeleton is an important transmitter of sound. The auditory nerve from the ear to the brain is also connected with the balance system of the inner ear. Balance, movement, body awareness, the perception of sound, language, and thoughts are strongly connected (www.tomatis.com). Rudolf Steiner describes auditory perception as a stream coming up from the body towards the head, as opposed to the visual process streaming from the head down. The structure of the ear with eardrum, hammer, anvil, stirrup, oval window, and cochlea is similar to the structure of the leg: foot sole, lower leg, knee, upper leg, and intestines (Steiner, "The Ear," Dec 9, 1922). Auditory perception takes place in the lower part of the human being. The understanding of what one perceives takes place in the rhythmic system. The memory is imprinted into the metabolic processes of the head. All auditory experiences are imprinted in the etheric processes of the head. Therefore there is a big difference between visual and auditory memory.

In contrast to the ear, which is like a limb, the architecture of the eye is similar to that of the brain. Both are isolated organs within a bony cave. The retina can be seen as brain substances pushed towards the back of the eye by spiritual currents, leaving open space that could be filled with selfless, almost etheric, substance: the vitreous humor (Steiner 1909 lectures).

The connection between visual and auditory, so important in the process of learning to write and to read, takes place in the rhythmic middle system. Hence the importance of working with the breathing when one is giving educational support.

In these 1920 lectures (*Balance in Teaching*), Rudolf Steiner builds up a new picture on the earlier theme of the forces of antipathy and sympathy, terms he used a year earlier in the *Study of Man* lectures. The visual element is connected with the plastic-architectonic (antipathy) forces that work from the head down. The auditory, musical-speech (sympathy) forces work from below up.

After this description of the body, Steiner continues to explain how the visual and the auditory are related on a higher spiritual level. In the spiritual world, sound is color. Those familiar with eurythmy will have learned this. The tones of the major scales in the world of the soul are red and yellow, while the tones of the minor scales are blue and violet at the other end of the color spectrum. All single speech sounds have their own color: H—yellow, M—indigo, T and D—light blue, V and W—red, R—orange, and so on.

When the human being speaks, his soul life, which is an individual, microcosmic, and intimate invisible world of color, is concentrated in the larynx and appears as audible sounds, words, and sentences. In speech, the supersensible colored vibrations of the astral body become audible. When we perceive speech, the audible is the outer physical vessel, yet inwardly we are able to visualize what we hear. There is a constant process of reversal: color—sound—color.

The opposite happens in the process of visual perception. In the spiritual world, the creative forces behind every visual object are sounds. It is the Divine Word, the Logos, that spoke and created the visual perceptible world. Behind the world of moving visual colors in the atmosphere the sounds of the spiritual world are hidden. Color is cosmic feeling becoming visible; likewise, our personal feeling life consists of inner colors.

Audrey McAllen, in her recently revised book *Sleep: An Unobserved Element in Education,* points to the spiritual reversal of physical movement describing the relationship as a cubic organization. What we perceive as movement lives in the spiritual world as moral virtues. Going forward in the spiritual world is aligned with the moral virtue of *beauty;* going forward in the human being himself is aligned with *courage. Truth* in the spiritual world is revered as movement from above to below; in the human soul it is *temperance.* (For more detail, see chapter 11 on the cube.)

We know from Rudolf Steiner that in the perception of (letter) forms the sense of self-movement is involved; the sense of sight just gives us the perception of color. In contrast to that, producing a sound or speech also produces movement. Here again we see the importance of a proper development of the movement system in the first seven years and in educational support lessons. From this complicated lecture (*Balance in Teaching* lecture 3), we learn of the importance of the mirroring processes in perception—the importance of the physical breathing process where outer perception is carried into the inner light process of the soul life.

Constitutional Aspect

The mirroring sequence described above is the process in the structural body of nerves, muscles, and skeleton. The constitutional physical body is also vibrating. There is the will to perceive outer sense impressions; the will to look or hear actively, being interested in the outer world. On the constitutional side, the will of the Ego directs the eye in order to track the written line of words or to perceive colors. Also on the constitutional side, the other supersensible members mirror the will impulses of movement. This process Rudolf Steiner described in the medical lectures (see 1909 lectures and *Education for Special Needs*). It is clear that in reality the human being is a unity. Educational and medical support can go hand in hand.

Character of the Exercises in the Extra Lesson

To conclude this chapter, we can sum up the characteristics of the exercises developed by Audrey McAllen and published in *The Extra Lesson.* The Extra Lesson, however, is not a fixed set of exercises; it is much more so a concept. Having learned the background and principles one will become able to create new exercises. New times and new generations will come; new educational support will be needed. The archetypal character of the Extra Lesson exercises makes it possible to use all exercises for all children, as well as for older students and adults.

The following is a synthesis of research done by Uta Stolz in Germany:

1. The Extra Lesson exercises have an archetypal character. Therefore they can be used for all children and are not just for a specific teacher with a specific child, nor do they address specific temperaments.

2. The exercises are developed according to the archetypal laws of the neurological and movement development of the first seven years, or are steps in this neurological development. Neurological and movement development produces skills for learning.

3. The movements of these exercises are related to the movement patterns in the human being and the earth as has been indicated by Rudolf Steiner in 1909 lectures entitled "Anthroposophy."

4. In these exercises we find a rhythm between stretching and lifting movements, between tension and relaxation. They help the integration of the postural system (the sense of balance and the sense of self-movement).

5. By means of this rhythmical element and by repeating the exercises for several weeks or even months, the movements start to penetrate and activate the etheric body of the child, the carrier of habit patterns. The etheric body will become enlivened; the child will look healthier. These exercises are not purely physical training or patterning. The rhythmic repetition often requires help from the teacher to motivate the child.

6. Rudolf Steiner indicated in the 1909 "Anthroposophy" lectures that in the sense of self-movement the astral body moves in the opposite direction to that of the movements of the physical body. The movements through which the astral body is activated contain the archetypal patterns of the spiral or lemniscate. Through these, the movements of the exercises are dynamic and rhythmical. Other archetypal elements that are used are the straight line and the point within a circle, both pictures of the Ego organization. The six-pointed star and the five-pointed star are archetypal pictures of the incarnation of the human being.

7. Rhythmical repetition of the exercises forces the astral body to connect itself properly with the physical and etheric body. Often the day-wake consciousness is somewhat diminished as a result of the exercises, but far more the sleeping will, the subconscious, is activated by the exercises. The child will incarnate more properly into his body. Sometimes

only then will personality or constitutional problems of the astral body (the lower and not the objective astral body) become visible.

8. The Ego is called upon by the lifting element in the movement patterns. The eyes need to follow the movements of the limbs if possible and the feet need to be kept parallel if possible. In the rhythmic movements there needs to be a pause. The astral body can come to rest and the ego can imprint the movement pattern into the etheric and physical bodies.

9. A minimum age is given for each exercise.

---

1. Walter Holtzapfel, *Children with a Difference.*
2. Armin Husemann, unpublished lecture at the Kolisko Conference in Lahti, Finland August 2, 2002.
3. To help former Waldorf teacher Walter Johannes Stein with his doctoral dissertation, Rudolf Steiner wrote a letter explaining from a spiritual point of view how after-images are created. Stein had noticed that, after looking at a yellow sheet of paper for a while and then swiftly removing it, a blue after-image appeared on the light background and not a violet one as is commonly stated. Dr. Steiner wrote as follows:

    You must put the perceptual process before yourself in its totality: What happens when I perceive yellow?

    1. Objectively in the eye itself: *enlivened yellow.*
    2. The ether body of the person in the subjective act of perception penetrates into this enlivened yellow; thereby the yellow that is permeated by the outer ether and therefore enlivened becomes *dead yellow.* In the eye it is, therefore, dead yellow because its life has been dispelled by the inner life (ether body). Hence the subjective observer has an image of yellow enlivened from within—instead of outer enlivened yellow—but this image included the "corpse" of yellow. So far the process is objective-subjective. But with this, only an inner living yellow would be created, about which the "subject" would know nothing. He could only *experience* his own subjective-objective element, but not consciously.
    3. Now the astral body of the "subject" penetrates into this subjective-objective newly enlivened yellow. By means of this enlivened yellow, the astral body creates the *enlivened "blue."* This blue is actually created within the organism, but does not extend spatially beyond the organism.
    4. The following elements are therefore present:
        1. The astrally-created image "blue,"
        2. the effect of this astral image on the ether body as a subjective life process,

      3. physiologically the physical process in the eye—working inward but not outward—as blue.

    All this, however, does not become a matter of Ego consciousness. The Ego only *knows* when inwardly the "yellow" which was first enlivened in the eye is toned down—then you have:

      1. Toned down life in the yellow by the Ego,

      2. conscious appearance in the astral body of the no-longer-living yellow,

      3. the astrally-produced image "blue" remaining unconscious because it is "overlit" by dead yellow,

      4. its effect in the ether body,

      5. the physiological process in the eye.

    Now, if the object from which the yellow emanates is removed, the actuating of the astrally-produced "blue" is not a spatial entity but stems from the astral body and only its physical effect remains in the organism.

Published in *Rudolf Steiner's New Approach to Color on the Ceiling of the First Goetheanum* by Daniel van Bemmelen; also published in German in *Farbenerkenntnis* by Rudolf Steiner (GA291a).

4. Rudolf Steiner says, in *Broken Vessels*, lecture 3 (Dornach, September 10, 1924:

    In ordinary life, when we see, we are stimulated from without and we receive the stimulus into ourselves. It goes as far as the ether body, and the ether body creates the conscious experience. For example, with the eyes: When you see, the external stimulation occurs in the Ego, then this penetrates the astral body and then penetrates the ether body. Then the ether body communicates the whole conscious experience to you by pushing in every direction—in a certain sense pushing against the physical organization. The conscious experience comes about in the pushing. The physical body pushes back, and the pushing back—the repulsion by the physical body—is the actual experience you have in your eye. There is the constant interplay between the ether body and the choroid and retina of the eye. What the ether body does in the choroid and retina is what appears as optical experience, and it is the same for all the senses.

5. Daniel van Bemmelen, *Rudolf Steiner's New Approach to Color on the Ceiling of the First Goetheanum*.

6. In earlier private notes, Audrey McAllen used her initials AEM. W. Holtzapfel uses the word FORT.

Chapter 10

The Handedness Pattern Assessment and the Flower Rod Exercise

The Handedness Pattern assessment is not intrinsically meant for checking dominance. Rather, it shows the educational support teacher the relation of the child to the supersensible currents and the imprinting of the mirroring possibilities. Among the complicated sets of mirroring possibilities, the Ego needs to be able to guide the process of perception, reflection, refraction, and reversal. All currents in the supersensible system need to be under the control of a properly incarnated and anchored Ego organization. The individual must be able to live freely between the left and right, the above and below, and the front and back of his body. The Ego is anchored within the body like a sort of supersensible gyroscope that controls movement and balance. If the Ego is not so anchored, the sensory process can be disturbed by rotation and/or reversal of letter sequences or sound sequences.

The results on the Handedness Pattern assessment need to be read and interpreted with the 1909 diagram of supersensible currents in mind. Also keep in mind all the information given in chapter 3 on the Right-angled Triangle exercise.

In the Handedness Pattern assessment, the student ideally starts tracing the forms from the top downward, following the currents of the Ego. This gives the impression that the Ego is anchored in the structural physical body.

If a student works from the bottom up, which is the direction of the astral body, it indicates that the structural body and movement system are not properly under the guidance of the Ego. Said differently, the astral body is pushing too strongly upwards, which is indicated by the movement direction of the astral current (from bottom to top). This overly strong pushing of the astral body can cause overstretched gestures in the movement system. The opposite gesture is also possible when the astral organization cannot sufficiently penetrate the structural body and stretch it. Then the student even has difficulty in using his Ego to lift his own body weight. The weight of the physical body will be strongly experienced and a lack of lifting quality in the movement system will be evident. The legs will fall heavily back to the floor. Doing the Weight Lifting exercise (*Extra Lesson* 135) will confirm this condition.

When both hands or both feet need to be used for tracing a circle, the student might not keep them together; he might split and trace the forms with symmetrical movements. This shows a midline problem or residual symmetrical movement patterns. The left and right sides of the body do not collaborate properly. These are symmetrical movement patterns belonging to the 3-to-5-year-old development. This movement pattern will be even more pronounced when the second chart with the form with the vertical midline is presented. This outer symmetrical mirroring interferes with the inner reflection on the soul level.

When the student has problems in tracing the forms mirrored on the horizontal midline, the situation can even be more difficult. This movement sequence shows in movement the relation between the head and trunk. Head and trunk are not yet in a proper relation to one another. This goes back to an earlier stage of movement: creeping and crawling, or homolateral and crosslateral movement patterns. Integration of the vertical midline barrier might be a problem.

With the second and third charts, some students will trace the mirrored forms as if they were a circle, ignoring the vertical or horizontal midline. They continue their movement and do not stop, following the tendency to make circles. This might indicate that perception is still somewhat immature. The kindergarten child experiences the world as a unity; the faculty of keeping a distance and analyzing a sense perception appears when the child is ready for school.

A mixed use of left and right arms or legs will indicate that the Ego has not yet found its anchor in the physical organization and current. A student can alternate between the use of left or right limbs. There can be discrepancy between the use of upper and lower limbs, which might indicate a structural blockage in the spine or the hips. In these cases, if the astral body is insufficiently under the control of the Ego, it will disrupt the inner convex and concave mirroring processes, thus disturbing the student's inner gyroscope for awareness of space and movement. Other observations from the First Educational Support Lesson will confirm the movement patterns shown in this handedness pattern.

Within the soul, these problems shown in the movement system will affect the feeling life. The improperly functioning organization of the structural physical body is not supporting the soul life. The Ego that is not properly anchored within the structural physical body will have problems controlling the soul life.

Observations and Conditions that May Be Indicated

Natural, mature movement patterns:
movements from top to bottom—control of Ego
movements from left to right—current of the physical body, which anchors the Ego
circle traced clockwise—natural movement direction for a right-handed person showing that the inner "gyroscope" is functioning properly

Tendency to mixed movement patterns:
mixed choice in the use of limbs
different starting points
inconsistent movement directions

Midline topics:
symmetrical movement patterns
change of limb at the midline
ignoring the second half of the symmetrical form
avoiding crossings within the forms (very immature pattern)

Direction of movement:
problems with consistent movement direction (direction might change frequently)
movement from right to left (direction of the current of the ether body)
continual movement from the bottom up (current of the astral body)

Flower Rod Exercise

A properly working mirroring system will be revealed by a nicely done Flower Rod form drawing exercise. One can recognize the currents of the astral body streaming from the head via the middle system into the area of the metabolic system. The concave and convex mirroring aspects show the process of taking outer sense impressions into the inner life of the soul. The vertical straight line (rod) represents the forces of the Ego anchoring itself in the physical structure and imprinting threefold sense impressions into the memory of etheric body.

The Flower Rod form drawing can also give a picture of the processing of visual information. The eyes receive the outer stimulus; through the optic nerves this input is transmitted to the visual center in the brain, left eye to right brain and right eye to left brain.

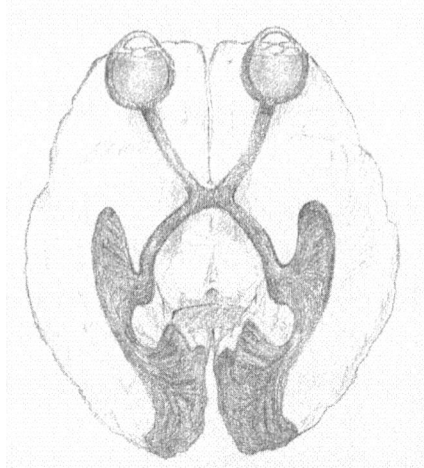

In the above illustration of eyes, optic nerves, and primary visual cortex, one will immediately recognize the archetypal architectural form of the Flower Rod. The Flower Rod Exercise can demonstrate whether the student is able to perceive outer visual input, take it into the inner soul life, and reproduce it. This is the process a student goes through when, for instance, copying text from the blackboard into a notebook. This is the interplay between sentient body and sentient soul (the lemniscate form) controlled by the Ego (the straight line).

Difficulties in doing this form drawing can indicate problems in the structural physical body (see examples of the different ways this drawing can be performed in *The Extra Lesson* 51–54). Is the skeleton aligned properly? From this perspective we look at the straight line as a picture of the Ego forces working in the spine. The lemniscate is always a picture of the astral body spiralling. There may be alignment problems in the hips, back, or shoulders.

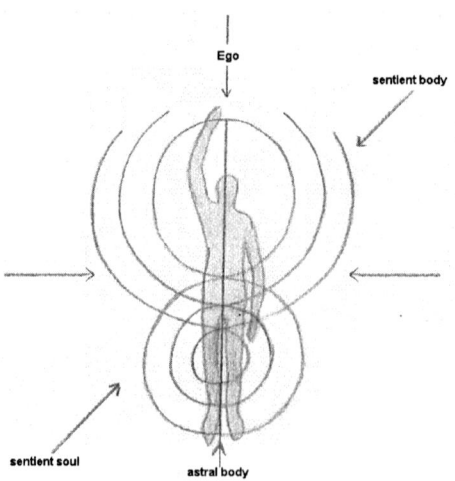

There could also be a developmental problem. If neurological and movement development has been delayed and vertical and horizontal midline barriers retained, this may reveal a delayed functioning of the corpus callosum. We could imagine the Flower Rod form drawing as a cross section of the skull. Then we see the currents of the astral body running from the eyes, crossing, and reaching the occipital lobes of the brain at the back of the skull.

Difficulties with this form drawing can also indicate certain constitutional problems. There can be breathing problems. This can also be shown by curved lines that are drawn closely together when crossing the straight line at the middle section of the drawing. The bodily constitution can either be too hardened or too weak and watery (see Cross Assessment, *Extra Lesson* 29–32).

Difficulties can appear in the bottom section of the drawing, showing that the imprinting into the memory is interrupted. If the lines do not reach the midline, sense impressions are not properly imprinted into the etheric. If lines cross over in the middle section and end on the outside (see *Extra Lesson* 53, bottom left illustration), outer sense impressions are hardly taken into the inner soul life and therefore are not imprinted. If lines curl up inwardly into spiral forms not reaching the midline, the etheric and physical bodies are too hardened to receive an imprint of the sense experience so that the inner mirroring process is blocked.

The student's sense organization may not be fully opened toward the sense world. This too can be seen as a problem in "breathing light," insufficient opening toward the surrounding outer world.

In cases where the student closes the top part of the Flower Rod so there is no opening towards the outer, I have learned to read this as a kind of "deafness" in the senses—not being open toward the sense world. This can also be caused by insufficient breathing. Rudolf Steiner explains that the sense organs need to be looked at as organs of will, like the limbs. The senses imitate the vibrations in the outer sense world, not only the ear drum vibrating from the outer stimulus of sound, but also the eye imitating the outer interplay between light and darkness in perceiving color. In the sense of self-movement, we register subtle movements that we imitate with our body when we perceive outer movements. In cases where this openness towards the outer world is blocked, the Flower Rod will be drawn closed at the top.

This exercise shows what the student demonstrates in movement performing the Copper Ball exercise (*Extra Lesson* 122–126). We see the Ego line from head to toes and the astral body moving from concave to convex. It shows the supersensible currents running through the physical body. Bringing this Flower Rod exercise into relation with the 1909 diagram of currents building up the structural body will teach the Extra Lesson teacher to recognize the problems in the supersensible organization of the student.

Cross Assessment

The Cross Assessment (*Extra Lesson* 29) gives us an indication of the astral body's affinity either to the etheric body or to the physical body. The astral body can have affinity for the nervous system. This is the structure of the physical body.

This structure of skeleton, muscles, and nerves has the shape of the cross of St. George (+). The St.George cross is a combination of the static vertical and horizontal lines (see Rudolf Kutzli, *Creative Form Drawing*). The astral body here immediately comes into contact with the physical element of the nervous system, and therefore the student is able to react quickly and reflexively to outer situations. However, in cases where the Ego is not properly anchored in the physical body, the astral body connects itself too strongly with the physical organization. This can result in muscle cramp, the inclination of the astral body to press its reverse movements into the movements of the physical body, for example, when a student reads the letter sequence ALM as AML. Eye tracking is hindered by an insufficiently integrated vertical midline, and the sequence of letters and sounds is partly reversed. The astral body gives the movement system too strong a tendency to stretching movements. One can help to overcome this problem with exercises to produce a healthy balance between the stretching and lifting movements. This supports the Ego to gain control over the overly strong astral body. All exercises from *The Extra Lesson* help the Ego to anchor itself in the physical structure and thus gain control over the astral body.

The cross of St. Andrew (x) is formed by two dynamic diagonals. When this cross is chosen in the Cross Assessment, it indicates the affinity of the astral body for the dynamic processes of the etheric body. The reaction of the student to an outer sense impression will be a little delayed, because the astral body passes through the etheric body before it connects with the outer physical sense impression. In cases where the Ego is not properly anchored in the physical body, the astral body connects itself too strongly with the etheric organization. The etheric organization will be pumped up by an astral body that is working too strongly. The result can be that the student has difficulties with abstract thinking and memory from sixth grade upward because outer sense impressions cannot be properly imprinted into the etheric body. The etheric body produces a watery constitution, and outer sense imprints are washed away. There is no tendency in the astral body to properly find the connection with the physical structure.

To rebalance this condition, one needs to support the stretching movements so the astral body incarnates into the physical body. Then one also needs to support the incarnation of the Ego and establish a healthy balance between stretching and lifting. The Copper Ball exercise, the Rod Rolling exercise (*Extra Lesson* 137), and the Bouncing Ball exercise (*Extra Lesson* 136) can bring about this balance. Other exercises like the Right-angled Triangle exercise are often necessary also.

The choice of crosses hardly ever changes. Already in kindergarten one can find the two archetypes in the way the children draw a person—square trunk with the arms and legs at right angles (+ cross) or with diagonally outstretched arms and legs (x cross).

Reflections based on Audrey McAllen's personal notes:

From the time between death and rebirth, in the experience of Kamaloca (see Steiner, *Outline of Esoteric Science*), the astral body contains and brings the elements of pride and passion. Pride is the desire for self-experience; passion is the desire for the sense world. Improper development in the first seven years, such that the Ego is not properly anchored in the physical structure to control the human organism, allows the astral body to connect too strongly to one of the currents. This imbalance causes the natural movements of left and right hands to reverse.

Passion and pride are at work in the souls of the human being. It was Buddha who formulated the reason why the human being had to suffer from illness, aging, and death. Illness, aging, and death are caused by birth. Birth is caused by desire, desire comes into being through delight, which comes forth by means of the sense world. That is how the wheel of incarnation turns. It is all caused by passion. The inner counterpart of passion is pride, the desire for self-experience. In the words of the mythology of Ancient India, this is caused by the evil spirit Mara and his hosts. This is Lucifer at work in the astral body, in the blood.

Ahriman is at work in the subconscious realms of the ether body. Ahrimanic forces contract the ether body (Steiner, *Balance in the World and Man*). Ahriman works in the nervous system and in intellectual thinking. The physical body dries out and hardens—the image of the goat's hoofs. In the soul life, this brings about fear.

PRIDE	PASSION
+ St. George cross The astral body drives into the physical current of left side of the human being.[1]	x St. Andrew cross The astral body drives out the etheric current on the right side of the human being.
FIRE Ego weakened, unconsciousness, materialism, inability to move will in matter	**THIRST** craves substances (desires requiring physical organs), longing for water, restlessness, too little engaged in substances soul drowns in "processes"
difficulty in building up forebrain with the two-petalled lotus extreme: imbecile despair, fear of water	activity in building middle system by 16-petalled lotus weak mysticism, childishness; overeats, fears fire
warm & dry—**draws*** choleric+sanguine cold & dry—**holds/contracts*** melancholic	warm & wet—**consumes*** sanguine+choleric cold & wet—**drives out*** phlegmatic
"There will be gnashing of teeth."**	"There will be weeping."**

chart by Audrey McAllen
* based on W. F. Zeylmans van Emmichoven's *The Foundation Stone*
** addition by the author from the Gospel of St. Luke

Weeping and the gnashing of teeth represent the condition in which the Ego is not able to keep balance between the forces of Lucifer and Ahriman, the opponents of humankind. In the Gospel of St. Luke we find two healings on a Sabbath day (Luke13:10 & 14:1-11). We can find here how the Christ Being balances out and heals the working of the opponents of humanity. One will find the same archetypal images in the Oberufer Christmas plays (Harwood, *Christmas Plays from Oberufer*). In the Paradise play, the devil shouts in jubilation at the idea of the married couples in which the man hangs himself and the woman drowns herself. At the end of the Three Kings play, the Roman centurion wished he had known what King Herod was intending to do. He wishes to hang himself from the highest tree or drown himself in the deepest sea. In the Grimms' fairy tale "Bearskin," two of the three sisters meet their end in the same way, by drowning and hanging.

The astral body pressing on the physical body or pushing the etheric body can be observed in the student's movements in the Moving Straight Line and Lemniscate Exercise (*Extra Lesson* 147–150). The pushing can be shown when the student strongly pushes or pulls the block crayons up or down the paper. It is also shown when the rigid left side of the body takes over the movement of the right side, with symmetrical or opposite movements. This is as if the too dry left side sucks in the fluid element of the right (etheric) side of the body. Often in these cases we see too strong muscle tension—a hypertonic gesture.

The astral body pushing or inflating the etheric body can be shown when the student has low muscle tension hypotonic gesture. Here is a lack of stretching movements. The right-hand movements overpower the left side; round and weak forms appear. One can also use the choice of color to build up an inner picture of the student's condition.

Chapter 11

The Cube as a Reversal of Three-dimensional Space

When working with the anthroposophical picture of the human being that stands behind Waldorf education and the work with the Extra Lesson, we need to take into account that the creative forces of the spirit are working behind the physical sense world. In the Extra Lesson work, we support the students' ability to develop proper spatial orientation and body geography; we support the incarnation of the Ego into the physical body. Behind the world of the senses is hidden the creative world of the spirit. People experience a barrier between the outer world (object) and the inner world of one's own soul (subject). From the time the child says "I," he starts to experience that these two worlds are separated from one another. Human thinking can build a bridge between the inner psyche of the subject and the objective outer world (see Rudolf Steiner *The Philosophy of Freedom*).

What we experience visually as color in the outer world (the macrocosm), in our souls is connected with feeling (the microcosm). There is a deep connection between these inner and outer elements. The objective outer sense impression of color in the outer world—revealing the creative powers of cosmic feeling—is linked to the individual and subjective feeling life of like or dislike, as we have explored in chapter 7 (Qualities of the Colors). Rudolf Steiner states that behind what we perceive as color is hidden a creative world of spiritual sounds (*Balance in Teaching*). Spiritual beings create movements of sound behind the veils of our visual sense experience of color. What we perceive as color is a reversal of the creative sounds from the spiritual world, reversed once again as feeling in our individual, inner, spiritual soul world. This is the path of visual sense information.

In the realm of the auditory, what we perceive as sound, language, and thought concepts is brought to our ears by the Angels, Archangels, and Archai respectively (Steiner 1909 lectures). In the spiritual world these sounds are created as spiritual movements of color. The sounds we perceive are a reversal of colors within the spiritual world. In the individual human soul live our feelings, thoughts, and intentions of will. They live as the invisible colors of our feeling life within our psyche. When we want to express our feelings, these inner colors move upward and are dammed up by the larynx. There they are reversed into sounds and words. Something similar happens when we hear someone speak. We perceive sounds, and inwardly we are able to visualize what is spoken to us. I hear the word *horse,* and I can inwardly picture a horse. This is the reversal from the auditory into the visual, and vice versa. This is a very important phenomenon that definitely needs more research in relation to dyslexia.

In a eurythmy performance, the audience can experience visually what is hidden behind the world of sound perception. One listens to music, poetry, or a tale in prose; on the stage one sees eurythmists embedded in colored light and costumed in layers of colored veils, performing movements expressing the quality of sounds and moods. In the art of eurythmy, the auditory is made visible.

When dealing with spatial orientation, one could state that the outer three-dimensional world is created by white-green light. This light creates the luciferic illusion of the three-dimensional outer world we live in. This is perception of color by means of the sense of sight. This gives us the image of color perspective. We perceive form and linear perspective by means of the sense of self-movement. One could imagine that only we human beings, through our vertical position, are aware of the three dimensions of space. Animals and even the young child that is still creeping and crawling live in the two-dimensional plane. The young child needs to explore the third dimension after learning to stand upright and walk. The eyes that start focusing bring the consciousness of the human being into perspective. It is when the left and the right eye start working together around the age of two and a half years, that the child says "I." The consciousness of the human being is part of three-dimensional space. There is a connection between the inner soul life of the human being and the three dimensions of the outer physical world. Through the position of the eyes, most animals are not able to bring together in one picture the vision of the left and right eye and will not experience perspective (the third dimension).

Spiritually, the directions of space are created by movements of morality. In language, one will recognize moral virtues connected with the different spatial directions. One can be straightforward, upright or not quite right, sinister (*sinister*, 'left side' in Latin); one can keep things back or face problems head on or stand on firm ground. The verb "to fail" is close to the verb "to fall". In German you have *fallen* and *fehlen*, in Dutch, *vallen* and *falen*. These words certainly have to do with the Fall from Paradise. To be upright in German is *aufrecht*, in Dutch *oprecht*. The French know the expression *être droit.* In the different languages one will find inner soul moods are expressed in words related to spatial orientation. (Uta Stolz, an Extra Lesson teacher in Germany, has given special attention to this point.)

Throughout history humanity has had to discover and explore three-dimensional space. In very ancient times the day-wake thinking consciousness we have nowadays was not yet developed. People had a dream consciousness. In the age of exploration (15th–17th centuries), the ability to focus on the horizon developed. In art, people began to understand the laws of linear perspective. This brought the day-wake consciousness of the Ego, enabling it to perceive the physical, concrete outer sense world from a greater distance. In the art of painting, people began to use cobalt blue to color the sky; previously the background was gold. Natural science and materialism began to dominate the feeling life of humanity. The skeleton of the human being grew taller and therefore heavier. The Ego learned to connect more strongly with this physical structural organization, lifting it out of gravity, and therefore the soul went through a change of consciousness.

Spatial dimensions as such gradually came into appearance during the prehistoric world evolutionary process. When earth only consisted of warmth, there was no spatial dimension at all. What is the dimension of warmth? It could only be a point. Warmth is the bridge between the spiritual and the physical. Then, when light came into being, the first dimension appeared. Light is linear; at least it appears as linear. Light seems to move in a straight line. The third evolutionary step brought the element of water and the second dimension into being. This is the two-dimensional plane we know from the surface of water and of the leaves of the plants. Only with the evolutionary process of condensation did the element of the physical appear as three-dimensional space (see Ernst Marti, *The Four Ethers*).

Movement and Virtues

As mentioned before, movements in the different spatial directions are connected spiritually with moral elements. We can learn to understand this by imagining that when we move forward this asks inner *courage* of us to go into the future. Leaning backward and enjoying the beauty of the surrounding world can fill us with *joy*. The feeling of *faith* can arise in our souls when we look up to the heavens. This is the inner moral force that lives in our astral body. It is the current from below upwards. What comes from the past, what was created and now forms the living world around us, is filled with *wisdom*. This wisdom is the current of the ether body, moving from right to left. Moving from left to right is the current of the physical body. We share the physical structure of our body with all human beings; here within lies *righteousness*. The Ego teaches us *temperance*. These are the six virtues connected with the spatial directions experienced by the human being (see chapter 7). In Audrey McAllen's diagram of the cube (p. 156), one will find these six virtues connected with the currents of the human being.

To gain some understanding of the virtues connected with the currents in the world, we need to look at what Rudolf Steiner says in his lecture *The Pre-earthly Deeds of Christ* (March 7, 1914 GA 152) and in the lecture cycle *Christ and the Holy Grail* (GA 149) about the early stages of humanity.

At the end of the Lemurian period, after the event that we know as the Fall, the human being was tortured by his sense impressions. A beautiful object would give him enormous feelings of desire; other things gave him tremendous feelings of dislike or hate. The human soul was the victim of these sense impressions. This condition was caused by the intrusion of the luciferic beings. Their desire was to keep the development of creation at the Old Moon stage. On the Old Moon, there was only a two-dimensional world; the concrete physical was not yet developed. Rudolf Steiner describes the Old Moon planet as consisting of a substance similar to cooked spinach (*Outline of Esoteric Science*).

On the Earth planet, after the Lemurian period, human beings and the animals were still kept in the horizontal plane. The Christ Being came to rescue the human being. A part of the human soul—the soul of Adam—had been held back from the Fall by the higher gods. The Christ Being connected with this pure soul element and brought the human being into the vertical position. In this vertical position, the human being was no longer victimized by sense impressions but could maintain some distance, learning the difference between outer and inner, object and subject.

Human beings had to migrate from Lemuria to Atlantis, and there a new danger arose. Through the influence of luciferic and ahrimanic beings, the functioning of human organs was brought into disorder—the senses, the heart and the blood rhythm, the lungs—for the human soul was filled with forces of animal passion and covetousness. The senses became too vulnerable to sense impressions, which were terribly painful. Because of that condition, the human being could only produce dreadful sounds created by forces from the lower instincts. To rescue humanity for the second time, the Christ Being connected with the pure soul element to enable the human being to produce vowels. Then human beings were able to sing, to vocalize (see *The Pre-Earthly Deeds of Christ*).

Later in the Atlantean period, human soul forces of thinking, feeling, and willing were in danger of becoming disconnected and falling into disharmony. For the third time the Christ Being, with the help of the pure human soul, intervened to enable human beings to use consonants. With this new capacity they could describe outer objects.

We see in this historic overview that the highest spiritual forces—the Ego of the Christ himself, in connection with the purest soul forces of Atman, Buddhi, and Manas (Spirit Man, Life Spirit, and Spirit Self)—give humanity the forces to stand upright and to speak, to express inner feelings and give names to outer objects. The highest spiritual and soul forces rescue the human physical body (of senses), the etheric body (life processes), and the astral body (thinking, feeling, and willing). Reading this, one can understand that the spiritual currents of movement building up the world can be connected with the virtues of *hope* for the physical body of the senses, *love* for the etheric body, and *peace* for the astral body. The Christ, who during his three years incarnated in Jesus of Nazareth and connected with the spiritual organization of the earth planet, is the world's Ego. He is *truth*; His sentient soul is *beauty*, and His sentient body is *goodness*.

When the Christ Being incarnated and lived on earth until the Mystery of Golgotha, becoming a living human being, he offered humanity the capacity of thinking. That was in the Greco-Roman cultural epoch when philosophy appeared. The birth of Christ on earth is described in the Gospels. The pure soul of humanity, who did not know sin and thus was totally innocent and filled with love, is described by St. Luke. St Matthew, however, describes the birth that was expected by the Wise Men from the East. They were μαγoζ. Magus is the name given by the Babylonians (Chaldeans), Medes, Persians and others to the wise men, teachers, priests, physicians, astrologers, seers, and interpreters of dreams. One could say that they were initiates in the Persian mysteries who expected their master Zarathustra to reincarnate. Rudolf Steiner says that the Ego of Zarathustra, through successive incarnations, developed the highest possible forces of a human Ego, which however also carried the results of the intrusion of Lucifer and Ahriman. It had experienced the development of humanity through history.

The Gospel of St. Luke describes the moment when the personal element of the Zarathustra soul and Ego come into connection with the pure, innocent soul forces. This is the scene of the twelve-year-old Jesus in the temple. The priests and scribes in Jerusalem are amazed by the boy. They were used to lucid and keenly intellectual discussions of the Torah, the Jewish law and scriptures. Then, for the first time they experienced great wisdom mixed with the greatest love. This was totally new. Later, at the baptism in the River Jordan, the highest Sun Spirit incarnated into this complexly prepared body of Jesus of Nazareth. This is the imagination of the Holy Grail, the cup that can feed and cure because it receives the forces from the highest Holy Spirit.

When we observe a one-year-old child learning to stand and walk, and who will later learn to speak and think, we still see the result of the pre-earthly deeds of Christ. The forces with which the child before the age of three learns to stand, walk, speak, and think are the forces of the Higher Ego and soul. When the child says "I", the lower personal ego comes to self-consciousness. The higher forces withdraw into the realms of the subconscious. They are at work in the supersensible organization—the sense of life, the sense of balance, and the sense of self-movement (1909 lectures).

What Rudolf Steiner describes to us as anthroposophical Christology is the world archetype of every human being. In the lecture *The Invisible Man within Us* (February 11, 1923), he shows that the lower ego, astral, etheric, and physical bodies penetrate into the nutrition and growth processes of the human body. Before birth, these forces are at work in the embryonic envelopes of the baby: the chorion (lower ego), the allantois (astral body), the amnion (etheric body), and the yolk sac (physical body).

The higher Ego and the pure soul, consisting of Atman, Buddhi, and Manas, work as forces of destruction. After birth, the higher Ego works directly into the nerve-sense system. The higher Ego flows into the objective astral organization and goes directly into the lungs with the oxygen. It also works into the etheric body, which encounters destruction through oxygen in the form of carbonic acid in the blood.

In this complex picture of the working of the human supersensible sheaths, one can easily recognize the structural and constitutional elements Audrey McAllen described. The *cube diagram* is an image of the Holy Grail, the archetype of the way the higher and lower supersensible sheaths work in the human being. Note that in the lecture cycle *Deeper Insights into Eduction* Rudolf Steiner speaks about this to teachers. He explains that sense impressions are a direct working of the outer physical. In breathing, outer etheric forces come into the lungs with the air. The pulse of the blood rhythm is the astral body.

Some readers will have studied the 1909 lectures and gone on to study the lectures Rudolf Steiner gave a year later when he shared his anthroposophical insights of the soul. They will have wondered why Rudolf Steiner gave a different diagram of currents that year later. He showed the Ego coming from above, as in the year before. But then the physical is carrying the soul from below. The current from the left, that in the text he calls the etheric, is the past. The opposite current from the right, that in the text he calls the astral current, is the future. Later, in *Study of Man*, Steiner used different terminology for the same elements. What comes from the past he named *antipathy*, what comes from the future he named *sympathy*. The diagrams and content he brought in the second lecture of *Study of Man* correspond with the content of the 1910 lectures.

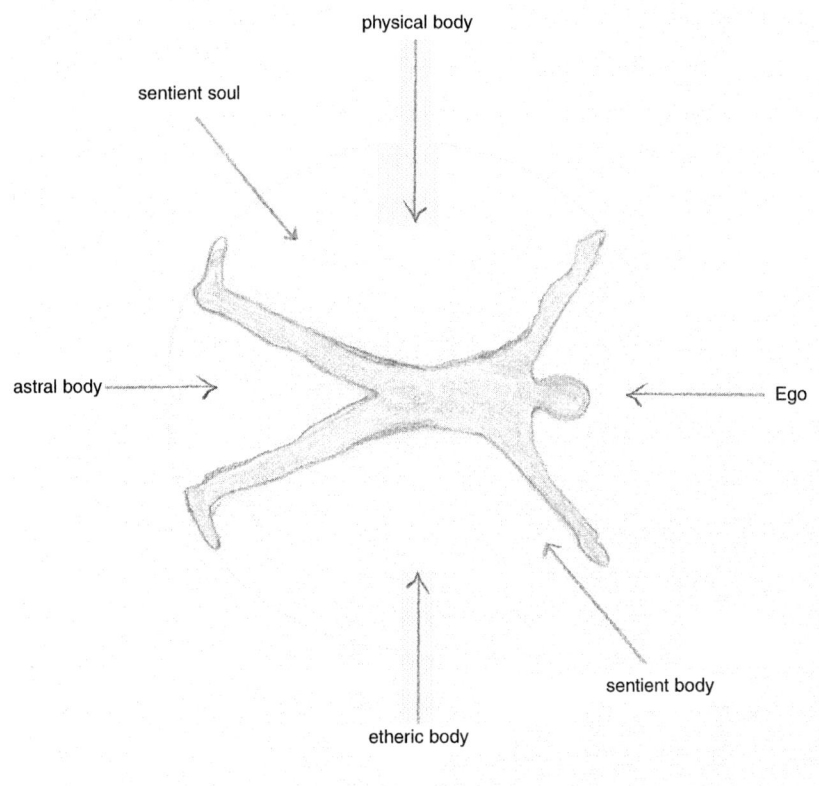

Currents of the Human Being

Now we take the principle of the mirroring process and try to approach the cube as a reversal of three-dimensional space. Let us move from the dimension of space to the dimension of soul to the dimension of the moral virtues "where space becomes time," as Gurnemanz says to Parsifal in Wagner's opera when they enter the Grail Castle.

The 1909 diagram of currents building up the human structural physical body can be seen as a reflection of the creative forces behind world evolution. In the Norse myths, the world was formed by the gods out of the body of the giant Ymir. Until the Fall from Paradise, the forces of the world and of the human being were one, as when the pregnant mother and the baby she carries form a living unity. One can make a reflection of the diagram Steiner gave and find the spiritual currents forming the body of the earth. Note that in the history of mapmaking the

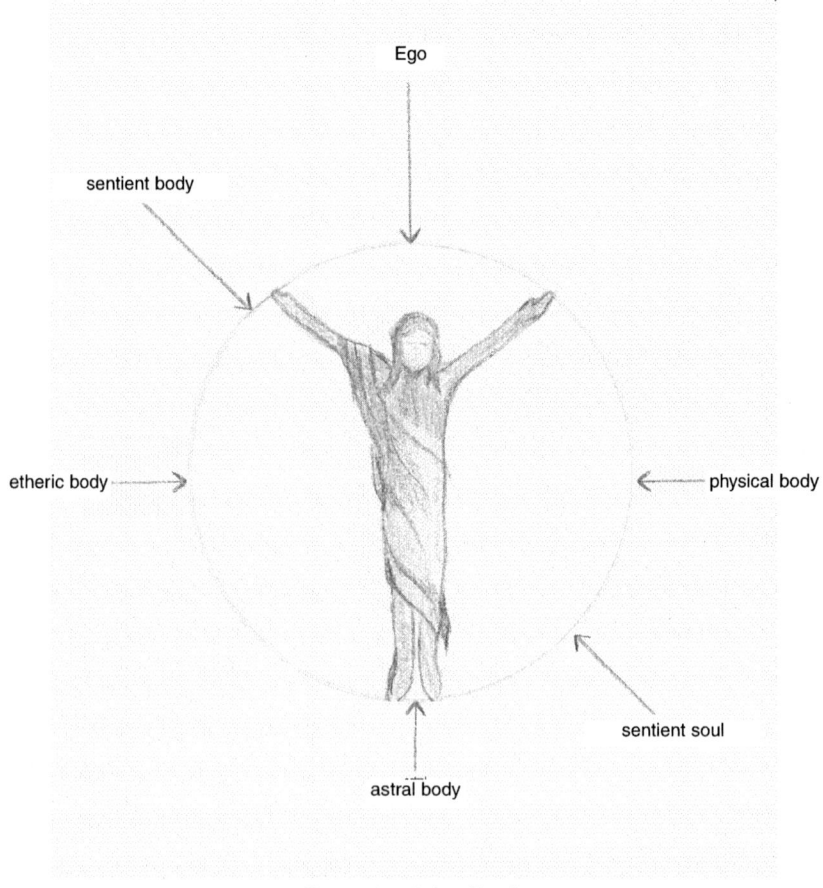

Currents of the Earth

east was originally put at the top. In older times one was "orienting," that is, looking for the Orient—the east. After the Renaissance, people got used to having the north at the top of a map. This all has to do with the change of consciousness as described above.

From the individual human standpoint we have become a diagram of the earth from an onlooker's point of view, as in medieval mapmaking when the earth was illustrated as the body of Christ.

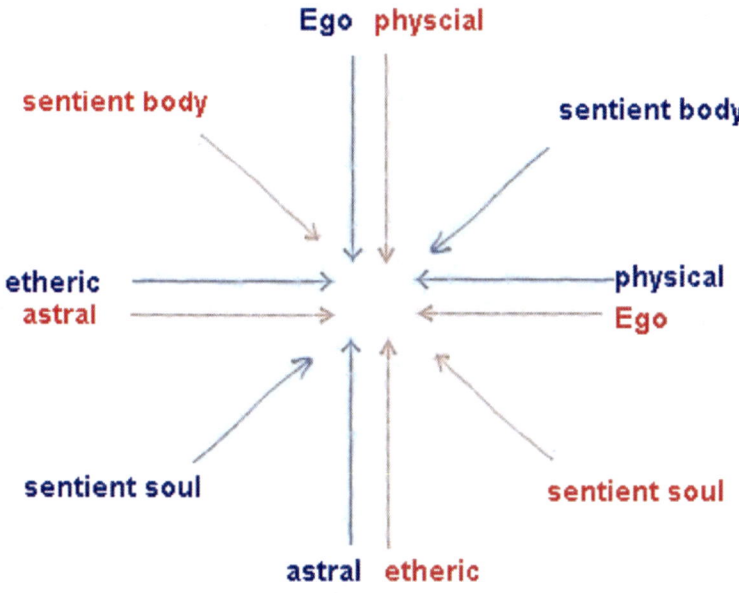

Currents of the Earth (blue) and the Human Being (red)

Combining the two diagrams of currents in world and human being, one comes to an overview map of twelve currents of movement. In the diagrams, these currents are projected as lines, but one has to think of them as planes of movement—movements that in the spiritual world of the soul, where space has become time, are twelve moral virtues.

This two-dimensional projection of three-dimensional orientation in space can be reversed into an astral map. Reversing means, as we already have learned, turning inside out. The center will become the periphery and the currents will move in opposite directions.

Projection of the Supersensible Currents in Man in Relation to those of the World

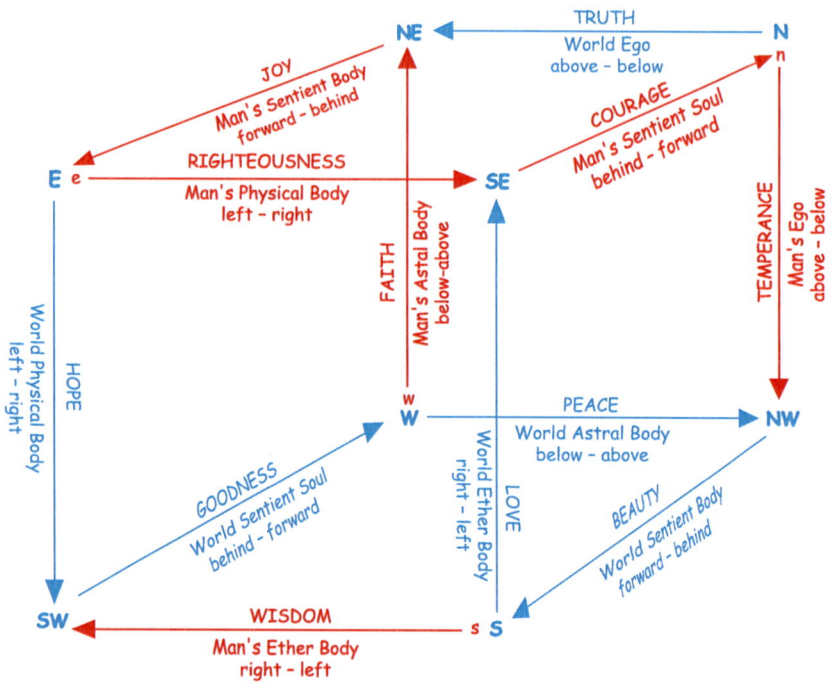

This is how Audrey McAllen came to the Cube as the spiritual moral map she published in her book *Sleep*. She wants to show the Extra Lesson teacher that helping the child to incarnate into three-dimensional space not only has a physical connotation but also helps the students to find their connections with the spiritual creative forces that are at work behind the scene of the outer sense world. We can follow the currents and see what vortexes these planes of movement create. It is not to be seen as a static picture, but as an image of creative forces.

The twelve ribs of the cube correspond in number to the twelve signs of the Zodiac, the domain of the formative forces. The three-dimensions of the cube lead us into distances of infinity where the forces of the Holy Trinity are at work as divine thinking, feeling, and willing. The cubic form of the New Jerusalem in the Book of Revelation represents the end result of the completed earth stage of evolution, when the human being will reach the spiritual heights and will offer these results to the spiritual world. The New Jerusalem will have walls as high as they are long and as they are broad, with twelve gates. This is an image of the Holy Grail, where the results of the human experience in three-dimensional space and the spiritual development of the Ego within the physical world will be imprinted in the course of evolution. It is then that physical space will have become time.

Inside himself the human being also carries an inner cube, as Rudolf Steiner says (*Balance in the World and Man* lecture 2). This one is located in the chest and is the inner free space where God the Father breathed the spirit into Adam. Only here are we truly human. This cube acts as an inner gyroscope for our movement system and orientation. It is the inner reversal into the individual soul life. One can look at the large cube as representing movement as spiritual moral virtues. The reversal of this is in the physical sense world, where the Ego focuses to a point creating three-dimensional space. The small inner cube represents a reversal into the inner soul element of the individual.

Often in circles of people interested in spiritual science, one can meet fear of the physical element. We have to keep in mind the spiritual law that the highest spiritual Hierarchies are connected with physical forces like gravity. The human being can only develop self-consciousness while living in the physical world. The importance of a healthy incarnation as a result of a proper first seven-year development cannot be underestimated. The result will be that experience inside the three-dimensional physical world will be imprinted into the etheric body of the individual human being and of the earth itself. Rudolf Steiner expresses the importance of this as follows (*The Gospel of St. John in Relation to the Other Gospels*):

> Through the entrance of Christ into the body of Jesus of Nazareth, the individuality of Christ gained dominion over the bony structure itself with its physical and chemical processes. As a result, there once lived on earth a body able to use its forces in such a way that it caused the spiritual form of the bony structure to become embedded into the evolution of the earth. The sum of everything that man has undergone would be irretrievably lost, unless he were able to incorporate the noble form of his bony structure into the evolution of the earth, as an evolutionary law of which he could by degrees gain mastery. No vestige of earth-future evolution would be carried over into the future if the bony frame were not preserved. The form of the bony structure conquers death in a physical sense.

This is the mystery of the Holy Grail (see drawing on next page).

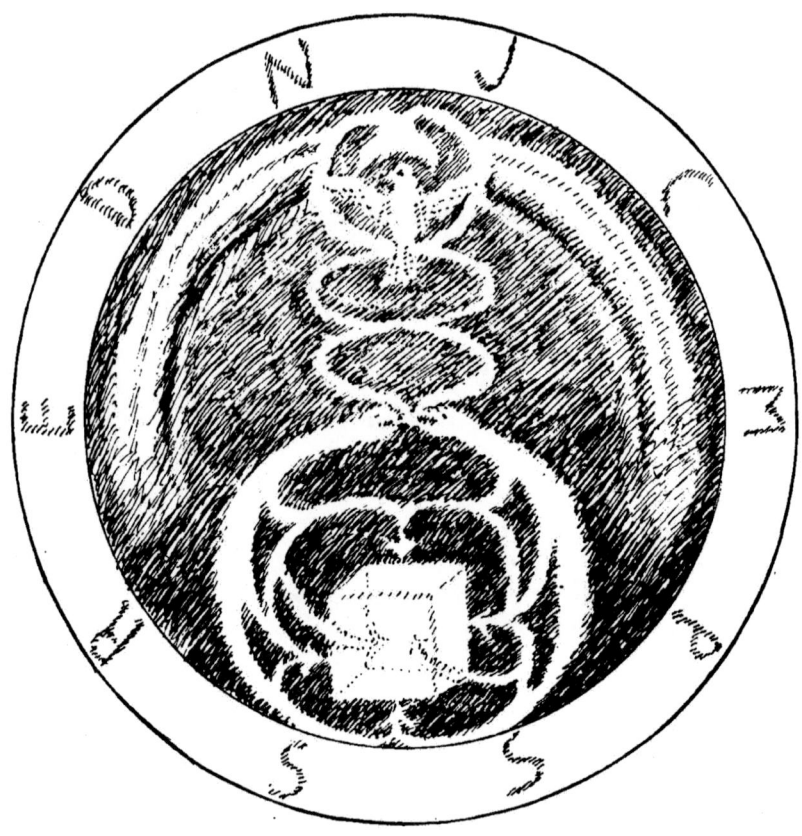

7th Apocalyptic Seal

Sketch by Daniel van Bemmelen
from a painting by C. Rettich, after a sketch by Rudolf Steiner
© Verlag am Goetheanum, Dornach Switzerland

Chapter 12

The Divine Architecture of the Structural Physical Body

In the evolution of the earth and of the human being, the physical structure of the human body was to be developed step by step. Its development corresponded with the developmental circumstances of the body of the planet earth itself. According to Rudolf Steiner, Plato's picture of Atlantis was a description of a period in the earth's evolution when the atmosphere was still filled with the element of water as mist and dampness. The earth's surface was not as solid as it is nowadays. Neither were human bodies yet condensed into a physical bony structure. During this time the sense organs were created. For example, the eyes were created by the light of the sun. Rudolf Steiner describes the sunlight penetrating the cloudy earth atmosphere and burning, as it were, the organs of sight into the delicate structure of the human body (*Egyptian Myths and Mysteries*). They appeared as a kind of brand made by the sunlight, taking in the laws of light. Likewise, the ear was created by sound. Into the delicate structural body the different sense organs were imprinted from without. The skeleton was formed by the spiralling movements of moon and sun going through the signs of the zodiac. These movements were imprinted into the structure of the spine with its vertebrae.

At the end of this Atlantean time the mists and moisture in the atmosphere started condensing. The elements of air and water were separated; it started to rain. This situation was not only described in the Bible story of Noah and the Ark but in all mythologies. In India there is the story of Manu; in Greek mythology there is the story of Deukalion and his wife Pyrrha. When we take the biblical description of the Ark seriously, we read that its dimensions were 300 cubits long, 50 cubits wide, and 30 cubits high (Genesis 6:15). It is hard to imagine the Bible is describing a boat here. According to spiritual science, it wasn't. These measurements were an indication of the proportions of the structural physical human body prepared for the time after the deluge. The proportions 300:50:30 will give us the image of a large coffin containing a human body with arms outstretched above the head.

The Ark was three storeys high, and Noah had to take with him into it two of every sort of living thing, male and female. This can be read as the astral body incarnating into this structural physical body (Steiner, *Occult Signs and Symbols*).

We have to take into consideration that it was Moses who wrote the Book of Genesis. Moses was initiated in the Egyptian Mysteries. That the Lord told Moses to cast his rod to the ground and it became a snake, is a symbol for the fact that Moses was initiated into the spiritual forces behind the creation of the physical body on Old Saturn. The Bible story (Exodus 2:10) tells us that Moses was raised by the Pharaoh's daughter, after she found him in a basket in the river Nile. The floating basket on the river Nile itself is an archetypal picture of an initiation rite. The image of the basket can be seen as a sort of sarcophagus in which the initiate was laid during the three days of initiation. A sarcophagus definitely was more than just a coffin. In this illustration we see the inside of the lid of a sarcophagus with Nut, goddess of the heavens, with outstretched arms and stars, moon, and sun all over her body.

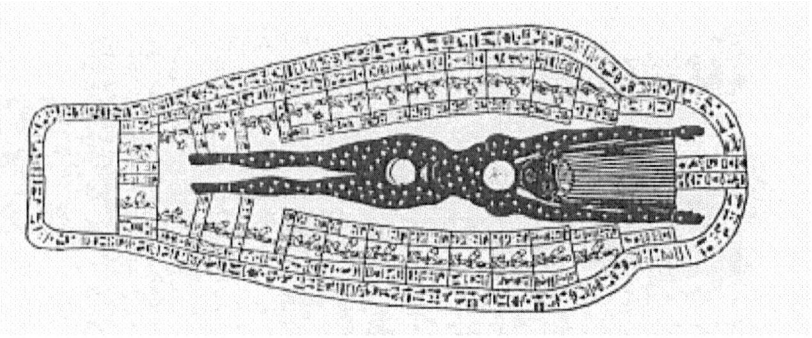

Being an Egyptian initiate, Moses must have taken up knowledge of Egyptian temple architecture. This architecture was, as the Roman architect Marcus Vitruvius Pollio (90–20 BC) articulated it centuries later, based on the proportions of the human body.

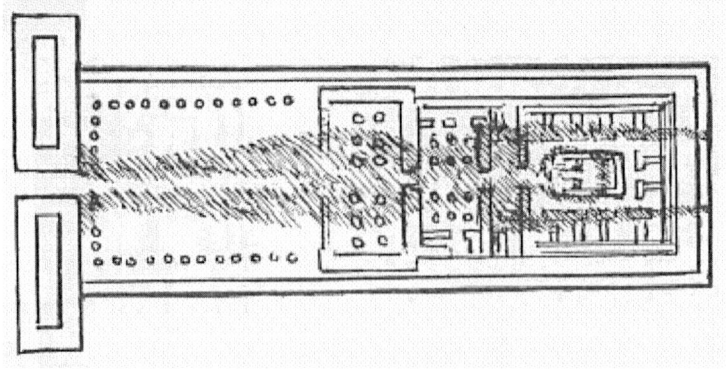

Egyptian Temple Based on Human Form

One entered the temple between two large pylons. The first court was a peristyle court, which means it was not covered by a roof and had pillars around it. This court was accessible to the public and used for sacrifice and temple healings. The middle part was covered by a roof which was supported by beautifully sculptured columns decorated with color. The third part was the inner building, only accessible to the high priests. This was where the statue of the Godhead was, as the high Ego of the temple. Like the human skull, it was closed and dark. Projecting a figure of the human body onto the temple floor plan, one can clearly distinguish the threefold structure of limbs, middle system, and head. The French author R. A. Schwaller de Lubicz published a great deal of his research on this topic in *The Temple of Man: Sacred Architecture and the Perfect Man*.

Temple architecture corresponded with the Golden Ratio, which is also derived from the proportions of the human body. The above-mentioned Marcus Vitruvius Pollio inspired Leonardo da Vinci to make his famous drawing of the *Vitruvian Man* showing the geometric harmony of the olden Ratio in the human structure.

The Egyptian sacred knowledge of architecture was taken up by Moses when he constructed the tent of the congregation and the ark of the covenant. The detailed description is in the Book of Exodus.

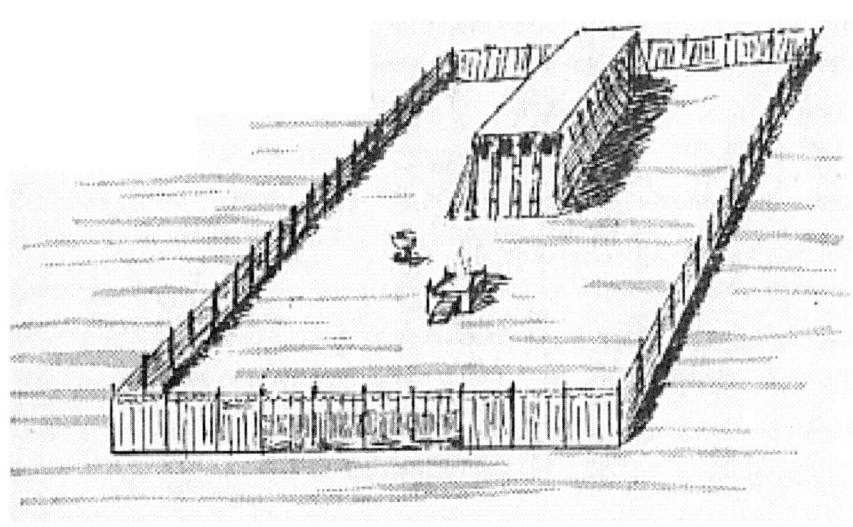

Courtyard and Tabernacle

Later, when King Solomon built the temple in Jerusalem, again the proportions of the human body formed the foundation of its architectural structure. As at the entrance of the Egyptian temples, this temple in Jerusalem had its famous two pillars Boaz and Jachim.

In medieval cathedral architecture, one can recognize the Christianized, yet similar, principle. A beautiful representative of this is the famous cathedral at Chartres in France. Let us compare the floor plan of this cathedral with Rudolf Steiner's diagram of 1909. Normally medieval churches are aligned facing east. Chartres is the one exception; it is oriented northeast, towards the rising sun of midsummer, probably in the tradition of the Celts.

Facing the altar in the east, one will meet the archetypal Ego. The portal on the left, north side of the transept, is decorated with sculptures representing the Old Testament. The portal in the south has sculptures representing the Last Judgment. The prominent color of the left rose window is blue; the right rose window gives a mainly red impression (see illustrations, pp. 77–78). One will recognize the principle of the Eye Color Affinity.

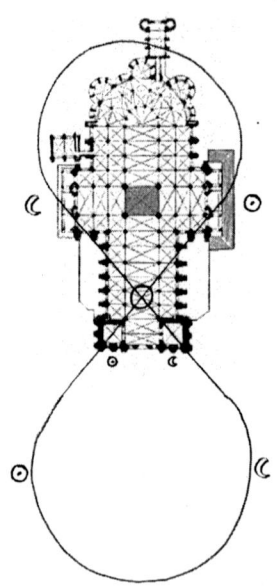

In the west the the main entrance of Chartres cathedral has two towers. Normally they would have been symmetrical, but in Chartres they are shaped differently. The left tower, called the Michael tower, is richly decorated and has a sun sign on top. The right tower, called the Gabriel tower, is much simpler and has a moon sign on top. If one draws a diagonal line from the north portal to the Gabriel tower and another one from the south portal towards the Michael tower connecting the elements of the Old and New Testaments, one will notice that right where these diagonals cross is the famous labyrinth. Here we see the principle of reversal we have met in the chapters on Eye Color Affinity and Mirroring.

In addition to the linear aspect in architecture, one also can trace the development of the curved line or circle in the history of architecture. In the Greek temple one can picture the center of a circle in the middle of the

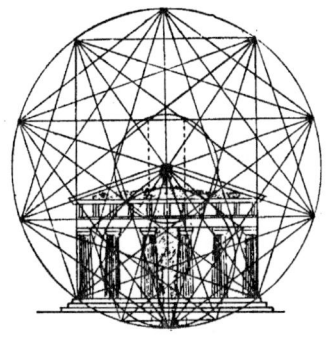

architrave. In children's early drawings, by the time the child says "I," he will be able to draw a circle with a dot as a center. In the Greek temple one can recognize the Ego in the triangle, representing the spiritual soul aspect, while the rectangle represents the physical and life bodies. The large upper part of the circle is still above the building as if at that time the Greek experienced their spirit and soul still strongly connected with the gods and the heavens.

In Roman times, humanity was already more deeply incarnated into the body. The Pantheon, built by the Emperor Hadrian, shows the circle with its center inside the building. The cupola is carried by a cylinder. Here one can experience the Ego point as center of this huge building.

Originally the inside of the cupola was covered with gilt bronze coffers. These coffers reflected the sunlight coming in through the 9-meter-wide opening in the center of the roof. The building is like an immense eye looking upwards to the heavens. The light was reflected by these bronze plates to the floor as to the retina in the eye.

The curved line is definitely one of the characteristics of Roman architecture. The Romans used this element in building huge constructions like aqueducts and stadiums. Later, after the Crusades and under the influence of Arab culture, the Roman arch vault narrowed into the Gothic arch. The Arabic architecture the Crusaders met in Jerusalem had the pointed arch as a main principle. In his book *Chartres: Sacred Geometry, Sacred Space*, Gordon Strachan beautifully illustrates this process. It might very well be the architectural expression of the ahrimanic influence on the human organism and soul. As Rudolf Steiner points out, this influence presses together, shrivels up, and hardens the ether body and therefore the physical body. This dried out condition of the physical and life bodies creates the ability of intellectual thinking (Steiner, *Balance in the World and Man*).

Architecture of the First Goetheanum

Rudolf Steiner combined the linear and curved principles in architecture in his design for the First Goetheanum that consisted of two interpenetrating cupolas, creating a lemniscate form. The building was aligned towards the East. The proportions of the two cupolas were set according to the Pythagorean theorem with the ratios 3:4:5, using the principle of the Egyptian twelve-knot rope. These proportions nearly equal the ratio of $\sqrt{1} : \sqrt{2} : \sqrt{3}$, the diagonals of a cube. Earlier we learned that Pythagoras studied in the Egyptian mysteries and that the basic root of his theorem is the picture of the three godheads Osiris, Isis, and Horus, representing physical, etheric, and astral bodies.[1] The hypotenuse in the building formed the distance between the centers of the small and large cupola. The bores or radii of the two cupolas were in the ratios 3:4. Simply from this one can understand Rudolf Steiner's saying that the First Goetheanum was a house for the soul. As in the Egyptian temple, these proportions coincide with the proportions of the human body with outstretched arms. One can think of the Right-angled Triangle exercise.

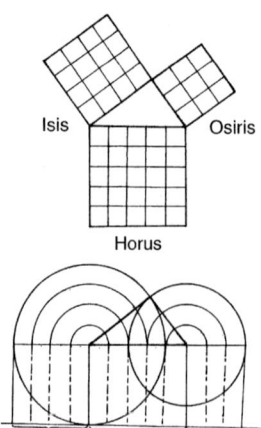

The construction of the First Goetheanum was begun in 1913. One can assume Rudolf Steiner used the insights he shared in 1909. Entering the building from the west, one passed the colored windows, following the current of the astral body meeting the current of the Ego from the east. There was the stage, where the Statue of the Representative of Humanity was planned as the statue of the Godhead, placed in the Holy of

Holies. The small cupola had no windows; it was surrounded by offices and backstage rooms. The small cupola is the head, the large cupola the trunk, of the human figure. The crossing point where the lectern stands is the heart and shows the crossing of the muscles of the thorax, making possible the rotation of the body.

The roof of the small cupola was supported by two sets of six columns. The large cupola had seven columns on each side. When one draws lines from the columns of the small cupola, crossing the center of the building, they end in the spaces between the columns in the sets of seven columns of the large cupola.

Here one can have the impression that the columns show the relation between the twelvefold sensory process of the nerve-sense system

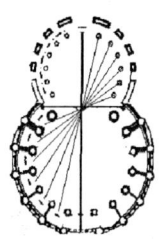

and the sevenfold processes of the metabolic system. The sense impressions in the nerve-sense system are taken up by the rhythmical element in the middle system, where the human soul can connect sense perceptions with feeling. For memory, there is the imprinting in the etheric processes of the metabolic system, represented by the six non-physical intervals between the seven columns of the large cupola. The Extra Lesson teacher can recognize here the shape and also the main principle of the Flower Rod exercise. All that has been described about this in the foregoing chapters can be found in the architectural structure of this building.

When we project the proportions 3:4:5 of the First Goetheanum onto a cross section of a human head, we will find that the small and large cupolas correspond to the proportions of frontal brain and cerebellum. The intersection in the center of the head is where the pineal gland and the pituitary gland are located. In this cross-section once again we can recognize the principle of the Flower Rod exercise. One can trace the outer sense impressions coming in from the main entrance in the west going into the inner realm of the building, as they do when they are being transformed into the inner life of the human being.

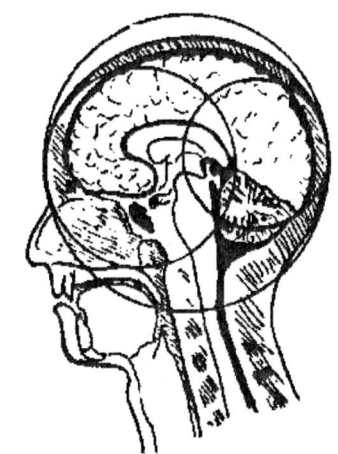

As the Pantheon's structure is like a large eye looking up to the heavens, the large cupola with its colored windows also depicted the structure of the eye. The large red window in the entrance hall, the porch, is like the frontal part of the eye with cornea, aqueous humour, pupil, iris, lens, and so forth. Outer light is received by the eye as it is in a camera obscura; however, the impact of this outer light needs to be destroyed by the human organism. The red window is the only one in an active color. The other windows inside the main hall of the large cupola were in the sequence of green, blue, blue-violet, and rose pink on both sides. These passive colors are bound to the elements basic to the outer sense world: earth, water, air and fire. It is a resonance of outer sense impressions. The inner processes within the sense of sight were brought into consciousness here by the colored shadows, the complementary colors.

In chapter 9 on the mirroring process, we mentioned the process of mirroring from convex to concave for the sense of color perception. In the First Goetheanum the convex aspect of the astral body was made visible in the colored windows and the complementary colors and colored shadows in the large cupola. It represents the astral body working inside the etheric body. The outer aspect of the astral body, connected with sense perception and imprinting into memory, was found in the painting on the ceiling of the small cupola. These paintings represent Spirit Memory and, according to Rudolf Steiner's indications, they were supposed to be done in the counter-colors. This is the inner and concave astral mirroring of color. The artists at that time were not able to follow Rudolf Steiner's indications, as Ms. Bruinier reported. Later the painter and first Dutch Waldorf teacher Daniel van Bemmelen attempted to do so. His work is published on color plates in the book *Rudolf Steiner's New Approach to Color on the Ceiling of the First Goetheanum*. The painting showed the different cultural epochs in the development of the human being.

Projecting Rudolf Steiner's Statue of the Representative of Humanity proportionately onto the floor plan of the First Goetheanum, one can immediately recognize the gesture of the last part of the Copper Ball exercise. Again all that has been described about this exercise in the foregoing chapters can be found in the architectural structure of this building. The Copper Ball exercise not only recapitulates neurological and developmental steps, but it also gives the student an inner picture in movement of the cultural history of humanity. This is, so to speak, the "Practicing of Spirit Memory" that Rudolf Steiner referred to in the Foundation Stone Verse (see Zeylmans, *The Foundation Stone* or Bamford, ed. *Start Now!*).

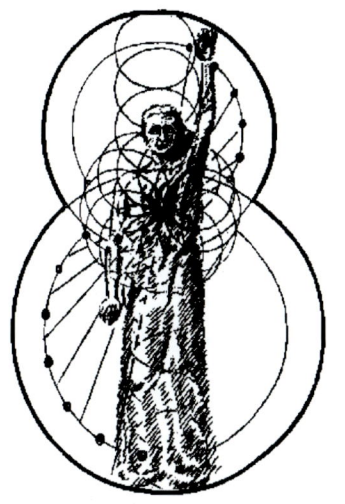

© Verlag am Goetheanum, Dornach, Switzerland

In the early 1990s, I discovered the architectonic principles of the First Goetheanum in the Extra Lesson exercises. I phoned Audrey McAllen asking her, "Audrey, did you know this?" The answer was, "Oh, did you discover that? I didn't know it was there. I only can tell you that at the time I was working with these students, I was meditating the building. I could visualize it inwardly as if I were walking through it. I never thought it would come out like this in the exercises."

Sharing these insights with the reader, I hope the respect for the gift Audrey McAllen gave to Waldorf education will be deepened—that in the Extra Lesson practitioner courage, faith, and joy will grow. Audrey McAllen's concept of the Extra Lesson offers insights and exercises in movement, drawing, and painting connected with and based on the spiritual architecture of the human being. The Extra Lesson concept is deeply rooted in the anthroposophical knowledge of humanity.

The First Goetheanum — painting by Katharina Eisleben
reproduced by permission of Walter Keller Verlag

Appendix A

Notes on *The King of Ireland's Son*
by Joep Eikenboom

In chapter 12 on the sacred architecture and the First Goetheanum, I tried to give in an artistic way some images to deepen the understanding of the Extra Lesson backgrounds. This was as seen from the view of the plastic-architectonic arts. That is the stream of antipathy, the stream of the visual. In the arts of music and speech, we have the opposite—sympathy and the auditory stream. In Padraic Colum's beautiful story *The King of Ireland's Son*, the concept behind the Extra Lesson exercises is given in a wonderful way.

Structural and Constitutional Physical Body

When you read this story for the first time, the complex structure will not be revealed at once. There are three main storylines: First there is the story of the King of Ireland's Son. Secondly there is the story line about Gilly of the Goatskin. And interlinked with the stories of these two main characters, there is The Unique Tale. The first story line tells us the adventures of the structural element in the human body. The King of Ireland's Son is, in contrast with the main characters in most fairy tales, the eldest son. Therefore he carries the family heredity (Karl König, *Brothers and Sisters*), not only of his parents but of the complete evolution from Old Saturn, Old Sun, Old Moon, and Earth. He is not an easy boy. The King and his Councilor *let him have his own way in everything*:

> His hound at his heel
> His hawk on his wrist
> A brave steed to carry him whither he list.

Always pay attention to the different animals in the story: hound, hawk, and steed all represent different aspects of thinking. The King of Ireland's Son is the eternal "spirit-I," as Audrey McAllen calls it in *Reading Children's Drawings*. The story line of the King's Son therefore always points in the direction of the nervous system, muscles, and bones.

The King's Son has two younger stepbrothers, Dermot and Downal. All three share the same father, but the King of Ireland's Son's *mother had died before she could guide him*.

The second storyline is about the personal constitutional element, here put upon stage as Gilly of the Goatskin. This is the personal "soul-I," the threefold soul that lives in the sevenfold processes of the organs.

Fedelma, the Enchanter's Daughter

Right at the beginning, the King of Ireland's Son, whose name is never mentioned, meets his main opponent: the Enchanter of the Black Back-Lands. He doesn't recognize him as his opponent right away; however, the old man he meets, the Old Fellow, is playing cards with himself, his right hand against his left hand. The symmetrical movement pattern is a picture of the loose connection of the Enchanter's Ego with his physical organization. One should pay attention to small details like the one when the Old Fellow is playing while sitting on a heap of stones. This small detail points toward the physical element. The old fellow invites the King's Son to play cards with him. The Enchanter is able to pay the wager in a wonderful way. After winning two times, of course the King's Son loses the third game. The Enchanter reveals himself as the King's enemy: *"I have done him injury. And the Queen who is your father's wife I have done injury too,"* he says. The penalty the Enchanter puts upon the King of Ireland's Son is the following: he needs to find the Enchanter's dwelling place and take three hairs out of his beard within a year and a day, or lose his head. Earlier in the story the King of Ireland's Son had sung the lines:

> I put the fastenings on my boat
> For a year and for a day,......

The theme of the three hairs we know from the Grimms' fairy tale "The Devil with the Three Golden Hairs." According to Rudolf Meyer in his book *The Wisdom in Fairy Tales*, the three golden hairs represent the solutions to all the riddles of life the young human being is facing at the beginning of puberty.

The King and his Councilor do not know who the Enchanter of the Black Back-Lands is. Nevertheless, they fear the danger for Ireland if the King's Son does not go and seek him. When he leaves, his stepmother does not allow him to take with him his hound, hawk, and horse. Hound, hawk, and horse all three are imaginative representations of human thinking. The Prince is given a horse that was lame in one leg and short in the tail. His thinking is hindered, maybe through materialism. One will find the imagination of the lame and short-tailed horse once more later in the story.

On his journey, the King's Son witnesses a fight between an eel and an eagle. Eel and eagle might point to the two aspects, lower and higher, of the zodiacal sign Scorpio, this sign of the November sun that sends the forces of death. The formative sound of this sign is "S" that penetrates deepest into matter and forms it (see Audrey McAllen, *The Listening Ear*).

The King's Son helps Laheen, the Eagle, and as a reward the eagle shows him how to reach the dominion of the Enchanter of the Black Back-Lands. The higher force of Scorpio helps the Son of King Connal to enter the physical stream where Ahriman holds dominion.

Laheen the Eagle tells the King's Son to travel first with the sun before him and then with the sun at his back. That means he is told to travel East, facing the current of the incarnating Ego and also a journey into the direction of the future. At a lake he will discover three swans, one with a green scarf in her mouth. Green is the color of the incarnating Ego.

The three swans appear to be three daughters of the Enchanter. The youngest daughter helps the King's Son. Her name is Fedelma. The other two are called Aefa and Gilveen. As is common, one can recognize the theme of threefoldness, which in fairy tales mostly has to do with the three different soul elements: the sentient soul, the intellectual soul, and the consciousness soul. Here, however, Aefa represents the sentient soul poisoned by Lucifer; Gilveen represents the intellectual soul poisoned by Ahriman. The Enchanter gives three tasks to fulfill. Fedelma helps the King's Son, but the other two sisters are both interested in marrying the King's Son. Every night the King of Ireland's Son sleeps in a dry narrow water tank. This water tank is an image of the sarcophagus, a sign that here we are reading of an initiation.

With the help of Fedelma, the King's Son fulfills his three tasks. He has to catch Whitefoot the Fawn. Fedelma gives him the Shoes of Swiftness, the element of thinking. Secondly, he needs to thatch the shelter for the Enchanter's beehives with the feathers of birds. Fedelma helps him, and her blue falcon gathers him all the birds. This is in the element of air, the breathing, the middle system where human feeling life is located. The last task is the riskiest: he needs to go down into a well and bring the Enchanter the Ring of Youth. This well is the metabolism, where the ever-rejuvenating forces of the human being are located. The big difficulty is that Fedelma only can be of help to the King's Son if he kills her and uses the bones of her skeleton as steps to go down into the well. Here we see the imagination of the consciousness soul. The Ego can only awaken in the consciousness soul and develop self-consciousness when it is properly supported by the forces of the structural physical body, the skeleton. The King's Son finds the Ring of Youth and brings the bones together again. One thing is not in place: the joint of Fedelma's little finger. Of the five fingers of the hand, the little finger is the carrier of the forces of heredity (see Norbert Glas, *Die Hände offenbaren den Menschen*). It is the least flexible finger, for its muscle is connected to the muscle of the ring finger. Anyone who has the experience of learning to play the piano and working on a typewriter or computer will know this phenomenon. The broken little finger gives the King's Son the key to finding Fedelma as his bride.

Aefa sits at a spinning wheel. She has a little mouth, a hooked nose, and her eyes are crossed. This is caused by the influence of Lucifer on the (sentient) soul. She advises the King's Son to escape, escape from physical reality and flee into illusions. When the King's Son tells her he wants to marry Fedelma, she sends her cat (cat-o'-the-mountain) to seize him.

Gilveen is little, has a face that is brown and tight like a nut. In her tower are the wisest books of the world, she says, in which the King's Son surely will find a way to the Enchanter's country. When the King's Son tells her he wants to marry Fedelma, Gilveen's lips draw together and her chin becomes like a horn. She whistles through her teeth and instantly everything in the room begins to attack the King's Son. Here one recognizes the ahrimanic element within the intellectual soul and the etheric body.

Happily together at last, Fedelma and the King's Son leave the Enchanter's dominion on the back of the Slight Red Steed. The Red Steed is the element of will within the thinking. At the Hill of Horns the Little Sage of the Mountain melts lead to make them two rings. Lead is the metal of Saturn, the planet of the physical structure.

While the King's Son and Fedelma are traveling, they tell each other stories. Then the King's Son is filled with weariness and must sleep. Fedelma takes his head upon her lap and the King's Son falls asleep. Fedelma is kidnapped by the King of the Land of Mist. She sees to it that the King of the Land of Mist tells her how the King of Ireland's Son can find her. Fedelma's blue falcon listens in and reports to the King's Son: he must conquer the King of the Land of Mist with the Sword of Light. Fedelma can be taken out of slumber if one cuts a tress of her hair with a stroke of the Sword of Light. The King's Son wants to return to the Enchanter's country, but he finds a message that Fedelma has written. He enters the Wood of Shadows, the land of death. He perceives shadows and creatures and goes after some of them. He hears them whisper louder and louder, and the shadows surround him. Then he hears a voice from under the ground, calling: "Shout out your own name, Son of King Connal." The shouting of his own name brings back self-consciousness. The shadows stop and the King's Son can travel further. Then he goes back to his father's castle.

The adventure in the dominion of the Enchanter of the Black Back-Lands can be seen as an initiation in the realm of the astral body. The Land of Mist and the Wood of Shadows could very well be the realm of the etheric in which the King's Son is not yet ready to be initiated at this point of the story.

The King of Cats Came to Visit King Connal's Dominion

The story line of the King of Ireland's Son continues, and at this point the second story line starts. It is the story of Gilly of the Goatskin, the representative of the constitutional picture of the human being. The King's Son is trying to find the King of the Land of Mist. The story that the King's steward tells the King's Son contains elements that point in the direction of the lower astral body, influenced by the Fall. It is this lower astral body that carries the lower animal character. The human astral body contains the whole animal kingdom, but in the human being the activity of the Ego should be able to suppress this so this can become the element of thinking within the soul. Rudolf Steiner points out that these formative forces of antipathy, working from the head downward, have the tendency to make the human body animal-like and the trunk works to counteract this process (*Foundations of Human Experience* lecture 12). The astral forces of sympathy at work in the blood from below upward carry the lower levels of will—instinct, impulse, and desire—which have the tendency within the human being to arouse bestial behavior like that of a snake, wolf, or fox. Treason, murder, and craftiness need to be conquered by singing and making music (*Balance in Teaching* lecture 2). It is this astral quality that will surprise the second grade teacher after the lovely fairy-tale mood the class has in first grade. At the end of the story about the King of Cats, a war between elves and men and even among the men of Ireland is threatening. At the end of this war, the eagle and the cat become figures of stone. This story is continued at the end of the book when the history of the Fairy Rowan Tree is told as part of Gilly of the Goatskin's adventures.

The Sword of Light

The quest of the King of Ireland's Son now continues. He finds the Gobaun Saor, the Builder and Shaper of the Gods. It is forbidden to tell where he found him! "Show me first your will, your mind, and your purpose," says the Gobaon Saor. The King's Son has to guard the Gobaun Saor's anvil for a few nights. For three nights a creature comes out of the river, a Fua, which engages the King's Son in combat. Then the Gobaon Saor reveals where the Sword of Light can be found. It is in the Palace of the Ancient Ones under the Lake. The King's Son finds the Lake with an island in the middle. His Slight Red Steed swims towards the Black Island, covered with ashes up to the horse's knees. He enters an opening in the black rock, travels through a hundred passages and reaches a wide hall. The Sword of Light is hanging from the roof.

This scene can be compared to the one in the Grail Story when Parsifal reaches the Grail Castle. The black island in the middle of the lake could be an image of the brain floating in the brain fluid. In the center of the brain are the pituitary and pineal glands. The Sword of Light is hanging there shining, like the light of the higher Ego.

The King's Son pulls the sword down and flashes it about. He sees twelve women sleeping with great gemmed cups in their hands. He drinks from the bubbling water in the cups. The twelve women represent the twelve cranial nerves or the twelve senses, as we know them from the Grimms' fairy tale "The Sea-Hare." The King's Son's spirit grows haughty. He meets the one-eyed Swallow People. The one eye, as with the Cyclops, Polyphemus, stands for the old clairvoyance. The Sword of Light loses its brightness, because an ass rubs its hoof against it. The Sword turns black and loses its spiritual light.

The Gobaun Saor can brighten the Sword. This is not easy, however, and he wants the King's Son to find the Unique Tale—and what comes before its beginning and what comes after its end.

All elements in the story line of the King's Son point to the structural body. The ahrimanic element is met. Ahriman, or Mephistopheles, is present in the realm of the etheric and heredity. In the soul, this is the element of the intellect. Through his working, the etheric body is squeezed together so that the physical body dries out. Therefore the nerves, brain, and skeleton of the structural body can become brittle, the muscles stiff.

The King's Son visits the Old Woman of Beare to find the Unique Tale. There he meets Gilly of the Goatskin who wants to tell him the Unique Tale. Before the Old Woman of Beare lets them exchange the Unique Tale, the two boys have to count the number of her ox horns. These ox horns are in two pits. The King's Son starts counting the ox horns in the pit on the left-hand side of the house; Gilly is counting the ox-horns in the right-hand pit.

In fairy tales, the house is the archetype of the human body. Think of "Snow-white" or "The Wolf and the Seven Young Kids." The left-hand side of the body is twofold, where soul-spirit and life-body come together, the structural side. The right-hand side is threefold: thinking, feeling and willing. Structural and constitutional form a unity; the King's Son and Gilly need to work together.

Gilly of the Goatskin

Gilly never stirred out of his cradle till he was twelve years of age, says the story. This is the age when the soul awakens in the structural element and weight of the bony system. It is the age of the sixth grader, the Roman that will be able to do geometry and natural science. The fifth grader is like the Greek, living still in the muscular system, not yet so much connecting with the weight of the skeleton.

Gilly is nurtured by the Three Hags of the Long Teeth. The image of an old woman with long teeth we know from the Grimms' "Mother Holle". According to Rudolf Meyer, these long teeth are connected with ossification processes, which one can understand thinking of Gilly's age of twelve. In other fairy tales Mother Holle represents the life forces of the etheric world, the world of the elemental beings. In this story, we see this image appearing in a threefold way, which shows the threefold soul element imprinting from within onto the body of life forces.

Gilly for the first time leaves the house of the Three Hags of the Long Teeth. *He sprang across the cradle, over the threshold of the door, and out into the width and height, the length and the breadth and the gleam of the world.* This is an excellent description of the soul of a twelve-year-old.

In the constitution live the individual astral forces, brought into reincarnation from previous lives. In many fairy tales and myths these elements of the individual astral body are pictured as encounters with animals. These animals are qualities of the personality that appear as assistance in the biography or need to be brought under control of the Ego. In this story, Gilly encounters the weasel, an image of slyness. The frogs represent the ability to cross the threshold of the etheric (water) and enter the realm of the life forces (Grimms' "The Frog King"). The frogs in this story drag up pebbles from the river so that Gilly and the Weasel can build a stone wall. In this way the frogs also drag up the Crystal Egg, which appears to be a magic egg. The Crystal Egg fulfills Gilly's wishes. He wishes himself a nice little house and there it is. The house is an image of the total bodily organization, as in "Snow White," "Hansel and Gretel," and "The Wolf and the Seven Young Kids." Then Gilly wishes to see himself. This is the image of Narcissus. *There was a looking glass on the wall before him.* This is the brain as the mirror, the element in the structural body that gives the soul self-consciousness. One can also think of the mirror of Snow White's stepmother, whose self-consciousness has turned into jealousy and egoism. The weasel makes himself a home under the roof of the little house; the triangle of the house shape represents the spiritual soul element, or sometimes the brain. Rory the Fox, the lower earthly intelligence, takes away the Crystal Egg. Gilly loses the capacity to draw on the wisdom of the forces of the etheric world.

Gilly starts searching for the Crystal Egg and he encounters the Spae-Woman. He stays with her until he takes service with the Churl of the Townland of Mischance. This Churl of the Townland of Mischance rides *a bobtailed, big-headed, spavined, and spotted horse. He carries an ash-plant in his hands to flog the horse and to strike the dogs that cross his way.* One can take notice of the condition of the Churl's horse and the way he treats it and the dogs, all representations of the thinking. Two former servants of the Spae-Woman precede Gilly. He is the third. Here again one finds the theme of the threefold aspect of the soul. The consciousness soul succeeds in defeating the Churl of the Townland of Mischance. He works in the way Rudolf Steiner advises us to approach the element of the ahrimanic in our culture: defeat him by his own means. One has to take the materialistic way of thinking and follow the thinking process to the end. Then one will discover the spiritual. Gilly takes the orders the Churl gave him very literally. At the end the Churl is sorry he took Gilly as a servant. The Churl of the Townland of Mischance keeps his money in a stone chest. If Gilly will say he is sorry he made the bargain, he will lose a strip of his skin an inch wide from the neck to the heel. That is a strip of the skin along the back, near the spine, the vessel of the Ego-organization. This shows the ahrimanic character of the Churl.

Gilly returns to the Spae-Woman, who is the Churl's neighbor. This can make one think of Rudolf Steiner's indication that in the etheric Lucifer and Ahriman are each other's neighbor, left-right, above-below, front-back (*Balance in the World and in Man*). The Spae-Woman very well could be seen as the luciferic element in the etheric body.

The Unique Tale

At first this Unique Tale seems to be just an inserted fairy tale, but it forms an important element in the total story. We recognize elements we know from other fairy tales, like "The Seven Ravens" and "The Six Swans." It is the theme of the brothers and the little sister. The number seven always points to the seven life processes that correlate with the seven organs and the seven planets. It is the constitutional physical body involved here.

The queen said, "If I might have a daughter that would show such colors. . . ." Blue, yellow and white are the colors she wishes her daughter to show. Blue and yellow are the representatives of the soul forces of antipathy and sympathy (plastic-architectonic forces and musical-speech forces) during the first seven years. The daughter bears the guilt that her brothers have become swans. She wants to rescue them. She doesn't succeed. The Old Woman of Beare wants Gilly and the King's Son to bring her the rest of the story.

Gilly asks the Old Woman for a name. He must stand before her and strip off his goatskin. He appears to have stars on his breast, a sign he is the Son of a King. The Old woman doesn't give him a name. He first needs to find out what happened to the Crystal Egg. Both Gilly and the King of Ireland's Son will meet in the Town of the Red Castle. First the two youths eat slices of the Unwasted Loaf and drink from the Inexhaustible Bottle (life forces from the world of the etheric). The King of Ireland's Son stays with the Old Woman to practice his sword fighting skills. Gilly wishes the Old Woman seven waves of good-luck.

Then Gilly finds his house. Six robbers and a robber wife live there. This makes us think of the Gospel of St. Luke (11:14-28), wherein an unclean spirit takes seven other spirits with him, more wicked than he is. They enter, sweep, and decorate the house. Gilly becomes their captain. Then he learns what had happened to the Crystal Egg. It hatched and the Swan of Endless Tales came out.

This is what Gilly tells the Old Woman of Beare. She gives him the name Flann.

The Town of the Red Castle

In this town Gilly (now Flann) and the King's Son meet the robber Mogue and Dermot and Downal, the King's Son's stepbrothers. Also they meet again the Gobaon Saor (helper of the King's Son) and the Spae-Woman (helper of Gilly—Flann). This Builder of the Gods and Reconciler of the Gods, as they call one another, could be seen as high spiritual forces that help the individual on the path of incarnation. We can think of Raphaël's painting of the Sistine Madonna. Here we see St. Barbara and Pope Sixtus showing the way to the child in his heavenly mother's arms. They represent the plastic-architectural and musical-speech forces, or antipathy and sympathy.

The King's Son meets the Enchanter of the Black Back-Lands, pursues him and learns what goes before the Unique Tale and what comes after it. The Enchanter is transformed into a wolf, the ahrimanic element we also meet in "The Wolf and the Seven Young Kids."

Flann (Gilly) encounters the Princess Flame-of-Wine and falls in love with her. He gives her three presents: the Rose of Sweet Smells, the Comb of Magnificence, and the Girdle of Truth. We think of the three gifts Snow-white receives from her stepmother: the poisonous comb, the stay-laces, and the very poisonous apple. The stepmother attacks the middle system, the head, and the metabolic system. Likewise, thinking, feeling, and willing are involved here in this story. Flame-of-Wine, however, is not worthy to receive Gilly's gifts. She is jealous, prideful, and selfish. Together with her sisters, Bloom-of-Youth and Breast-of-Light, she appears to be the un-purified astral body. It is the lower astral body of the constitutional side, influenced by Lucifer, which is the cause of illness, pain, and death.

Flann learns from the King's Son that he can rescue his mother Sheena and her seven brothers whenever the maid he loves gives him seven drops of her heart's blood.

The King of the Land of Mist

The King of Ireland's Son now has the Sword of Light again and goes on his way to conquer the King of the Land of Mist and rescue Fedelma. The imaginations tell us that the King of the Land of Mist has power over the structural body and over that part of the astral body (Fedelma) connected with it. The river (of Broken Towers) is an image we also find in Goethe's fairy tale "The Green Snake and the Beautiful Lily." It is the border between the sense-perceptible and the supersensible world. The King of the Land of Mist's castle has seven gates and courtyards. Think of the sevenfoldness in Rudolf Steiner's diagram of the Lord's Prayer in connection with the Pythagorean theorem (see Steiner, *The Lord's Prayer*). The first four courtyards could then represent physical, etheric, astral body, and Ego. The last three, now under the power of the King of the Land of Mist himself, could be the three spiritual members. If this is true, the King of the Land of Mist appears to be an even higher evil being than Lucifer or Ahriman. It could very well be that we see here pictured the Asuras, the negative powers at work in the physical. Asuras, according Rudolf Steiner, are of the hierarchy of the Archai, high beings that did not complete their development. In our time of the consciousness soul, which has its basis in the physical body, these beings for the first time in evolution enter the realm of the human soul. The King of Ireland's Son is able to conquer the King of the Land of Mist with the use of the Sword of Light, the force of the higher Ego. Then he can liberate Fedelma. They then return to the place where the whole story began. The higher Ego wins.

The House of Crom Duv

For Flann (Gilly), this is not yet the case. He returns to the Three Hags of the Long Teeth and then becomes prisoner of Crom Duv, the Giant. Here he meets a maid that will love him. It is Morag the byre-maid. Her face is pitted and her hair is bushy. She is staying with the giant because she wants to get berries from the Fairy Rowan Tree, which can cure her. Again Flann encounters different animals, aspects of the lower astral body—a dangerous bull, cats (2 x 12 senses)—and Rory the Fox (lower intelligence) reappears. Morag possesses a Little Red Hen and she milks the cows. Morag also has two stepsisters, Baun and Dilla. Also here the sentient soul and the intellectual soul are not very much interested in their younger sister: the consciousness soul. They were raised in the Spae-Woman's house. They leave there and reach the Three Hags of the Long Teeth. In the dominion of King Senlabor, they meet Dermott and Downal, the King's Son's stepbrothers. More and more the two story lines interlink.

The story of the Fairy Rowan Tree gives an image of a tree of life. The tree is from the dominion of the Elves. Morag puts red ribbons across the cats' necks, which prevents them from seeing. The blood-forces in the senses (luciferic passion) need to be brought under control. Flann can pick two berries of the Fairy Rowan Tree. Flann and Morag hide, but Crom Duv chases them with an iron spike, representing the iron in the blood. They escape.

The Spae-Woman

Flann and Morag reach the house of the Spae-Woman. The King of Ireland's Son and Flann appear to be brothers. Of course, the structural body and constitutional body should match perfectly. Morag hands Flann seven drops of her heart's blood. The seven Swans can be saved.

Now Gilvina, one of the other daughters of the Enchanter of the Black Back-Lands tries to win Flann's love. She tries to kiss Flann, and makes him forget Morag. Also Aefa reappears. Morag has three gifts to conquer the power of Givina. The gifts are all technical appliances which attract Givina's attention (remember, she represented the ahrimanic element). At the end the Little Red Hen wakes up Flann's memory. He recognizes Morag, the purified astral body of the constitution.

The King of Ireland's Son marries Fedelma and Flann marries Morag. Also Aefa and Gilvina find husbands; likewise, Baun and Dilla marry Dermott and Downal. All characters in the story are related. The story is about the human being given here in a fairy tale form. It is the complex picture of the human being that Rudolf Steiner made accessible to us as concepts for our work.

Summary
- The King of Ireland's Son represents the structural element of the human being in history and spiritual development.
- Gilly of the Goatskin represents the constitutional element of the human being in history and spiritual development.
- In fairy tales, the stepmother is often the antipole of the loving father. Think of Snow White and Cinderella. The Unique Tale is the story of The King of Ireland's Son's stepmother, Queen Caitingern. She is Sheena, Gilly's mother. The Unique Tale is the story of Mother Earth. Like the constitutional side of the human being, she is suffering from the Fall.

- In this light, the King of Ireland could be seen as the Father God element. As he says in one of the early chapters: He doesn't know he has enemies.

May it be clear that the story of The King of Ireland's Son is the story of humankind!

Appendix B

Intrusion of the Adversarial Powers
by Audrey McAllen

Lecture given September 1988
in The Hague, The Netherlands;
recorded and transcribed

I think that there are many kinds of attitudes and even misunderstandings about our two friends Lucifer and Ahriman. They always turn up in unusual places. I was watching a performance of *The Tempest*. There is a scene toward the end with Caliban and two drunken sailors. They see this monster and begin to tease him. And suddenly I realized: These are our two friends in disguise!

I think it is important that one begins to spot them. I have found another very unusual place where I would never dream of finding them. They were so changed and so lifted up that they were completely transformed. Only when one goes to the background of history could one begin to see: Oh, here they are again—in the [painting of the] Sistine Madonna. If you look at Pope Sixtus and at St. Barbara, they are a metamorphosis on a very high level; you need the biography and history of these two people to recognize the metamorphosis.

But tonight I want to speak about Lucifer and Ahriman in connection with our work and with twofold man.

We have threefold man, which has to do with the development of consciousness: thinking, feeling, and willing. And we have the twofold man, which Steiner says is represented by the head and the trunk; these make up the heredity body. I want to speak about the forces, the soul-forces, which, as it were, build up the physical body of the human being: antipathy and sympathy.

In *Study Of Man [Foundations of Human Experience]*, Steiner speaks about antipathy being that force that we bring with us from the spiritual world. It begins to work in the formative forces so that finally we are able to think. It is that power that transforms into our conceptual thoughts. Then we have the stream of sympathy; this is the power, coming towards us from the future and into which we plunge our will. And between the interaction of these two forces arises the realm of feeling; this we educate from age 7 to 14.

I think we can connect these two forces quite clearly with the Eye Color Affinity. The eye-color-affinity for the left eye is blue, a color that spreads out and leads us back. That is the force of antipathy coming from the past. The force of sympathy we can see manifested in the color red; this color is connected with the right eye. This color comes towards us; it has a center, a focal point. It is a color in which our will forces are working. One must say that with the right eye we perceive movement, and with the left eye we have the perception of the picture. Those are the two faculties of the two eyes.

In a lecture ["The Cosmic Origin of the Human Form"] Steiner speaks about the Sun and Moon uniting before our birth. We dive through the center into incarnation. The image of this in our body is the pupil of the eye. Then they separate again, forming our two eyes. We now can see that the Eye Color Affinity is connected with Sun and Moon—on the left side the forces of antipathy and on the right side the forces of sympathy. When we find the red and blue in the drawing of a man, with a blue jacket and red trousers, the soul is working in the "house" of the physical body.

Let us now see how these two beings Lucifer and Ahriman are working in connection with these forces. The Father God created these two beings in the very, very far historical time. They are evolved beings and they have been allowed to enter into the stream of evolution in order that man should find his freedom.

When the forces of antipathy are exploited—are taken hold of too strongly—so that the objective element is exceeded, they then can turn from the kind of thinking that is intelligence into the intellectual. And if the sympathy forces are exploited, they enter too deeply into our will; this pushes us too deeply into the earth. It weighs us down. And we can see how the intellect can become *cold* and the weight can lead us into the realm of *darkness*.

When we incarnate, we come into the light—into the world, which is flooded with light. But we know that this light gives us empty space. The light comes about because our eye is darkened by Lucifer. But behind this outer, sensory light there is the Spiritual Light. That is why our cathedrals and churches and also the Goetheanum have colored windows, because these colored windows keep back the white light and the colors come through—the astral light of the spiritual world, the sevenfold light of the planets. We have the contrast between the seven-fold light of the spiritual world and the white light that awakens our day-wake consciousness, which is the gift of Lucifer. We are, as it were, in this empty space as free beings. And so it is that in this empty space, in this world of the senses, we have the temptation that Steiner characterizes in *Occult Science*.

There are two ways in which this temptation takes hold of the soul. Inwardly Lucifer is able to arouse in us *pride*. Outwardly he arouses in us *passion*, passion for the senses. The power of sympathy can be taken hold of by the fact that we have gone through the temptation by Lucifer and obtained day-wake consciousness in the spatial world. We are then able to enter into the process of intellectual thinking, which becomes cold and remote. Or we can take hold of the process of sympathy with such passion that it leads us into weight and darkness. We need to keep these two aspects in mind when we are talking about children "being caught by Ahriman," because often we are confused in saying that the ahrimanic is the other side of the luciferic situation.

The outer world of the senses, the outer aspect of the opening of the eyes is related to the stretching man. And when a child becomes sort of hardened and remote and cannot get hold of his feeling life at all, it is that this seeing—this inner aspect of the Luciferic temptation, the pride—will rise up in the soul. This is all in the soul realm; it is all taking place in the astral element.

And now there comes a time that Ahriman enters in. He takes his forces and presses the pride and the passion down, out of our consciousness into the etheric body. This is where Ahriman works. He works in the etheric world, and in this way he suppresses the pride and passion, so that we are not aware of being proud and not aware of plunging into our senses. He presses that down into instinctive life, which is between the habits of the etheric and the organic functioning of the physical body as such. So one thinks of it as the second layer—this suppressing.

And what keeps it there below our consciousness? It is *fear*, the ahrimanic fear. Fear is working in the soul so that we will not recognize the luciferic influence in the soul. The ahrimanic fear keeps this luciferic temptation below our consciousness. The polarity of fear is love; we are told in the Gospels that perfect love casts out fear.

Hate is the polarity of desire. And love and fear are a polarity. Hate and desire are, as it were, a lower aspect of the pure aspects of antipathy and sympathy, which are, for example, working in the eye. The eye is pure—it is selfless. It allows the sense world to enter into ourselves in such a way that like and dislike are in balance, because the forces of antipathy that belong to the nerve-sense pole and the forces of sympathy that belong to the life processes are in perfect balance in the eye. And it is because in the eye there is a perfect balance between Lucifer and

Ahriman that love can stream out of the eyes. Hence this polarity of love and fear. It is the ahrimanic element of fear that keeps the luciferic temptation below our consciousness. In this realm, in the etheric and physical bodies, there Ahriman comes in and begins to work in the soul. He offers us power. In the element of antipathy, Ahriman offers us power. Whereas on the sympathy side, where the passion lies, he allows Lucifer to enter in and give us glory.

If you look at the *left* side of the body in relation to the supersensible currents (1909 lectures), the incarnation process gets in deeper and begins to harden the body. The astral body begins to press too strongly. A brittleness of the physical body occurs.

On the other side, the *right* side, you can get a child who cannot get in because Ahriman allows Lucifer to enter. Then you get the soul being sucked out. With the astrality being sucked out, you get an extra amount of fluid. All the fluid processes are stimulated then, and the soul begins to drown. You get the drowning on the right side and the burning on the left side. You know in our Christmas plays is said, "The woman will drown—bubble, bubble—and the man will hang himself."

When these forces work too strongly, then the Ego cannot keep this in balance. This is what causes the clockwise and counterclockwise movements to be overstimulated and to go in opposite directions and overtwist. I wonder if you have seen this in the Handedness Pattern (*The Extra Lesson* 42–51). It is in the left leg where the trouble starts. We have a nursery rhyme:

> Goosey, goosey gander
> Whither do you wander?
> Upstairs, downstairs,
> In my lady's chamber.
> There I met an old man
> Who would not say his prayers.
> I took him by his left leg
> And threw him down the stairs.

Among the birds, the goose represents the heavy metabolic system. So in the nursery rhyme, we have the overcoming of the ahrimanic and the process connected with Lucifer and Ahriman.

Now, we can say that the physical body—the structural body—comes to us from Old Saturn. The whole of ancient Saturn was warmth. And warmth is characterized by Rudolf Steiner as *intensive movement*. We can understand that a little child is born to move. Maria Montessori spoke of this. But, for example, by the TV-box, through the sense impressions—the electronic light on the sense impressions—this warmth is compressed. The precious Saturn warmth is becoming cold as too much light drives out this warmth. It is the excess of light. And Ahriman, working in the ether body, is trying to seize the power of the Father God. It is the matter, the physical world, that is the gift of the Father God. The Father God is the bearer of the etheric and physical world, where Ahriman tries to rob the Father God of his possession, the human being, and bind the human being to the earth.

One can conclude thus:
You remember, this morning I spoke about the currents of the ocean—how my father taught me that it is the deepest current that will control the ship and pull it where the current goes. [During the morning lecture Audrey told anecdotes about her father, who was a sea captain.] Connecting ourselves with that deepest current, that is important. And it is in connecting ourselves with the deepest current—which we know is the Being that shines out not only with the sevenfold colors of the cosmos but also with the fivefold colors where the earth is impregnated with spirit—that we have the warmth shining in the darkness making the twelvefold colored light of the Word. This Word, the Logos, is the deepest current with which Anthroposophy and our school movement unites itself—the light, the twelvefold colored light of the Word that will not pass away. With that we can have confidence for the end of the [20th] century.

Appendix C

The Physical Body as Educator of the Soul
by Audrey McAllen

Concluding summary lecture given in November 1989
at a course for remedial teachers, therapists, and doctors
at Land en Bosch, The Netherlands
recorded, transcribed, and edited by the lecturer

Rudolf Steiner has described the physical body as the "sum total of the senses." In doing this, he is drawing our attention to something very specific, an aspect of the physical body—to which in our anthroposophical picture of man we have not paid sufficient attention.

When we think of our physical body, we usually associate it with something that has gone wrong and is causing us discomfort—or worse! This is the *process aspect* of the physical body. What Steiner is referring to is the archetype structure element, which goes back to Old Saturn at the beginning of our planetary evolution. Here at this time the senses were laid down, everything which during the following planetary stages would, on our present earth, metamorphose into the bones, muscles, and nerves. This is the *structural aspect* of our body.

This "structure" at the end of the Old Saturn period was so organized that inwardly it manifested as *smell* and outwardly could be apprehended, recognized, as a structure formed in such a way that it represented *egoity* in the cosmos. That is, it was formed in such a way that it could be a "cup" for the future ego the gods intended to create.

This evolution started in warmth. Today the primal archetypal warmth is contained in the blood. It is our blood[1] that is the connecting link between the two aspects of the physical body, its constitutional process of matter transforming activity on which our ego needs to "press" in order to obtain consciousness, and the structural cup that is to contain this ego so that it can know itself in space and inwardly visualize its structure [Steiner *The World of the Senses and the World of the Spirit*]. This is the basis for a healthy experience of the 9th-year crisis where one recognizes oneself as an I-ego and recognizes that the world is something separate from oneself.

In the parlance of modern research, this factor of spatial orientation and inward visualization of the body's structure—together with the integration of the postural system (i.e. vestibular and proprioceptive)— "is the basis of a fundamental psychological process, i.e., the ability to differentiate between external space and the body scheme which is actually the core of consciousness and the pivot of interaction between "ego" and "non-ego", subject and object." (F. S. Rothschild 1963[1]) This physio-psychological point in development, I would suggest, is the culmination of the first stage of childhood. It is when the second stage, the soul aspect, takes over from the first seven-year development that the rhythmic system is ready for use in education.

Class 1 and 2 are, in my view, a consolidation of the first seven years. They complete the coordination in the physical body, on which rhythmic movement is dependent. The birth of the independent ether body can now contain the soul forces of sympathy and antipathy and the faculties which are born out of the education of the physical body by the end of this period of development. The capacities children require when they come into class 1 are, in the words of neuropsychology:

- Purposeful equilibrium, body image, and the integration of the postural system (sense of balance and sense of self-movement), which are basic for the use of instruments or objects
- Independence of both halves of the body: to know your right hand from your left, how to turn right and left. (necessary for eurythmy)
- Learning to speak fluently
- Possibility of developing creativeness
- The capacity for higher level learning.[2]

Thus it is important that children are mature in these areas and that they are at least 6^1/$_2$ years old when they start school. *All the above needs time to consolidate.*

We have on the one side the contribution of the structural development—spatial orientation, and body schema. The other side is the constitutional development—the beginning of the regulation of heartbeat to breathing and the change from the head, which has been responsible for the digestive process, to that of the stomach. Medically we have researched this latter process. What can we learn about the structural development?

Steiner has pinpointed the moment of standing upright, but he has said little to teachers about the preceding stages. Here there is a large body of research material contributed by occupational therapists and doctors who have specialized in neuropsychology and in some cases have devoted a lifetime to the problems of children with learning difficulties. Obstructions to the neurological pathways from modern birth techniques, which we have been discussing, lead over into learning problems.

Here we have an example of world karma at work, frustrating the expectation of the normal [individual] incarnating process.

Let us look at the moment of standing with the concepts with which we are familiar: standing—movement—speech. This sequence leads over into the constitutional processes, a revelation of the working of ego into the astral and ether bodies and the forming of the total physical body according to the individual's life plan. We learn to read the psyche from its manifestation. On the structural side, the emphasis is on the archetypal, namely, that which is common to all people. We have the same number of bones, the same bone structure, muscles, etc. This has been the work of the gods through the evolution of our planetary system. It is difficult to see the archetypal medically, for as a doctor and in curative education one is faced with such terrible distortions. For the normal child and adult, we are given a "wrought work," which goes through a specific development which is the same whether one has a large-headed, small-headed, cosmic, or earthly type constitution.

This path of development nowadays needs more of our attention, because it culminates in the two psychological requirements for ego-awareness, namely, spatial orientation and body schema. How is this spatial orientation and inner picture of one's body attained? When the child raises himself into the vertical, he is free to move left and right, up and down, forward and back, and in these planes of dimension the signature of the threefold human being is implicit. Steiner defines them as the thinking plane, the feeling plane, and the willing plane [*Mystery of the Universe—the Human Being: Image of Creation*].

As soon as there is a duality, for example, left-right, then in their meeting the ego focus comes into play. Here again the body of Old Saturn is seen as the cup for the ego. Also we know from lecture 2 [in Steiner, *Deeper Insights into Education*]: through movement, the physical body is inserted into the ether body. It is via the sense of movement that the body schema is imprinted into the ether body. This imprinting process is the crux situation for the ninth-year crisis. This imprinting should ideally match the archetypal imprint, which the individuality is inserting into the ether body from within via the objective element in his astral body, which he has brought with him from his life between death and rebirth. Problems can arise if there is weakness or discrepancy from either of these imprinting activities.

Children with learning problems have difficulties just in this area of spatial orientation and the imprinting of the body schema, and it needs one-to-one help to make good this developmental gap, for it does not take place of its own accord after the change of teeth.[3] Here it is that the wonderful laws of movement within our body can educate the soul. For example, our modern life-style plunges the soul too strongly and one-sidedly into the movement system. In an exercise like the Moving Straight Line and Lemniscate, one can see how the movement laws inherent in the structure of the body take over and school the soul. All handwork, craftwork, and instrument playing also do this. In effect, all the exercises in *The Extra Lesson* address spatial orientation and body geography through the movement law defined by Steiner that *an astral current moves in the opposite direction to that of the ether and physical bodies* and *the astral body moves through the physical body during the day in a spiral*. [Steiner, *A Psychology of Body, Soul, and Spirit* lecture 2.] My researches show that this has a clockwise movement.

The facts of spatial orientation and body geography are well known in educational therapy, and there are many types of movement exercises devised to remedy this condition. We, in anthroposophy, have something unique to add because, from Steiner's indications in lectures given in 1909, the Extra Lesson exercises, which have been so effective, have taken into account the movements of the supersensible sheaths of the earth in relation to those of the human being. This objective element, which enables the soul to find its archetypal relationship to the earth, has been a consoling factor to the frustrations in the incarnating process that the individuality has experienced.

We need to be aware that the earth planet also carries in it the picture of the human being. Early Christian consciousness was aware of this, as one can see in medieval maps portraying the earth as the body of Christ. It is in the sheaths of the earth that the Christ—the ego of our planet—is now working.

The importance of imprinting the structural image of the human being into our ether body is highlighted in chapter 7 of [Rudolf Steiner's] *The East In The Light Of The West*:

> Mankind is entering a condition in which the etheric body is to a certain extent drawing itself out of the physical body again; but it must not be thought that it now receives spontaneously everything which in earlier times it possessed as an ancient heritage. If nothing else happened but its withdrawal, the etheric body of man would just leave the physical body and would retain in itself none of the forces, which it formerly possessed. In the future it will be born from out of the human physical body. If the human physical body did not add something to it, this etheric body would be empty, barren. The future of human evolution will be that men will, as it were, allow their etheric body to leave their physical bodily nature, and they will eventually have the possibility of being able to send it out empty.

What does that mean? The etheric body is the force-bearer, the energizer, of all that takes place in the physical body. It must not only provide forces for the physical body when it is entirely concealed within it, but at all times; it must provide forces for the physical body even when it is again partly outside it. If the etheric body is left empty, it cannot react upon the physical body, for it would then have no strength with which to react.

The etheric body must, after it has passed through the physical body, have obtained its forces from within the physical body. The forces with which the etheric body can react again upon the physical body must have been drawn from within the latter. The task of present day humanity is to absorb into itself that which can only be acquired through activity in a physical body. That which is gained within the physical body accompanies evolution, and when man in future incarnations lives in organisms wherein the etheric body is to a certain extent released from the physical body, he will experience in his consciousness a kind of memory through the partially liberated physical body.

Where do we see the archetype for this imprinting? It is in the Gospel accounts of the Resurrection where the Christ shows his disciples the imprint of the wounds of the nails in His hands and feet and that of the spear in His side. Here we see the physical imprinted into the ether body, a new phenomenon in earthly history [Steiner, *The Gospel of St. John and its Relationship to the Other Gospels*].

Nowadays everything connected with our physical structural body is exploited. External research has discovered the intelligence secreted in the body, and this has been used in sport, in education, in commerce. Our sensory organization is stimulated in every possible way. In consequence, the movements of our astral body cannot maintain their balancing activity, and so we get all kinds of tensions in our muscular system, and these in turn block the neurological pathways that carry the stimulus to the brain for the soul to use.

I want again to link this with planetary development. We are told that at the end of the Saturn evolution, the planet manifested inwardly as smell. Steiner connects the sense of smell with the consciousness soul [*A Psychology of Body, Soul, and Spirit* lecture 2]. This is the soul member into which the ego awakens between age 35 and 42. The consciousness soul gives the faculty of recognizing that the Spirit has organized the body we live in and that the same Spirit has created the world [*The Michael Letters* November 2, 1924]. This secret we can see in the mosaics in the ceiling and the vestibule of San Marco in Venice. Furthermore, we know that the basis for the consciousness soul is the physical body whose education we are responsible for during the first seven years.

Again let us link this with Old Saturn evolution. In Saturn's body of warmth, the Archai were going through their "human" incarnation consciousness, and since that time they have maintained the connection with what is now our skeletal movement system. When we sleep our astral body and ego leave our physical and ether bodies, and it is necessary for members of the Hierarchies to maintain them. It is the spiritual structure of the physical body that the Archai protect so that we can pick it up again when we awake. Hence it is important that this sensory aspect of the physical body is recognized, because just at this point in time the Archangel Michael is ascending to the rank of an Archai and, thus, entering into connection with the will forces of the Godhead that created the sensory structural body of man on Old Saturn.

During the Old Moon evolution, we know that certain ranks of the Hierarchies endeavored to separate these will forces from the intention of the progressive gods. This rebellion was defeated. Now, in our time, the same attempt is being made to separate the evolution of man from the primal creative beings of our universe.

This is something we have to take very seriously, for our senses have a twofold activity. By day, they are used by us for perception of the world; by night, their function is to revive the formative forces of our body so that we awake refreshed. All this comes under the domain of Michael as he enters into his new hierarchical rank.

I would like to read you something from lecture 10 of Rudolf Steiner's *The Gospel of St. John and its Relationship to the Other Gospels* (Kassel), which shows this wonderful connection between the Christ Being and Michael. One could almost say: what has the Christ done for Michael in preparation for this time, when he will become an Archai?

> Through the entrance of Christ into the body of Jesus of Nazareth, the individuality of Christ gained dominion over the bony structure itself with its physical and chemical processes. As a result, there once lived on earth a body able to use its forces in such a way that it caused the spiritual form of the bony structure to become embedded into the evolution of the earth. The sum of everything that man has undergone would be irretrievably lost, unless he were able to incorporate the noble form of his bony structure into the evolution of the earth, as an evolutionary law of which he could by degrees gain mastery. . . . No vestige of earth's evolution would be carried over into the future if the bony frame were not preserved. The form of the bony structure conquers death in a physical sense.

In our modern life we can see how this attack on Michael comes as an inability to use the body of the senses. One aspect is the very fact that the postural system, that is the vestibular system and proprioceptive system, is not so easily integrated by children about the time they say "I."

In these lectures called *Deeper Insights into Education* that Rudolf Steiner gives [to the teachers at the first Waldorf school] at Stuttgart [Germany], he says: if we understand Michael's struggle with the dragon in a particular sphere that we are working in now, we are working for the healing of humanity in the future.

And to integrate the human being and the world as part of this developmental process, this is really the whole reason for our earth incarnation. This is why we are here on the earth, because it is only from the earth that we can gain the forces for the future. Again from the lectures on the Gospel of St. John, Steiner says:

> At the moment of Golgotha the Logos began to unite with the earth, the earth aura changed. Anyone who understands the profound meaning of this mystery will feel not only that one's physical body is united with the physical earth, but that one's psycho-spiritual being is united with Christ Himself, how Christ as the Spirit of the earth flows through one's body.

These are the thoughts I would like to leave with you for your future work and its development.

---

1 Research by F. S. Rothschild, quoted in *Neuropsychological Fundamentals of Learning Difficulties* by Julio de Quiros, MD. PhD. and Orlando Schrager, MD. Novato, CA: Academic Therapy Publications, 1979. Also quoted in *Learning Difficulties*, edited by Mary Ellen Willby, p. 16.

2 de Quiros, op.cit., Chapter 2, Section 12, page 27.

3 Audrey McAllen, Report on a two-year research project on children with learning problems in Waldorf schools, 1985–87. Margaret Wilkenson Trust Archives. The Secretary, Rudolf Steiner House, 35 Park Rd. London NW16-XT, U.K. and Rudolf Steiner College, Research Dept., 9200 Fair Oaks Blvd. Fair Oaks, CA 95628, U.S.A.

Appendix D

The Earth as a Picture of the Human Being
by Audrey McAllen

Lecture given September 22, 1990
in Dordrecht, The Netherlands;
recorded and transcribed

It is always a great privilege to see so many of our Waldorf teachers all come together. And it has been one of the joys of going round the world and seeing so many of this enormous Waldorf college, because you all belong to the same Waldorf school college. There is this big one, up there of which you are all a part. We only see bits, but every night you are all present one with the other. Do not forget it. There is a constant interchange between the northern and the southern hemisphere and between the west and the east in sleeping. So we all have the possibility of inspiring each other through our inner work, through our observation of the children, and through the gifts that Rudolf Steiner has given us of the concepts that we need from the spiritual world in order to meet the requirements of our time. I am sure that the colleagues that I have met in the southern hemisphere, and those I have just been with in Finland, would like me to give you their greetings.

I want to bring to your attention an aspect of anthroposophical research that is not so usual in our educational approach—namely, the picture of the human being that is contained in the earth, and especially with the interconnection between our movement system and the movements that are always taking place in the body of the earth itself.

One's Ego always needs something to press on. And that is why we are on the earth. Let's look a little bit at the developmental stages of this pressing that the Ego needs. You see, as soon as the child is born modern psychology comes out saying: Oh yes, the mother and child have to bond together. They encourage that babies be cuddled and nursed and rocked. What is that doing? That is pressing, as it were, on the whole nerve-sense apparatus. Through the mother, being conscious of what she is doing, the whole Ego-organization of the child is gradually awakened. And many children with psychological problems have missed this first pressing: being played with, being bounced on daddy's knee, being carried on his back. All these first pressures are the way in which the Ego begins to experience itself.

And, of course, as soon as the baby has come out of the womb into the air, he is hungry. I remember being quite amazed when I read in a lecture by Rudolf Steiner that we do not take food to nourish us. That is not the important thing. What we take in food for is to break it down, to demolish it. And in that breaking it down, the Ego has something to press on. And, as you know yourselves, when you are tired, if you eat something, you immediately feel better. It is not just because you have increased the sugar content of your blood, but it is because your Ego has been called on. So instead of saying, "I am hungry," I say now, "My Ego needs something to press on!" I like the other things that go with it. So those are two basic pressings that the Ego needs.

Another one comes when we stand up, which is basic to the human being: this pressure against gravity that awakens our self-consciousness. We then pull ourselves against gravity into the upright position. It is this vertical position that makes the difference between the animal kingdom and the human kingdom on earth. This standing, this pressing against gravity, is a vital element for the waking of our Ego. Gravity is one of the important processes in the first seven-year development.

I want, in this connection, to enlarge our picture of the terms "ether body" and "formative forces." Very often they are assumed to be the same. They are terms that we use indiscriminately meaning one or the other. As time went on, it dawned on me that there must be a difference between the formative forces and the ether body. Then there was published in English the translation of Ernst Marti's book called *The Four Ethers (Die vier Äther)*. Ernst Marti was one of the early Arlesheim doctors. I do recommend that you read this book, because it is a most beautifully clear description of the four ethers and their work, how they work together in general.

The ether body of the earth—what is it? It is a globe of life around the earth. It is in a drop form. Although it has the curve of the sphere, it assumes flat surfaces. That is what we see outside in nature, but that is just the one archetypal element of the ether. However, there are four ethers—and they each have specific tasks—together, working in an organism. They bring about certain forms and processes that can multiply themselves. But the four ethers, Marti says, by themselves cannot bring forth a special leaf or a special animal or even a human being. Something else has to come and enter into the activity of these ethers in order that a species can develop. These are the *formative forces* (in German, *Bildekräften*).

Marti says: Where do these formative forces come from that take hold of the ethers and prevent them from expanding and expanding to the periphery? That is what the ethers want to do. They want to fly off in lovely big bubbles. That is why children like blowing bubbles, because they see it going on and on, this pulling out to the periphery of the etheric forces. How are they formed, so that they stay on the earth? Ernst Marti describes how it is the twelve constellations of the zodiac that send their forces and hold the ethers together in specific ways so that the specific plants appear, the animal kingdom with its members appear, and finally the human being. So the formative forces are really those forces that mould and sculpt the etheric body in which the individuality is working in the first seven years.

And now, this is the important thing Marti added: there is a *thirteenth* formative force. That formative force comes from the earth. It is the force of gravity with the related aspects of electricity and magnetism. Without that we should be, as it were, a floating human being. We would not be rooted on the earth. That thirteenth force, the force of gravity, is the one that we need to awaken our Ego and our will forces. Without having to press against gravity and lift ourselves into the upright position, our Ego and our self-consciousness would not awaken.

We are, as teachers, meeting children who have lost touch with gravity forces in their early development. I do not want to go through a long recital, but I will just tell you one or two aspects where this loss of contact with gravity takes place in our ordinary upbringing of children today. As soon as the child manages to begin to struggle into the upright position, somebody comes along with a baby walker. So the child is then forced into the upright position, but he cannot maintain it so he falls forward and grasps hold of the bars and then he totters along on the tips of the toes. Those of you who are physiotherapists, I am sure, already get children with distortions of the muscles at the back of the legs, because the children are prematurely lifted out of their own will against gravity. Then they do not really get this upright position in the whole of the structure of their body. It is very interesting, if you watch mothers lifting their babies, to see how they put the baby's feet and how the gesture of the body is. This conditions them. I was watching a baby in the hairdresser's the other day, and mother lifted it and you could see: immediately the toes went down. And it stayed on the toes before it could get its foot down. One knew that baby had been brought up in a baby walker. And then you have the playpen, which keeps the child in so he does not crawl enough, but pulls himself up and hangs, which is not his true gesture of lifting himself against gravity. And the other one that is so prevalent is the toy: the tricycle or the pedal car. Almost before the child can walk, his little legs are lifted out of gravity onto the pedals of the tricycle, and he makes quite contrary movements to those movements that are balancing movements in walking.

That is one of the things that our modern life-style does in depriving the child of the first experiences of integrating with the gravity of the earth. So we have children coming into our classes—and this is whether they have learning problems or not—who have disturbances in balance and movement. We have the tasks of re-educating their bodies, so that they find again their relationship to gravity, so that the individual Ego can awaken and, therewith, self-consciousness.

This is a widespread problem. Many, many movement programs are devised to meet disturbances in the balance-vestibular system, or self-movement-proprioception, and the postural system. You can have all sorts of programs worked out to meet these specific disturbances. But what one has tried to do through anthroposophical knowledge is to recognize that, through this interference, somewhere or other the soul has felt frustration. Deep in the subconscious, because their intention is to incarnate properly, they have been frustrated by our life-style. There is something deep in their soul of resentment and even fear. And although you could make a program that remedies these deficiencies, they do not necessarily touch this resentment or the fear that had been engendered because of the frustration they have had at these points of incarnation. This is where our insights in anthroposophy can help, not only to remedy that which is specific, but to help the whole situation, the whole child.

How has that come about in the set of exercises that are called the Extra Lesson?

We have to remember that the human being has specific sheaths; we have the physical body, the etheric sheath, the astral sheath, and the Ego. But the earth also has supersensible bodies. The earth has an ether body; the earth has an astral body. And, since the Mystery of Golgotha, these sheaths of the earth have become a cup into which the Ego of the Christ Being now lives and operates. Within these forces of the earth, the power of the Christ is living and working.

This reality was deeply present in the souls of, for instance, the map-makers of the Middle Ages. We in England have the last remaining map made in the early part of the thirteenth century [Mappa Mundi, Hereford Cathedral], and this map shows not only the earth, but the history of the earth. At the northern top there is the picture of the Christ, and the whole of the land masses of the earth are pictured there as the body of Christ. We have to remember that this is a present reality in our time. We can look then at the earth, and we can begin to see how in man and in earth there are the same laws of structure and movement at work.

Those of you who are old scholars of our schools know that in class 10–11 you do map making, and in your geography you learn about the structure of the earth from north to south. In the North Pole it is all ice and water, and then the land is around the arctic sea—just as we have the open fontanel in the infant's skull, which does not close for some time. Then we have the structure of the skull.

And now our feet that we walk on: In the Southern Hemisphere, there is the landmass of Antarctica and all around this the great oceans. If we look at the human being, you see, from that point of view, we have our feet on which we press against the earth, but all around here—around the legs—is really where we are paddling, moving in the etheric body of the earth. Here, the lower leg is Waterman, our feet are Fishes, and the knee is Capricorn. In this wonderful structure of the knee, the kneecap is loose. It is not attached—it floats on the structure of these two bones. It is there, Steiner says, that the ether body of the earth interpenetrates the personal ether body of each of us.

We have this picture all around in the body of the earth; we have all these oceans around in the southern hemisphere, whereas in the northern hemisphere we have all these land masses. We have the mountains of the Americas going from north to south, and the great ranges of the Himalayas and the Alps go from east to west. So we have a cross. Here we have this picture of the human structural system that is imprinted also there in the structure of the earth on which we live.

Even our consciousness is reflected in the earth in the way it moved historically from east to west. In the east you have the wisdom of the past—everything that has been given us by Lucifer in China, coming over into India and then into Persia, Babylon, Egypt, and Greece on to our modern consciousness, which is going west over England into the Americas. You have this stream of consciousness that belongs to the awakening. The time of complete dream slowly awakening to self-consciousness, just as we have in the child, the sleeping into the dreaming into the waking—the willing into the feeling into the thinking. We have that mirrored in the movement of culture from east to west.

Now, we have another way of looking at this. Earth and man—they fit together. How is this? We are again indebted to Rudolf Steiner for these observations. In the 1909 lectures called "Anthroposophy" [*A Psychology of Body, Soul, and Spirit*] he says: if we stand looking toward the east, we have this landmass of the Northern Hemisphere on our left side, Asia, Europe, North America. The forces that have created the Northern Hemisphere landmass are the same ones that are creating and forming the left side of the human being. And this goes right back to Old Saturn, to the time when our physical body was entirely a warmth organism, and all our senses were like buds embedded in this warmth. At the end of the Saturn evolution—and this is so important—the whole of the warmth body of Saturn, which was our earth to be, was organized so it could bear an Ego. So it is the structural body that is the cup for the Ego—that is to carry it. Here we see how this pattern has come about in our present time.

But on the right side, the Southern Hemisphere, there is all this water mass. And it is from the right side, Steiner tells us, that the forces of the ether body are playing—the watery that takes hold of the mirrored image of the physical body on the left side and impregnates this left side. And the right side has to be twice as strong in order to carry the weight of the left side of the human body.

So we have this interconnection with the earth itself. I am only doing this part of the picture, because it gets more and more complicated as we go on. It is better that you read it up yourselves in the four lectures called "Anthroposophy." [Berlin 1909]

What I now want to point out is the interconnections of our own movements with those that we see reflected to us in the earth through the currents of the air and the water. Air and water are the representations of the astral and the etheric element in the physical sphere. I want you to explore the movements of your arms and legs on the left and the right. I suggest that you all stand up. Everything in *The Extra Lesson* is done from the center of the self, from inside out, so you are not to stand as onlookers. How does the natural movement of your right arm take place? You are going in a clockwise direction. Now try the other side, you are going now in a counterclockwise direction. So up here, in the arms, you have clock and counterclockwise movements.

What happens below the equator, as it were? I suggest you take a few steps forward and just notice how your legs swing. Try to feel how the hip makes your leg move. Which way is your right leg going? It is going counterclockwise, which is opposite to your right arm and hand, isn't it? And your left leg is going clockwise. You see this incredible balance between these two movement systems. And our Ego keeps them all going together. You can see how, if you went in the opposite direction with your legs, you would literally be pulled in half.

Now you see, life is complicated—nothing is simple. Steiner tells us that there is a very special law, which takes place between the physical and etheric—which are, please, a unity—and the astral body. The astral body moves always in the opposite direction to that of the physical and etheric [1909 lectures]. There is always a balancing process between the movements of your physical and etheric and the movements of your astral body.

And now, can you see what is happening with many children? The astral body is pushed too tightly in and cannot release itself in the movement, and so they lose their balance. Or it can be sucked out too much, and again they lose their balance. So this law [of the direction of movement of] the physical and the etheric and the astral body is most important for everything that we have to do with the children in movement.

I want to show you how wonderfully the earth sustains us. What a wonderful planet we are living on! This planet has been created by the Hierarchies through three incarnations of this earth. And the physical-structural body has also been created through the planetary incarnations of our earth. We have not done it! It is the work of the gods that we are working with in the whole nervous system, the muscles, and the bones. That is not our work; it is the gift of the Hierarchies. And it is mirrored again in the gift of the planet earth, which gives us our will forces and our awakening of self-consciousness.

Now look, in the Northern Hemisphere we have currents that are blown by the winds and moved by the revolution of the earth and its axes. We have them going clockwise, whereas here in the southern hemisphere we have them going counterclockwise [page 28 of this book]. If you think of that in the upper part of our body, it goes in the opposite way to [the directions of movement in] the human being. But can you see that in this way the astral movements of the earth are balancing, entering into the countermovements of the astral body that are taking place. We are there supported by the earth, and we are freed in the upper part of our body. We are free beings because of this support from the astral body of the earth. We are then able to "do our own thing."

But if we look down here below the waist, we find that these movements from north and south work in the same direction as our legs. Our left leg inward, going clockwise the same as the currents of the earth's Northern Hemisphere. And our right leg is going counterclockwise in the same way as the currents of the earth's Southern Hemisphere. In this way we are drawn into the gravity forces. There we are in the same position as the earth. This is the tension of the incarnation process. And if something is going wrong there, then, as it were, we are kicked out of the earth. We cannot make our way deeply enough into gravity in such a way that we can walk firmly on the earth—and breathe in our karma for the life we have to lead. That is all being moulded into us through the formative forces in the first 21 years of our life. Therefore it is so important that our muscles work properly as we walk—and that our structure is such that we can carry this body gracefully through the forces of gravity—and at the same time be freed up here to do our task on earth.

I think this is a picture that is important for you to carry when you are concerning yourselves with these exercises from *The Extra Lesson*—because in every way they are calling on the clockwise and counterclockwise movements in the human body and also on the movements of the spiral. Many of these things came to light first through the problem the child had and then, secondly, through the study of domestic movements like sweeping, wringing, dusting, polishing the floor. All these things one looked at to see how they were done. Nobody gets on their knees nowadays and polishes the floor, but that was done for generations and imitated by the children. All these movements, these activities, were working so that the astral body was properly assimilated into the nervous system, patterning the brain so that the intelligence of the human being was organized. All our domestic movements were intelligence-making. All our cooking things and our musical instruments are, as it were, another projection of these movements that belong to the body. And we make the music of the spheres, or we try to hear and reproduce that.

The exercises that you can use from *The Extra Lesson* are speaking, then, a deeper language to the child's soul. They are telling the child of fundamental spiritual facts, things that he learned with the Hierarchies before birth, things that he longs to bring himself into connection with during his sleep. And it is because they do these movements in their waking life—that are then inlaid—that when the child's soul expands in sleep, the angel of the child can be operative and help to reform what has gone wrong through the results of our modern lifestyles.

This, I think, is the offering that anthroposophy has to give, when we search for the answers to children's problems.

One question that is often asked me is: Why do you do all the exercises with all the children? Why don't you differentiate according to each individual's needs?

It is because one is addressing the whole child. All the exercises have something to say to the problem of balance, to the problem of self-movement, to the problem of the integration of the postural system, also for the developmental stages.

You have heard about the horizontal and the vertical midline. Well, with the Counting Star, for instance: You have to be very particular with all the exercises, especially the Wool Winding, the Ball Bouncing and beanbag exercises, that the feet are kept exactly parallel. You do not allow the child to slump down on either hip; see that they really stand centrally. When you do the Counting Star, here you are working to get rid of the midline barrier through crossing over. You are touching and counting as you go, and that engages speech and hand coordination. You are also going constantly in this big clockwise direction of the spiral that integrates all the other spiral movements during the day, as our astral body infills the physical-etheric.

In each exercise you will find many, many of the problems of the modern child addressed. Nevertheless, the whole thing is not static. Out of your own working, you will find things that may address particularly the vestibular system.

In our little remedial conference last week, someone brought folk dances. There was a lovely one from Russia, called "The Troika," where you were all in threes, and then you put your arms around your shoulders and whirled round—absolutely lovely for the vestibular system! And then you had to go in a chain in and out the three—lovely for all the neck muscles! You could say: That differentiates the vestibular system.

If we can make our colleagues understand this kind of thing, then we hope they will not be so reluctant to do folk dancing in their main lessons. Integrate it into the geography or the history lessons. We've got all the medieval dances, which address the rhythms and the walking together. These things then can heal, because all folk music has come out of the earth—the interconnection of the movement system with the movements of the earth, the geology.

We shall find things that will address what is specific. I do suggest that you work together in the way that, when somebody has a new idea, a new exercise, you then examine it together to see whether that is something that belongs just between that teacher and that particular child or whether it is something that is archetypal and can then be used with all children. That is your research. In this way the whole body of remedial work can grow. The merit is that at the moment you can start with the exercises from *The Extra Lesson* that give you a firm foundation on which to begin. And if you do the exercises yourselves as well as when you teach them to the children, they will train you and awaken your perception. I know this because of what the other colleagues who are using them in other countries have told me. That is the best training: to *do* the exercises. Then it awakens your own creativity and you will know what to do next.

So, with that, I would like to take my leave of you and wish you everything that is good to your endeavors to help children with learning problems.

Bibliography

GA number for works by Rudolf Steiner refer to the volume number in the bibliographical survey of the complete works of Rudolf Steiner in German. For out-of-print items, the reader might inquire at the Rudolf Steiner Library (65 Fern Hill Road, Ghent, NY 12075, Tel. 518-672-7690, Fax 518-672-5827, e-mail: rsteinerlibrary@taconic.net) or the Rudolf Steiner House Library (35 Park Road, London NW1 6XT, e-mail: rsh-library@anth.org.uk). Books published in Vancouver by Steiner Book Centre are held in the archives of Anthroposophic Press (also known as SteinerBooks) and sometimes reissued as Archive Editions. Books published by St. George Publications in Spring Valley, NY are now the property of Rudolf Steiner College Press, Fair Oaks, CA.

Acton, Loren, cited in *The Home Planet* edited by Kevin Kelley. Reading, MA: Addison-Wesley, 1988.

van Bemmelen, Daniel. *Het Eerste Goetheanum*. Zeist, The Netherlands: Uitgeverij Vrij Geestesleven, 1979.

———. *Rudolf Steiner's New Approach to Color on the Ceiling of the First Goetheanum*. Spring Valley, NY: St. George Publications, 1980.

Boos-Hamburger, Hilde. *Gespräche mit Rudolf Steiner über Mahlerei*. Basel 1961.

Collot d'Herbois, Liane. *Colour*. Driebergen, The Netherlands: Magenta Group, 1985.

———. *Light, Darkness, and Colour in Painting Therapy*. Dornach, Switzerland: Verlag am Goetheanum, 1993.

———. *Mahlen in Schichten* (Painting in Veils). Owingen/Überlingen, Germany: Iona Schülungstätte für künstlerische Therapie, summer 1990. Translated from German by Ineke Rijsdijk.

Colum, Padraic. *The King of Ireland's Son*. Edinburgh: Floris Books, 2002.

Davis, Ronald. *The Gift of Dyslexia*. NY: Penguin Putnam, 1997.

Glas, Norbert. *Die Hände offenbaren den Menschen*, (The hand reveals man). Stuttgart: J. Ch. Mellinger Verlag, 1994.

Govinda, Lama Anagarika. *The Way of the White Clouds: a Buddhist Pilgrim in Tibet*. London: Hutchinson, 1968.

Harwood, A. C. *Christmas Plays from Oberufer*. London: Rudolf Steiner Press, 1973.

Hauschka-Stavenhagen, Margarethe. *Fundamentals of Artistic Therapy Based on Spiritual Science*. Spring Valley, NY: Mercury Press, 1997. (*Zur kunstlerischen Therapie*. Boll, Germany 1971)

Holtzapfel, Walter. *Children with a Difference*. E. Grinstead, Sussex, UK: Lanthorn Press, 1995. (*Seelenfleg-bedürftige Kinder II*)

Husemann, Armin. "The Living Body as Visible Word." Unpublished lecture at the Kolisko Conference in Lahti, Finland, August 2, 2002.

Kirchner-Bockholt, Margarete and Erich. *Rudolf Steiner's Mission and Ita Wegman*. London: Rudolf Steiner Press, 1977. (*Die Menschheitsaufgabe Rudolf Steiners und Ita Wegman*)

König, Karl. *Brothers and Sisters: A Study in Child Psychology*, 2nd ed. Blauvelt, NY: Garber Communications, 1991.

———. *The First Three Years of the Child*, 2nd English edition. Edinburgh: Floris Books, 2004.

———. *Embryology and World Evolution*. Camphill Books, 2000.

Kranich, Ernst Michael. *Die Formensprache der Pflanze* (Planetary influences upon plants). Stuttgart, 1970.

Kutzli, Rudolf. *Creative Form Drawing*. Stroud, UK: Hawthorn Press, 1989.

Lehrs, Ernst. *Man or Matter*. London: Rudolf Steiner Press, 1985.

Marti, Ernst. *The Four Ethers*. Roselle, IL: Schaumberg Publications, 1984.

McAllen, Audrey. *The Extra Lesson*, 6th ed. Fair Oaks, CA: Rudolf Steiner College Press, 2004.

———. *The Listening Ear*. Stroud, UK: Hawthorn Press, 1989.

———. *Reading Children's Drawings: The Person, House and Tree Motifs*. Fair Oaks, CA: Rudolf Steiner College Press, 2004.

———. *Sleep: An Unobserved Element in Education*, 2nd ed. Fair Oaks, CA: Rudolf Steiner College Press, 2004.

———. *Teaching Children Handwriting*. Fair Oaks, CA: Rudolf Steiner College Press, 2002.

Meyer, Rudolf. *The Wisdom of Fairy Tales*. Edinburgh: Floris Books, 1988.

Nash-Wortham, Mary and Jean Hunt. *Take Time*. Stourbridge, UK: Robinswood Press, 1988.

Peipers, Felix. *Farbentherapie*. Beiträge zur Rudolf Steiner Gesamtausgabe, Vol. 97, Dornach 1987.

de Quiros, Julio, MD, PhD and Orlando Schrager, MD. *Neuropsychological Fundamentals of Learning Difficulties*. Novato, CA: Academic Therapy Publications, 1979.

Rienks-Läser, Rösli in E. Leonora Hambrecht. *Liane Collot d'Herbois Erinnerungen von Freuden und Schülern*. Dürnau, Germany 2003.

Schwaller de Lubicz, René A. *The Temple in Man: Sacred Architecture and the Perfect Man*. Rochester, NY: Inner Traditions International, 1981.

Schwenck, Theodore. *Sensitive Chaos*. London: Rudolf Steiner Press, 1996.

Steiner, Rudolf. 1909 lectures. Part I of *A Psychology of Body, Soul, and Spirit*.

———. 1910 lectures. Part II of *A Psychology of Body, Soul, and Spirit*.

———. "Anthroposophy." Part I of *A Psychology of Body, Soul and Spirit*. Hudson, NY: Anthroposophic Press, 1999. (GA 115)

———. *Balance in Teaching*. Spring Valley, NY: Mercury Press, 1982. (GA302a) Also published by Robinswood Press as *Meditatively Acquired Knowledge of Man*.

———. *The Balance in the World and Man: Lucifer and Ahriman*. First published by Rudolf Steiner Publishing Co. 1948, second impression by Steiner Book Centre, N. Vancouver 1977. (GA 158) Three lectures given in Dornach, November 20–22, 1914. Alternate title: *The World as Product of the Working of Balance*.

———. *Broken Vessels*. Hudson, NY: Anthroposophic Press, 2003. (GA 318) Formerly published as *The Pastoral Medical Course*.

———. *Christ and the Spiritual World and the Search for the Holy Grail*. London: Rudolf Steiner Press, 1963. (GA 149) Six lectures given in Leipzig December 28, 1913 to January 2, 1914.

———. *Colour*. London: Rudolf Steiner Press, 1992. (GA 291) The edition published under the same title in 1982 contained three additional lectures and selections on the subject of color from Steiner's notebooks.

———. "Cosmic Being and Egohood." Lecture given in Berlin June 20, 1916. *Toward Imagination: Culture and the Individual*. Hudson, NY: Anthroposophic Press, 1990. (GA 169) Seven lectures given in Berlin June 6–July 18, 1916.

———. "The Cosmic Origin of the Human Form." Lecture given in Oxford, England, August 22, 1922. (GA 214) Published in *Planetary Spheres and Their Influence on Man's Life on Earth and in the Spiritual Worlds*. London: Rudolf Steiner press, 1982.

———. The Curative Education Course. See *Education for Special Needs*.

———. *Deeper Insights into Education: The Waldorf Approach*. Spring Valley, NY: Anthroposophic Press, 1983. (GA 302a)

———. *Discussions with Teachers*. Hudson, NY: Anthroposophic Press, 1997. (GA 295)

———. "The Ear," *Spiritual Relationships in the Human Organism*. (GA 218) http://wn.rsarchive.org/Lectures/GA/GA0218/19221209p01.html

———. *Education for Adolescence*. Hudson, NY: Anthroposophic Press, 1996. (GA 302) Formerly referred to as "The Supplementary Course."

———. *Education for Special Needs*. London: Rudolf Steiner Press, 1998. (GA 317) Also known as "The Curative Education Course."

———. "The Education of the Child in the Light of Spiritul Science" part I of *The Education of the Child*. Great Barrington, MA: Anthroposophic Press, 1996.

———. *Egyptian Myths and Mysteries*. Hudson, NY: Anthroposophic Press, 1971. (GA 106) Twelve lectures given in Leipzig September 2–14, 1908.

———. *Faculty Meetings with Rudolf Steiner*. Hudson, NY: Anthroposophic Press, 1998. (GA 300a–c) Also published as *Conferences with Teachers*, Forest Row, East Sussex, UK: Steiner Schools Fellowship, 1986.

———. *Farbenerkenntnis*. Dornach, Switzerland: Rudolf Steiner Nachlassverwalltung, 1990. (GA 291a) A 1908 notebook.

———. *Foundations of Esotericism*. London: Rudolf Steiner Press, 1983. (GA 93a)

———. *Foundations of Human Experience*. Hudson, NY: Anthroposophic Press, 1996. (GA 293) Also published as *Study of Man*.

———. *The Gospel of St. John in Relation to the Other Gospels*. Hudson, NY: Anthroposophic Press, 1982. (GA 112) Lectures given in Kassel, June 24–July 7, 1909.

———. *Intuitive Thinking as a Spiritual Path*. Hudson, NY: Anthroposophic Press, 1995. (GA 4) Also published as *A Philosophy of Freedom* and *A Philosophy of Spiritual Activity*.

———. *The Invisible Man within Us: the Pathology Underlying Therapy*. Spring Valley, NY: Mercury Press, 1987. (GA 221) Lecture given in Dornach, February 11, 1923.

———. *Karmic Relationships: Esoteric Studies*, 8 vols. London: Rudolf Steiner Press, 1972–75. (GA 235, 236)

———. *The Kingdom of Childhood*. Hudson, NY: Anthroposophic Press, 1995. (GA 311) Lectures given in Torquay, England August 12–20, 1924.

———. *The Light Course.* Great Barrington, MA: Anthroposophic Press, 2001. (GA 320)

———. *The Lord's Prayer: an Esoteric Study*. Spring Valley, NY: Anthroposophic Press, 1970. (GA 96) Lecture given in Berlin, January 28, 1907

———. "Menschenwerde, Weltenseele und Weltengeist" Lecture given in Dornach, July 2, 1921. (GA 205)

———. *Man: Hieroglyph of the Universe*. See *Mystery of the Universe—The Human Being: Model of Creation*.

———. *The Michael Mystery*. Spring Valley, NY: St. George Publications, 1984. (GA 26) Also known as the Michael letters and published as *Anthroposophical Leading Thoughts*.

———. *A Modern Art of Education*. London: Rudolf Steiner Press, 1981. (GA 307) Lectures given in Ilkley, UK, 1923.

———. *Mystery of the Universe—The Human Being: Image of Creation*. Hudson, NY/London: Anthroposophic Press/Rudolf Steiner Press, 2001. (GA 201) Also published as *Man: Hieroglyph of the Universe*.

———. *An Occult Physiology*. Forest Row, UK: Rudolf Steiner Press, 1983. (GA 128) Eight lectures given in Prague March 20–28, 1911.

———. *Occult Science: An Outline*. See *An Outline of Esoteric Science*.

———. *Occult Schools in the 18th and First Half of the 19th Centuries*. London: Rudolf Steiner Press, 1965. (GA 233a) Lecture given in Dornach, January 12, 1924.

———. *Occult Signs and Symbols*. New York: Anthroposophic Press, 1972. (GA 101) Lectures given in Stuttgart, September 13–16, 1907.

———. *An Outline of Esoteric Science*. Hudson, NY: Anthroposophic Press, 1997. (GA 13) Also published as *Occult Science: An Outline*.

———. *The Pastoral Medical Course*. See *Broken Vessels*.

———. *A Philosophy of Freedom* or *A Philosophy of Spiritual Activity*. See *Intuitive Thinking as a Spiritual Path*.

———. *Practical Advice to Teachers*. London: Rudolf Steiner Press, 1976. (GA 294)

———. *Prayers for Parents and Children*, 4th edition. Forest Row, Sussex: Rudolf Steiner Press, 1995. (GA 40) (selections from *Wahspruchworte*)

———. *The Pre-Earthly Deeds of Christ*. First published in English by Rudolf Steiner Publishing Co., 1947. Second impression by Steiner Book Centre, Inc., N. Vancouver, 1976. (GA 152) Lecture given in Pforzheim, Germany, March 7, 1914.

———. *A Psychology of Body, Soul, and Spirit*. Hudson, NY: Anthroposophic Press, 1999. (GA 115) Lecures given in Berlin October 23–27, 1909, November 1–4, 1910, and December 12–16, 1911. (*Anthroposophie, Psychosophie, Pneumatosophie* Dornach, Switzerland 1980; sometimes referred to as "The Wisdom of Man, of the Soul and of the Spirit.")

———. *The Renewal of Education*. Great Barrington, MA: Anthroposophic Press, 2001. (GA 301) Lectures given in Basel, April 20–May 16, 1920, also referred to as "The Swiss Course."

———. *The Spiritual Guidance of the Individual and Humanity*. Hudson, NY: Anthroposophic Press, 1991. (GA 15) Three lectures given June 5–8, 1911 in Copenhagen.

———. *Study of Man*. See *Foundations of Human Experience*.

———. "Subconcious Impulses in the Human Soul." Manuscript. Lecture given in Dornach, January 14, 1917. (*Zeitgeschichliche Betrachtungen*)

———. The Swiss Course. See *The Renewal of Education*.

———. *The Temple Legend*. London: Rudolf Steiner Press, 1997. (GA 93)

———. *Theosophy*. Hudson, NY: Anthroposophic Press, 1994. (GA 9w)

———. *Verses and Meditations*. Forest Row, UK: Rudolf Steiner Press, 2004. (GA 40) (translation of selected verses from *Wahrspruchworte*)

———. *The World of the Senses and the World of the Spirit*. Archive Edition. Hudson, NY: Anthroposophic Press. (GA 134) First published by Rudolf Steiner Publishing Co. in 1947, second impression by Rudolf Steiner Book Centre, N. Vancouver 1979.

Strachan, Gordon. *Chartres: Sacred Geometry, Sacred Space*. Edinburgh: Floris, 2003.

Tomatis, Alfred. www.tomatis.com.

Wilkes, John. *Flow Forms: The Rhythmic Power of Water*. Edinburgh: Floris Books, 2003.

Willby, Mary Ellen, ed. *Learning Difficulties*. Fair Oaks, CA: Rudolf Steiner College Press, 1999.

Wilmar, Frits. *Vorgeburtliche Menschewerdung*. Stuttgart: J.C. Mellinger Verlag, 1979.

Witkin, H. A. "Personality through Perception: An Experimental and Clinical Study." Westport, CT: Greenwood Press, 1954.

Zeylmans van Emmichoven, Emmanuel. *Willem Zeylmans van Emmichoven: an Inspiration for Anthroposophy*. London: Temple Lodge, 2002. (*Ein Pionier der Anthroposophie*. Arlesheim, Switzerland: Natura Verlag, 1979)

———. *Who Was Ita Wegman? A Documentation, Vol. I 1876–1925*. Spring Valley, NY: Mercury Press, 1990.

Zeylmans van Emmichoven, F. W. *De Werking van Kleuren op het Gevoel*. Utrecht 1923.

———. *The Foundation Stone*. London: Rudolf Steiner Press, 1963.

Index

Appendices are not included in this index.
Pages for charts and illustrations are given in boldface.

age, appropriate for exercises, 39-40
Ahriman/ahrimanic, 4
    and lower astral, 9-10
    in ether body, 141
    influence on human expressed in architecture, 162
antipathy, 44, 70
    plastic-architectonic, 130
archetypal forms/patterns
    Blue Moon and Red Sun, chap. 6
    form variations, 81-82
    imprinted into body, 68
    moon and sun forms, 77-80
    picture of all human bodies, 37-41
    straight line and curve, 66
astral body, 2, 115
    affinity for etheric body, 41, 141
    anchored in metabolic system, 10
    and color, 43, 46
    and ego, 9
    and luciferic forces, 11
    and senses, 15-16
    countermovement of, 16, 18, **34**, 35-36, **38**, 43, 50-51
    current of, 21, 23, 40, 41, 49
    incarnating into physical (Biblical), 157
    in First Goetheanum form, 164
    inflating etheric, 143
    lemniscate as image of, 66, 138
    mirroring, 119-120, 135
    more independent in eye, 118
    moves in spiral, 23, 45, 63, 116
    nervous system as vessel for, 67
    of world (Cosmic Soul), 72
    penetrating physical, 26, 40-42
    prepared by Hierarchies, 6, 20
    pressing physical or pushing etheric, 143
    reflection and refraction in, 124
    reversal in, 120, 124-25
    too strong, 81
    working into etheric, 44, 46, 51-52
    See also sentient body; sentient soul

Bible references
    Exodus, 52, 158, 159
    Genesis, 4, 7, 157
    Luke, 8, 143, 149
    Matthew, 5, 8, 11, 19
blood
    and nerves in eye, 71
    connected with sympathy, 43
    opaque to spirit, 88
body geography
    development of, 6, 103
bones
    and structural body, 9, 11, 32
    become next skull, 120
    embedded into earth evolution, 155
    formed by antipathy, 43
Boos-Hamburger, Hilde, 107, 112n
brain, 2-3, 12, **24**
    and intellectual soul, 25
    brings inner and outer into consciousness, 64
    constructed by currents, 23-24
    differentiation/development, 5, 6, 11
    left and right halves, 72
    mirrors process of waking, 41
    similar to eye substance, 130
    skull impinging on, 82
    stimulated by breathing, 55
    See also nervous system
breathing
    connects with sense impressions, 114
    harmonizing of, 82
    importance for education, 55-57
    in Copper Ball exercise, 61-63
    light, 139
    perception carried into soul life, 131
    problems in, 139
    properly, 32
    teacher aware of student's, 44, 45
Buddha/Buddhist, on incarnation, 5

Cernan, Eugene, 86
chakras (lotus flowers), 6, 18
Christ, 76
    balances opponents, 143
    Ego of, 149
    gift of thinking to humanity, 149
    Judeo-Christian tradition, 7-8
    in meditation on Interpenetrating
        Triangles, 53
    pre-earthly deeds of, 148-50
    three years of, 14
    See also ego, World Ego
Collot d'Herbois, Liane, chap. 7
    Big Diagram mirrored, **91**
    Colour, 72, 85, 86, 90
    Light, Darkness and Colour in
        Painting Therapy, 88
    "Malen in Schichten", 103n
color(s), chap. 6, chap. 7
    after-image, 133-34n
    behind the light, 94-97
    blue and red, 43, 44, 68, 73-77
    blue and red in advertising, 73, **75**
    blue and red meditation, 77
    choice of for exercises, 39
    complementary, 119, 124
    connected with feeling, 145
    counter-colors, 100-101, 119, 164
    earth colors, 97-98
    engage astral body, 43, 85
    for Moving Straight Line and
        Lemniscate, 68
    in front of the light, 91-93
    in world creation and
        consciousness, 146-47
    movement of darkness around
        light, 114
    perception (2-dimensional), 126
    perspective, 126
    sound is color, 130
    theory (Goethe's), 72, 86
    See also reversal of auditory and
        visual
consciousness soul, 24
    and cortex, 25
    depends on ego anchoring in
        physical, 127
constitutional physical body, 9-13
    and planetary forces, 11
crook and flail, **66**

Cross Assessment, 139, 140-41
cube
    cubic organization, 131
    (reversal of 3-dimensional space),
        chap. 11, **154**

Davis, Ronald, *Gift of Dyslexia*, 127-28
dominance
    and Handedness Assessment, 135
    development of, 11
    strengthened, 40
dyslexia, 113, 121, 127-28, 146

ear
    and nervous system, 57
    and senses, 16
    built by sound, 21, 157
    resonates with movements, 114
earth
    currents of, 27-30
    evolutionary phases, 20
    migrations, 29-30
ego/Ego, 2, 115
    affinity for physical body, 41, 141
    anchored in etheric, 114
    anchored in metabolic system, 10
    anchored in physical body,
        10, 67, 127, 128, 140
    anchored in structural physical
        body, 120-21, 125
    builds body substances, 117
    current of, 34, 36, 41, 47, 48, 49
    day-wake consciousness of, 147
    focus to create 3-dimensional
        space, 155
    higher Ego 5, 6; carried by
        structural body, 10-11
    imprinting movement into
        etheric, 36, 45, 125
    in architectural forms, 159, 161
    incarnating into other sheaths, 6
    individuality maintaining balance,
        80
    infected by luciferic forces, 9
    lifts body out of gravity, 26, 46, 59,
        147
    lower ego, 5
    not incorporated in animals, 117
    perception of form, 126
    saying "I", 12, 19, 150, 161

ego/Ego (continued)
- self consciousness, 5, 7, 9, 14, 20, 66, 72, 155
- stand, walk, speak, think, 150
- straight line, 138
- transforms etheric and physical, 24
- working in the blood, 9, 23
- World Ego prepares vertical, 21-22
- *See also* astral body; etheric body; physical body; mirroring

Eikenboom, Erica
- Colors behind the light, **95**
- Colors in front of the light, **95**
- Colors in front of and behind the light, **96**
- Convex and concave color movements, **96**

etheric body, 2, 115
- and rhythmic system, 112
- and the senses, 15-16, 114
- astral moving through, 23, 40, 46
- current of, 22, 34, 36, 41, 49
- divided in 2 parts, 122
- early movements imprinted as habit patterns, 126
- educated by arts and religion, 36
- imprinting from Ego, 36, 64
- imprinting from physical, 126-27, 155
- memory in, 125
- mirroring, 119
- penetrates muscles, 118
- prepared by Hierarchies, 6
- pushes against physical organization, 134n
- reflection in (flat mirroring), 122-23
- too strongly connected with physical, 81
- *See also* astral body; ego; physical body

eurythmy, 25
- multisensory experience, 121, 146
- relation of visual and auditory, 130
- rod exercises, 31
- sevenfold exercise, 36-37
- weight presses downward (Triangle Rod) exercise, 52

evolution
- ascending and descending streams, 82-83

evolution (continued)
- of world and human being, 3-4

Extra Lesson (book), 2
- mirroring sequence, 122

Extra Lesson (concept/work), 1, 113
- and subconscious, 127
- architectonic principle of the First Goetheanum, 165
- characteristics of, 131-33, 145
- multisensory experiences, 66
- recapitulates first seven years, 6
- self-correction, 68

Extra Lesson/educational support teachers
- and warmth of room, 17-18
- diagnosing relationship to space, 69
- importance of breathing, 105, 130
- not jump to conclusions, 69
- observe bodily conditions from behind, 21
- possible conditions shown in Handedness Assessment, 137
- read elements in children's paintings, 111
- relate Flower Rod to diagram of currents, 139
- responsibility for study, 1, 4

Extra Lesson exercises, 2
- Ball Twirling, 26-27, 41, 68
- Blue-Red Perspective, 45-51, **47**, **48**, **49**, **50**
- Blue-Red Spiral, 43-45, 51
- Bouncing Ball, 141
- Copper Ball, 55-65, 139, 141, 164
- Dominance Form, 40
- Eye Color Affinity (Blue Moon and Red Sun), 39, chap 6, 102, 112, 160
- First Educational Support Lesson, 136
- Flower Rod, 64-65, **64**, 137-39, 163
- Interpenetrating Triangles, 52-53
- Moving Straight Line and Lemniscate, 65-68, 111-12, 143; recommendations for class teachers in, 67
- Person-House-Tree, 770, 82 102, 110
- Right-angled Triangle, 31-40, **34**, **35**, **37**, 43, 46, 48, 49

Extra Lesson exercises (continued)
   Rod Rolling, 59, 141
   Threefold Spiral, 26-27, 40-42, 43, 51
   Thumb Twirling, 68
   Triangle Rod, 52
   Weight Lifting, 135
   Wool Winding, 26-27, 56, 68
   See also Handedness Assessment
eye, 70-73
   and sense of self-movement, 121
   constructed by currents, 23-24
   controls hand movement, 44
   created by the light, 157
   different modes of seeing, 69
   focus of left and right, 146
   functioning shown in Flower Rod exercise, 138
   in Pantheon form, 161
   in First Goetheanum form, 164
   pair created by sun and moon, 80
   perception of light, darkness and color, 119, 121, 129
   resonates with movements, 114
   reversed eye-color-affinity, 77
   tracking of, 140
   See also light; sense of sight

feeling, 145
   and Holy Trinity, 154
   and horizontal, 33
   in animal kingdom, 116
feet
   control of left and right, 49
   exercise with woolen ball, 62-63
   movement of, 25-27, 41
first seven years
   and Extra Lesson, 6
   antipathy and sympathy in body forming, 43, 70
   (im)proper development in, 127, 128, 131, 141, 155
   incomplete development in, 126
   laterality developed (5-7 years), 61
   symmetrical stage (3-5 years), 61, 72
   too little movement in, 67
first three years, 5
   and bodily senses, 16
   individualizing physical body, 11
   stand up, speak, think, 18-19, 21

fourfold human being, 2, 114
   and Pythagorean Theorem, 33-34
   Rudolf Steiner on, 10

Govinda, Lama Anagarika, *The Way of the White Clouds*, 78-79
Grimms' tale of "Bearskin", 143

hands
   move in opposite directions, 61
   movement of, 41, 67
Handedness Assessment, 31, 135-37
Hauschka, Margarete, 86
   Fundamentals of Artistic Therapy, 88
Henry the Navigator
   square and triangular sails, 34
Holtzapfel, Walter, 113
   Children with a Difference, 133n
   mirroring letters, 123, 134n
Hierarchies
   Angels (air), 17, **19**, 145
   Archangels (fluid), 17, **19**, 20, 145
   Archai, 17, **19**, 145
   connected with gravity, 155
   creation by, 6, 10, 14
   guiding 6 sense organs, 17
   Thrones, 20
Holy Grail, 150, 155, **156**
Hunt, Jean, *Take Time* (beanbag exercises), 31

illness
   and karma, 10
   fever, 71
   luciferic influence on astral, 11
Imagination, Inspiration, Intuition, 18
Imprinting, chap. 9, 126-27
   of mirroring possibilities, 135

karma, in illness, 10, 115
kidney shape in drawing of moon 81
König, Karl, *First Three Years of the Child*, 6, 12, 60, 63, 126
Kranich, E. M., book in German on planetary influences on plants, 52
Kutzli, Rudolf, *Creative Form Drawing*, 53 140

larynx
   colors dammed by the, 145
   forming of, 12

laterality, 11
learning difficulties
   processing sense impressions, 113
Learning Difficulties, 113
   "Mirroring Process", 122
left (side)
   less flexible than right, 41
   movement of hands and feet, **25**
   Triangle exercise for left-sided, **37**
Lehrs, Ernst, *Man or Matter*, 69, 72
Leonardo da Vinci
   painted at 6 PM, 41
   Last Supper, 74
   Vitruvian Man, 63
lifting, 25-27, 58-60
   alternating with stretching, 66
   and gravity and levity, 66
   balance with stretching, 140-41
light
   and air on Old Sun, 20
   eye formed by, 21
   linear, 147
   perception of, 118
   See also color
liver, in transformation and metabolism, 11
Lucifer/luciferic, 4, 5, 7-8
   darkens the light, 53
   infecting human ego, 9-10, 14
   influence on astral body, 11
   passion and pride, 141-43
   Prometheus, 8

Marti, Ernst, *The Four Ethers*, 20, 116, 147
McAllen, Audrey
   early work of, 1
   Extra Lesson, 68, 69, 80
   "Everybody knows astral moves in spiral", 45
   "Look at currents as planes of movement", 50
   "Mirroring Process in Relation to Two- and Three-dimensional Space", 113
   Reading Children's Drawings, 1, 33, 70, 82, 107, 111
   Sleep: An Unobserved Element in Education, 66, 102, 107, 108, 131, 154
memory, 113, 114, 124, 127
   auditory and visual, 129

metabolic and glandular system
   activated by red sunrise, 77
   activity in the eye, 71
   and constitutional body, 9
   connected with sympathy, 43, 70
   etheric body in, 64, 114
   origin of, 7-8
   processes, 117-18
midline (barriers), 11
   problems of, 81, 136, 137, 140
mirroring, chap. 9
   and cube, 151
   appearance of mineral, plant and animal, 115-17
   astral, 119
   convex, 124
   difficulty in, 37
   Ego guiding, 135-37
   etheric, 19
   horizontal, 123
   in Blue-Red Perspective, 49, 51
   in sense of self-movement, 121
   in two-dimensional space, 122, 126
   of sense impressions by middle system, 64
   lens mirroring reversal, **125**
   palindrome of flat mirroring, **123**
   reflection in convex mirror, **124**
   reversal in cathedral form, 160
   reversal in concave mirror, **125**
   right side reflection in 3 steps, **123**
   sequence, 76, 122
   shown by Flower Rod exercise, 137
   See also Handedness Assessment
morality, movements of. *See* virtues
movement
   creates sound, 114
   development of, 12
   harmonizing of, 30
   laterality developed (5-7 years), 61
   lemniscate pattern, 27
   moral virtues in spirit, 130, 147-56
   Moro reflex, 59
   of hands and feet, **25**
   overcoming gravity, 12
   patterns in human, 11, 25-27, 126-27, 137
   reflexes, 58, 60, 62
   sound produces movement, 131
   spiritual reversal as cube, 131

movement (continued)
    system and painting, 43
    See also lifting; stretching;
        Handedness Assessment
muscles/muscular system
    and structural body, 9, 11, 32
    development of, 6
    lifting and stretching, 26, 58-60
    penetrated by etheric, 118
mystery (streams)
    inner and outer, 8-9
    mystery centers, 22, 52

Nash-Wortham, Mary,
    Take Time (beanbag exercises), 31
nerves
    and structural body, 9
    spinal, 9
    transparent to spirit, 88
nervous system, **24**
    and breathing, 57
    and structural body, 11-12, 32
    astral affinity for, 140
    formed by antipathy, 43
    formed by astral body/sentient
        soul, 25, 116
    mirrors waking process, 41
    receives sense impressions, 64, 114
    See also brain
neurological development
    motor and, 11
New Jerusalem and cube form, 154

Oberufer Christmas plays, 143

painting, chap. 4, chap. 7, chap. 8
    diagnostic painting of person in
        green and red, 101-103
    Grünewald altar painting, 105
    moral color exercises, 107-110
    secondary color exercises, 106-107
    technique, 105-106
    yellow sun in blue sky, 110, 111
Parsifal (opera)
    "where space becomes time", 152,
        154
passion, 141-43, **142**
Peipers, Felix
    colored light therapy, 76
    Farbentherapie, 83n

perception, 113
    carried into soul through breathing,
        131
    structural process of, 127
physical body, 2, 115
    and the senses, 12, 20, 113
    as vessel for ego, 6-7, 67
    astral affinity for, 140
    astral moving through, 23
    blueprint filled with substance, 7
    brought into tension, 15
    connection to soul-spirit, 55, 58
    constitutional, 9-13, **14**, 69, 103,
        115, 131, 139, 150
    current of, 22, 47
    destruction of foreign substance, 117
    eastern spiritual paths and, 6
    forces for spiritual development, 5
    in children's drawings, 12
    perception of form, 126
    pride, 141-43, **142**
    proportions of (Biblical), 157
    related to structure of Earth, 22
    structural, 9-13, 32, 46, 49, 68, 69, 103,
        120, 135, 138, 150, chap. 12
    See also spiritual beings; spiritual
        currents
planets, effects on flowers, 52
Pythagoras, Theorem of, 33-34, 42n

reading
    and 2-dimensional space, 37
    mirroring and, 123
    problems in, 126, 128
    teaching of, 16-17, 128-30
restlessness/nervousness, 41
reversal of auditory and visual, 145-46
rhythmic system/processes, 3
    and astral body, 9
    and breathing, 40, 56, 66, 114
    and reading and writing, 130
    and Waldorf education, 32
    connects sense impressions with
        soul, 64, 114
    See also breathing
right (side)
    movement of hands and feet, **25**
    Right-angled Triangle exercise for,
        35, **38**

Schwaller de Lubicz, R. A., *The Temple of Man: Sacred Architecture and the Perfect Man*, 159
Schwenck, Theodore, 45
Sensitive Chaos, 29
self consciousness. *See* ego/Ego
sense of balance (vestibular system), 5
   and Spirit Self, 16
   with eyes closed, 61-62
sense of ego of the other, 16, 18
sense of hearing, 16
   and Angels, 17
   and nerves, 129
   and senses of balance and self-movement, 126
sense of life
   and Spirit Man, 15
sense of self-movement (proprioception), 5, 126
   and direction of movement, 66-67
   and Life Spirit, 15-16
   form and linear perspective, 146
   helped by sense of sight, 68
   mirroring in, 121-26
   perception of letter forms, 131
   registering astral countermovement, 35
sense of sight, 17, chap. 6, 118, 121
   and archetypal images, 66, 68
   and sound, 130, 146
   complementary colors, 124
   See also eye
sense of smell, 17
sense of speech, 16
   and Archangels, 17
   and color, 130, 131
   in senses of self-movement and life, 126
sense of taste, 17
sense of thought, 16
   and Archai, 17
   in senses of self-movement and life, 126
sense of touch, 18
sense of warmth, 17-18
senses/sense organs, 15-19
   and constitutional body, 9
   built by outer world, 21
   "deafness" in, 139
   development of, 6

senses/sense organs (continued)
   gate of Garden of Eden, 7
   imitate movements of outer world, 114
   imprinted into structural body, 157
   move like limbs, 64
   process sense impressions, 113, 118-21
   right-left symmetry, 72
sentient body, 20-21, 23
   activated by diagonals, 35
   and sentient soul, 138
   current of, 47, 48, 49
   in eye, 71
   penetrating physical, 26
   pushing by, 67
sentient soul, 21, 23, 25
   and sentient body, 138
   in eye, 71
   pushing by, 67
   reacting to sense impressions, 26
skeleton
   formed by sun and moon through zodiac, 157
sleep
   experiences taken into, 66
   problems of, 41, 82
solar plexus, 9, 24
soul/soul life
   addressed by painting, 43
   after change of teeth, 70
   and astral, 15
   and cube, 155
   and perception, 113
   called upon too early, 81
   change of consciousness, 147
   experiences influence sleep, 66
   expression in front of body, 21
   incarnation of, **14**
   inner processes of, 19
   perception as rhythmic breathing, 71
   pour inward, 18
   problems in movement system, 136
   receives sense impressions, 114
   rescued by the Christ, 149
   threefold aspect of, 3
   See also color; feeling; thinking; will
spatial awareness, development of, 6

speech/speaking, 5
   and memory development, 29
   individualized, 11
speech organs
   development of, 6
spiritual beings
   and forces from zodiac, 11
   behind sense world, 7, 15, 20
   independence from, 7-8
spiritual/supersensible currents
   as planes of movement, 153
   astral map, 153
   building human body, 1, 5, 20-25, 34, 36-37
   building structural physical body (1909), 1, 20-25, **22**, 34, 152, 160
   forming nervous system and brain, **24**
   in Copper Ball exercise, 62-63, **63**
   in relation to time, 30
   of sentient body, 20
   of sentient soul, 21
   of the earth, 27-29, **152**
   of the earth and human being, **153**
   of the human being, **151**
   projection of human's in relation to earth's, **154**
   relation of child to, 135
   right-angled triangle as picture of, 36-37
   working in chemical substance, 56
spiritual forces building human body, 5, 19
spiritual members of the human being, 15-16, **19**
   Spirit Self (Manas), Life Spirit (Buddhi), Spirit Man (Atman), 6, 149, 150
spiritual senses, 18-19
standing upright, 16, 146, 149, 150
Stein, Walter Johannes, 118
   letter from Rudolf Steiner on afterimages, 133-34n
Steiner books and lectures
   Apocalypse of St. John, 118
   Balance in Teaching, 1, 57, 64, 73, 77, 110, 129, 130, 131, 145
   Balance in the World and Man, 83n, 122, 141, 155, 162
   Broken Vessels, 134n

Steiner books and lectures (continued)
   Christ and the Holy Grail, 148
   Colour, 76, 87, 88
   Cosmic Being and Egohood, 18
   "Cosmic Origin of the Human Form", 80, 83n
   Deeper Insights into Education, 46, 56, 57, 115, 150
   Discussions with Teacher,s 41
   "Ear", 129
   Education for Adolescence, 46
   Education for Special Needs, 46, 59, 114, 115, 120, 131
   Education of the Child, 2, 11
   Egyptian Myths and Mysteries, 157
   Faculty Meetings with Rudolf Steiner 57, 73
   Farbenerkenntnis, 52, 100, 103n, 106, 120
   Foundations of Esotericism, 10
   Gospel of John in Relation to the Other Gospel,s 155
   Invisible Man within Us, 150
   Karmic Relationships, 21, 41, 83n
   Kingdom of Childhood, 114
   Lectures for the Workers, 56
   Light Course, 117
   Modern Art of Education, 126
   Mystery of the Universe, 33
   "Occult Schools in the 18th and First Half of the 19th Centuries", 52
   Occult Signs and Symbols, 157
   Outline of Esoteric Scienc,e 7, 20, 78, 141, 148
   Philosophy of Freedom, 99, 113, 145
   Practical Advice to Teachers, 66, 98, 112n, 122
   Prayers for Parents and Children, 21
   Pre-earthly Deeds of Christ, 148, 149
   Psychology of Body, Soul, and Spirit (Berlin 1909, 1910, 1911), 1, 113, 151
      Part I (1909 lectures), 6, 15, 18-20, 35, 46, 71, 110, 117, 131, 132, 145, 151
      Part II (1910 lectures), 30, 73
   Renewal of Education, 126
   Spiritual Ground of Education, 112n
   Spiritual Guidance of the Individual and of Humanity, 5, 18

Steiner books and lectures (continued)
Study of Man (Foundations of Human Experience), 1, 19, 32, 55, 59, 64, 70, 71, 113, 114, 120, 122, 130, 151
Temple Legend, 79, 83n
Theosophy, 21
Verses and Meditations, 112
World of the Senses and World of the Spirit, 7

Steiner, Rudolf
- basic ideas of, 1-4
- caduceus diagram, **90**
- concave color diagram, **89**
- first Goetheanum building, 90, 162-65, **165**
- meditation on the hexagon, 106-107, **107**
- new way of painting, 106
- on after-images, 133-34n
- on constitutional body, 9-10
- prepare a month's lectures in five minutes, 119
- seventh apocalyptic seal drawing, **156**
- statue of the Representative of Humanity, 164, **165**

Strachan, Gordon, *Chartres: Sacred Geometry, Sacred Space*, 162

stretching, 25-27, 58-60
- alternating with lifting, 66
- and gravity and levity, 66
- and overstimulated senses, 67
- balance with lifting, 140-41

sympathy, 44, 70
- musical-speech, 130

thinking
- and Holy Trinity, 154
- and vertical line, 33
- antipathy and sympathy in, 44
- bridge between inner and outer, 145
- capacity of, 5
- reflecting the world, 14

threefold human being, 2-3, 33, 114-15, 122

Tomatis, Alfred, 57, 72, 129
two-dimensional world (Old Moon), 148
twofold human being, 113-114, 122

virtues
- and movement, 147-56
- morality movements create spatial direction, 146

walking, 16
warmth
- bridge between spiritual and physical, 147
- in meditation for Interpenetrating Triangle, 53
- linking constitutional and structural, 12
- on Old Saturn, 20, 147
water, 2-dimensional plane, 147
Wilke, Elly, 1
Wilkes, John, 45
- *Flow Forms: the Rhymic Power of Water*, 29
will forces/impulses, 3, 145
- able to move physical, 46
- and diagonal, 33, 37
- and Holy Trinity, 154
- antipathy and sympathy in, 44, 70
- free use of, 69
- interference with, 59
- of Ego, 65
- sun forces in, 80
- to perceive, 131
Witkin, H. A., "Personality Through Perception", 61
writing
- and 2-dimensional space, 37
- capacity for, 70
- direction of, 30
- problems in, 126
- teaching of, 16-17, 128-30

Zeylmans van Emmichoven, F. W.
- *De Werking van Kleuren op het Gevoel*, 83n
Zeylmans van Emmichoven, J. E.
- *Who Was Ita Wegman?*, 83n
- *Willem Zeylmans van Emichoven*, 112n
zodiac
- formative forces of 11, 20, 154

About the author

Joep Eikenboom has been a Waldorf class teacher in the Netherlands since 1980 and has worked with the Extra Lesson exercises since 1984. He has researched the roots of these exercises in the work of Rudolf Steiner, consulting extensively with Audrey McAllen, Liane Collot d'Herbois, and other educational support teachers. In 1989 he joined with colleagues in different countries to collaborate in founding remedial education teacher training programs, which have since been established in the United States, Australia, the Netherlands, Germany, Brazil, Spain, Hungary, and Ireland. Joep has taught in most of these programs, which helped in deepening the insights now expressed in this book.